新编英汉笔译教程

张林影 娄琦 编著

清華大学出版社
北京

内容简介

本教材除了简单介绍中外翻译理论和知识外，还通过英汉两种语言的对比和大量译例分析，介绍了英译汉的一些常用方法和技巧，使学生能够掌握英汉双语翻译的基本理论，能够掌握英汉词语、长句及各种文体的翻译技巧和英汉互译的能力。

本教材由14章构成，所讲的理论问题大致构成了一个基本完整的体系，可以帮助学生掌握翻译的基本原理、方法和技巧。教材坚持理论与实践相结合的原则，每个翻译理论都会结合一定数量的实例来进行阐述。大部分章节后都配有大量练习题。

本教材适合作为高等院校英语专业本科翻译课程教学使用，但从理论深度和材料难度来看，也可用作翻译专业本科和翻译方向硕士生的教材。

图书在版编目(CIP)数据

新编英汉笔译教程 / 张林影，娄琦 编著. —北京：清华大学出版社，2016（2024.2 重印）
ISBN 978-7-302-45601-8

Ⅰ.①新… Ⅱ.①张… ②娄… Ⅲ.①英语—翻译—教材 Ⅳ.①H315.9

中国版本图书馆 CIP 数据核字(2016)第 272886 号

责任编辑：施 猛 马遥遥
封面设计：常雪影
版式设计：方加青
责任校对：曹 阳
责任印制：沈 露

出版发行：清华大学出版社
网 址：https://www.tup.com.cn, https://www.wqxuetang.com
地 址：北京清华大学学研大厦 A 座 邮 编：100084
社 总 机：010-83470000 邮 购：010-62786544
投稿与读者服务：010-62776969，c-service@tup.tsinghua.edu.cn
质 量 反 馈：010-62772015，zhiliang@tup.tsinghua.edu.cn
课 件 下 载：https://www.tup.com.cn, 010-62781730
印 装 者：三河市龙大印装有限公司
经 销：全国新华书店
开 本：185mm×260mm **印 张：**14 **字 数：**205 千字
版 次：2016 年 11 月第 1 版 **印 次：**2024 年 2 月第 7 次印刷
定 价：49.00 元

产品编号：067925-03

作者简介

张林影，女，硕士，生于1979年8月，黑龙江牡丹江人，牡丹江师范学院副教授。发表核心和省级学术论文10余篇，出版著作2部。主持黑龙江省社科研究规划年度项目2项，黑龙江省教育厅人文社会科学研究项目1项，黑龙江省教育科学规划项目1项，牡丹江师范学院国家级培育项目1项，牡丹江师范学院省级重点创新预研项目1项，获得黑龙江省高等教育教学成果二等奖1项，黑龙江省外语学科社会科学优秀成果三等奖1项。

娄琦，男，博士，生于1964年，黑龙江牡丹江人，牡丹江师范学院教授。牡丹江师范学院应用英语学院院长。主持国家社会科学基金一般项目1项，黑龙江省社会科学规划项目2项，发表核心和省级学术论文20余篇，出版专著2部，教材2部，获得黑龙江省高等教育教学成果二等奖1项。

前　言

高校英语专业教学大纲要求高校翻译教学要使学生具备笔头翻译的基本能力。通过介绍各类文体语言的特点、汉英两种语言的差异以及各种不同文体的翻译方法，使学生掌握英汉双语翻译的基本理论，掌握英汉词语、长句及各种文体的翻译技巧和英汉互译的能力。按照大纲的要求，联系自身的教学实际，并结合多年的教学经验，《新编英汉笔译教程》历经七年的时间终于完稿了。

教材由14章构成，所讲的理论问题大致构成了一个基本完整的体系，可以帮助学生掌握翻译的基本原理、方法和技巧。教材坚持理论与实践相结合的原则，每个翻译理论都会结合一定数量的实例来进行阐述。大部分章节后都配有大量练习题，目的是通过大量实例来引导学生掌握英汉两种语言的差异，找出英汉互译的规律，以便学生通过实践熟悉翻译技巧，培养翻译能力。教材中所涉及的英汉翻译理论和实践等方面的问题具有普遍性，也基本上适用于汉译英。教材除了简单介绍中外翻译理论和知识外，还通过英汉两种语言的对比和大量译例分析，介绍了英译汉的一些常用方法和技巧。本教材适合作为高等院校英语专业本科翻译课程教学使用，但从理论深度和材料难度来看，也可用作翻译专业本科和翻译方向硕士生的教材。

本教材是黑龙江省教育科学规划青年专项课题(GJD1214076)、黑龙江省哲学社会科学研究青年规划项目(14C044)、牡丹江师范学院优秀青年骨干教师培养计划项目(SYJZ1701)、牡丹江师范学院国家级课题培育项目(GP201612)、牡丹江师范学院教育教学改革项目(14XJ-16008)的阶段性研究成果，并得到了以上项目的资助。

本教材由张林影、娄琦共同编著，张林影负责教材的统稿和前11章的编写工作，娄琦负责前言及后3章的编写、参考文献的编排和教材的校稿工作。

目　录

第1章

翻译概述

学习翻译究竟应该学些什么？

首先，学习翻译应该学习翻译的基本理论知识，如翻译的定义、翻译的意义、理论、翻译的本质、翻译的标准、翻译的过程、风格问题、翻译主体问题、翻译研究的主要流派及其思想、翻译理论和实践的发展历史。

其次，学习翻译应该学习翻译的基本技巧，了解词、句、篇章的翻译方法和不同文体的特点及相应的翻译方法。

通过学习翻译提高双语的综合应用和转换能力，加深对两种文化的理解，扩大自己的阅读范围，拓展视野。

1.1 翻译的定义

翻译是国际沟通的桥梁，也是相互理解的钥匙，据说西欧的文明归功于翻译者。季羡林教授也说，翻译是永葆中华文明青春的万应灵药。前中国驻联合国代表凌青先生说，从中国来讲，没有翻译工作，就没有中国和中国近代的革命运动，就没有中国成功的对外开放和四个现代化；从世界范围来讲，没有翻译，就没有世界和平，就没有各种国际交往，就没有一个共同繁荣的美好世界的未来。中国加入WTO后，翻译的重要作用更不可忽视。经济竞争是在交际中进行，而没有翻译在场，沟通就很难进行，沟通不成，生意就做不成。因此，翻译的作用，再怎么强调也不过分。

翻译既是一门艺术，也是一门科学，涉及两种语言，是一种语言社会实践活动，既有跨文化性，又有交际性。翻译能开发我们的智力、活跃我们的思想、丰富我们的语言、开阔我们的视野，从别的语言中汲取对我们有益的成分。通过翻译，才能把语言文化、人类文明推向一个更高的层次和发展阶段。

到底什么是翻译？关于翻译的定义很多。有人把翻译看作一门科学，因为它有自身的规律可循；有人将其看作一门艺术，因为它是译者对原文再创造的过程；还有人将其看作一门手艺，因为源语的信息需要用地道恰当的目标语再现。

翻译的过程就好比交通工具的换乘过程，两者之间有诸多相似之处，如表1-1所示。

表1-1　交通工具换乘过程与翻译过程对比

交通工具换乘过程	翻译过程
内容 (人员)	内容 (信息)
载体(运输工具1)　内容(人员)	载体(源语)　内容(信息)
载体(运输工具2)	载体(译语)

两者有如下共同点：

(1) 相似的目的：两种转换过程都是为了实现内容通过载体的变换从一端到另一端的传递。

(2) 相似的基本要素：第一要素内容，在交通工具换乘过程中是人员，而在翻译过程中则是信息。第二要素载体，在交通工具换乘过程中是车辆、船舶、飞机等，转换前是一种运输工具，转换后改为另一种运输工具；而在翻译过程中则是语言，转换前是源语(source language)，转换后是目标语(target language)。

(3) 相似的操作要求：第一，两者都要求内容不变。第二，两者都要求过程顺畅。

《现代汉语词典》将翻译定义为“把一种语言文字的意义用另一种语言文字表达出来”。

根据《剑桥语言百科全书》，“翻译”这个中性术语是指将一种语言(源语)里的词句的意思转变为另一种语言(目的语)的意思所发生的一切行为，不论其手段是说话、写字还是做手势。

在自动化数据处理中，翻译又被定义为：将计算机信息从一种语言转换成另一种语言，或将字符从一种表示转换成另一种表示。

牛津词典(*The Oxford English Dictionary*)对翻译的定义是：to turn from one language into another (从一种语言转换成另一种语言)。

新韦氏国际英语词典第三版(*Webster's Third New International Dictionary of the English Language*)对翻译的定义是：to turn into one's own or another language (转换成本族语或另一种语言)。

美国翻译理论家尤金·奈达(Eugene A. Nida)在《奈达论翻译》(1984) 中对翻译的定义是：Translating consists in reproducing in the receptor language the closest natural equivalent of the source-language message，first in terms of meaning and secondly in terms of style. (所谓翻译，是指在译语中用最切近而又自然的对等语再现源语的信息，首先在语义上，其次在文体上。)

英国著名翻译理论家泰特勒(Alexander Fraser Tytler)对翻译的定义为：A good translation is one which the merit of the original work is so completely transfused into another language as to be as distinctly apprehended and as strongly felt by a native of the country to which that language belongs as it is by those who speak the language of the original work.(优秀的翻译应该是把原作的优点完全地移注到另一种语言之中，以使译入语所属国家的本地人能明白地领悟、强烈地感受，如同使用原作语言的人所领悟、所感受的一样。——泰特勒，1790)

法国翻译理论家布朗绍 (Blanchot) 将翻译定义为：翻译是纯粹的差异游戏，翻译总涉及差异，也掩饰差异，同时又偶尔显露差异，甚至经常突出差异。这样翻译本身就是这差异的活命化身。

德国译学教授维尔斯(Wolfram Wilss)在*The Science of Translation*：*Problems & Methods*一书中说：

Translation is not simply a matter of seeking other words with similar meaning，but of finding appropriate ways of saying things in another language. Translating is always meaning-based，i.e. It is the transfer of meaning instead of form from the source language to the target language.(翻译不只是在另一种语言中寻找意义相似的其他词语，而是在另一种语言中

寻找表达事物的适当方式。翻译始终立足于语义，也就是说，是语义从源语到译语的转换，而不是形式。)

这说明了翻译是语义的翻译，不是语言形式的翻译，是运用另一种语言文字的适当方式来表达一种语言所表达的内容，而不是在另一种语言中寻找与一种语言中含义相似的某些词语或结构。翻译必须跳出原文语言层面的束缚，必须着眼于传达原文的内容和意义。

换句话说，翻译的基本单位应该是语篇，而不是词语结构。根据系统功能语言学家的观点，语言的实际使用单位是语篇这样的言语单位，而不是词语结构这样的语法单位。实际使用的语篇有可能是一个句子、一个句段、一个句群，也有可能是一个词语。翻译作为语言交际的一种形式，其实质是用一种语言的语篇材料代替另一种语言与其意义对等的语篇材料。翻译是运用一种语言把另一种语言所表达的内容和意义准确而完整地重新表达出来的语言活动。

文艺学角度的翻译定义：从文艺学的角度解释翻译，认为翻译是艺术创作的一种形式，强调语言的创造功能，讲究译品的艺术效果。所以文学翻译是“传达作者的全部意图即通过艺术手法影响读者的思想、感情”。茅盾将文学翻译定义为：文学的翻译是用另一种语言，把原作的艺术意境传达出来。

语言学对翻译的定义：卡特福德(Catford)认为，翻译是把一种语言(源语)的文本材料替换成另一种语言(目标语)中对等的文本材料；巴尔胡达罗夫(Barhudalov)认为，翻译是把一种语言的言语产物(即话语)在保持内容方面也就是意义不变的情况下改变为另外一种语言的言语产物(区分语言(langue)和言语(parole))；费道罗夫(Federov)：翻译就是用一种语言把另一种语言在内容和形式不可分割的统一中所业已表达出来的东西准确而完全地表达出来。

总的来说，语言学派和信息派强调的是话语的语际转换过程或信息的转换过程。文艺学派强调的是艺术意境的再创造，它的侧重点放在文学的翻译上因而并未顾及非文学作品的翻译。

广义的翻译指语言与语言，语言变体与语言变体，语言与非语言等的代码转换和基本信息的传达。

狭义的翻译是一种语言活动，是把一种语言表达的内容忠实地用另一种语言表达出来。

翻译是用一种语言把另一种语言所表达的内容、形式和风格忠实、流畅、艺术地再现出来的实践活动(言语和思维活动)。

不管如何定义，翻译都要经过原文理解(understanding)、信息转换(transfer)、译文重组/表达(restructuring/expression)、译文检验(testing)。

1.2 翻译的标准

翻译标准就是指翻译实践时，译者所遵循的原则，也是翻译批评家批评译文时必须遵循的原则。翻译标准是翻译活动必须遵循的准绳，是衡量译文质量的尺度，也是翻译工作者应该努力达到的目标。翻译标准是翻译理论的核心问题。但是，翻译界对此还没有完全一致的定论。

1.2.1 国内翻译标准

严复是我国清末时期的著名学者。他在《天演论·译例言》(1898) 中提出了“信达雅”三字标准(faithfulness，expressiveness and elegance)。“信”是指意义不违背本文，“达”是不拘原文形式，尽译文语意之能事以求原意明显。“信”“达”互为照应，不可分割开来。“雅”在今天看来是不可取的，因为这个“雅”是用汉字以前字法句法，即所谓的上等文言文。“信达雅”的翻译标准，在我国翻译史上独具意义，给后代的译界以有益的启发，在翻译界最具影响力、典范性，甚至成了中国人翻译西方语言文字的准绳。

1935年鲁迅在《题未定草》中提出“凡是翻译，必须兼顾两面，一当然力求其易解，一则保存着原作的丰姿”。这就是说，译文既要信又要顺(both faithful to the source Language and smooth in expression)。我国当代翻译理论家张培基等人在其《英汉翻译教程》中所提出的“忠实”“通顺”标准也属此类型。

1951年傅雷在《高老头·重译本序》中提出的“神似”说：“以效果而论，翻译应当像临画一样，所求的不在形似而在神似。”

茅盾喜欢忠实地传达原作的信息内容，忠实地传达原作的内容和风格，译文明白畅达。

1964年钱钟书在《林纾的翻译》一文中提出“化境”说。钱钟书提出：“文学翻译的最高标准是‘化’。把作品从一国文字转变成另一国文字，既不能因语文习惯的差异而露出生硬牵强的痕迹，又能完全保存原有的风味，那就算得入于‘化境’。”(钱钟书，1985：125)

林语堂总结并继承前人的翻译成果，提出了翻译的三大标准：忠实、通顺、美。他认为这不仅是翻译的标准，也是译者应有的责任：“忠实”是译者对原著者的责任，“通顺”是译者对中国读者的责任，“美”是译者对艺术的责任。三样责任心具备，然后可谓具有真正译家的资格。他提出，“忠实”的程度可以大致分为四等，就是“直译”“死译”“意译”“胡译”。

梁实秋提倡译文应在“信”的基础之上做到“顺”，强调“信”与“顺”的统一，即译文既对原文忠实，又通顺可诵。他说：“翻译要忠于原文，如能不但对原文的意思忠实，而且还对‘语气忠实’，这自是最好的翻译。虽能使读者读懂而误译原文，这种翻译是要不得的。既误译原文，而还要令读者‘硬着头皮’去懂，这是太霸道了。”“译者为了忠于原文，行文不免受到限制，因而减少了流畅，这是毋庸讳言的事，不过所谓忠，不是生吞活剥的逐字直译之谓，那种译者乃是‘硬译’‘死译’，意译直译均有分际，不能引为拙劣的翻译的借口。”

瞿秋白主张在翻译中大胆地运用新的表现方式方法，新的字眼，新的句法。

朱光潜提倡“近似”说。朱光潜认为：有些文学作品根本不可翻译，尤其是诗(说诗可翻译的人大概不懂得诗)；大部分文学作品虽可翻译，译文也只能译得与原文近似；绝对的“信”只能是一个理想，事实上很不易做到。在尽量保存原文的意蕴与风格时，译文仍应是读得顺口的中文。以相当的中国语文习惯代替西文语句习惯，而能尽量表达原文的意蕴，这也并无害于“直”。总之，理想的翻译是文从字顺的直译。

刘重德提出了“信达切”的标准：信于内容；达如其分；切合风格。认为：“翻译起来不能一律要‘雅’，应该实事求是，酌情处理，恰如其分，切合原文风格。”他还说：“所谓‘切’，指的就是切合原文风格，理由是原作风格有雅俗之分，人物对话也有雅俗之分，一律雅之，显属不妥。一篇文章或一部文学作品的思想内容，语言表达和风格的特点是一个完整的统一体，而文学翻译也必须是其完整的统一体的如实再现。”

谭载喜提出了翻译的“东张西望”法和译学内容的“瞻前顾后”法。

许渊冲提出了诗歌翻译的“三美”原则：许渊冲提倡文学翻译要做到“意美、音美、形美”(beauty in meaning，beauty in sound and beauty in form)，并在这一理论的指导下译出了举世公认的优秀文学译作。这一翻译原则的共同特点可以说是译文重神似非形似，语言必须美，即许渊冲先生所主张的 “words in best order” “best words in best order”(英国19世纪诗人柯勒律治(Samuel Taylor Coleridge)语)。这里必须指出，美学取向的翻译原则多适合于文学翻译，以此指导翻译实践的确产生了不少精彩的文学译作。但是，该原则对于不少人来说显得过于“高深”和“抽象”，同时也不太适合用来指导非文学作品的翻译实践。

无论是“信达切”“信达贴”“信达化”“神似”“化境”还是“翻译的最高境界是‘化’”“翻译必须重神似而不重形似” 等等，都以期修补、更新、完善我国大翻译家严复提出来的“信、达、雅”的翻译标准，可始终没有哪一种新提法能取而代之。因为“信、达、雅”言简意赅，主次突出，全面系统，完整统一。

“信、达、雅” 这条标准看来简单，真正在实践中很难做到，常会遇到顾此失彼的问题。在这个意义上说，这条标准仍具有相对的意义。就是自己的作品都很难令人满意，更何况是翻译，永远不会十全十美。

要达到完全的“信、达、雅”或“等值(效果)”只能是一种美好的理想或愿望，能达到七八成或八九成之忠实，已是十分不错的了。因为任何一种文字都有其声音之美，有其意义之美，有其传神之美，有其文气文体形式之美，作为翻译者常会顾其义而丢其神，得其神而忘其体，绝不能把义、神、气、体、音之美完全兼顾，同时译出。比如：

She was a striking looking woman，a little short and thick for symmetry，but with a beautiful olive complexion，large dark Italian eyes，and a wealth of deep black hair. (Conan Doyle)

译文：她貌颇美丽，肤色雪白，柔腻如凝脂，双眸点漆，似意大利产。斜波流媚，轻盈动人，而鬈毛压额，厥色深墨，状尤美观。形体略短削，微嫌美中不足。

为此，我们还是主张“忠实、正确、流畅”的翻译标准，尤其是对本科学生来讲，这个标准是切合实际的。

所谓忠实是指忠实于原作的内容，将原作的风格完整而准确地表达出来；

所谓正确，是指把原作的语言内容、立场观点、思想感情未经任何篡改、歪曲、遗漏、增减地表达出来；

所谓流畅，是指译文的语言一定要明白晓畅、通顺自然、逻辑清楚、符合规范。

比如：On one of those sober and rather melancholy days，in the latter part of Autumn，when the shadows of morning and evening almost mingle together，and throw a gloom over the decline of the year，I passed several hours in rambling about Westminster Abbey.

译文：时方晚秋，气象肃穆，略带忧郁，早晨的阴影和黄昏的阴影几乎连在一起，不可分别，岁将云暮，终日昏暗，我就在这么一天，到西敏大寺去散步了几个钟头。

1.2.2 国外翻译标准

以作者和读者为取向的翻译原则(the author-and-reader-oriented translation principle)既考虑到作者又同时考虑到读者，比较全面。十八世纪末英国著名翻译理论家亚历山大·泰特勒(Alexander Fraser Tytler，1747—1814) 在《论翻译的原则》(*Essay on the Principles of Translation*)一书中提出了著名的翻译三原则。

(1) 译文应完全复写出原作的思想(A translation should give a complete transcript of the ideas of the original work)。

(2) 译文的风格和笔调应与原文的性质相同(The style and manner of writing should be of the same character as that of the original)。

(3) 译文应和原作同样流畅(A translation should have all the ease of the original composition)。

在国外的译论中，引证的最多的是等值标准和等效标准。运用语言学成果科学严正地提出等值概念论体系的，是二十世纪下半叶开始的。其代表作有前苏联费道罗夫(Federov)的《翻译概念》，该书研究了等值翻译所运用的语言模式，从传统语言学模式发展到结构主义语言学模式，最后发展到各种模式的综合运用。等值标准不但要求译文与原文思想内容等值，而且要求语言形式上的等值。等效标准所追求的目标是：译文读者能和原文读者同样顺利地获得相同或基本相同的信息，包括原文精神、具体事实、意境风格等。

现代人已经把翻译的标准概括为言简意赅的四个字："忠实，通顺。"忠实指的是忠实于原文。译者必须准确而又完整地把原文的思想及内容表达出来，不可擅自增删或变意，要绝对尊重作者在叙述、说明和描写过程中所反映的思想、观点、立场及个人感情，决不可凭着个人好恶去肆意歪曲，要"保存着原作的丰姿"；通顺指的是译文的语言必须合乎规范、通俗易懂。译者应该使用大众化的现代语言，力求译文朴实、通畅、清新、生动。

1.3 翻译的分类、方法与过程

1.3.1 翻译分类

既然翻译的性质可从不同的角度来定义，那么同样翻译也可从不同的视角来分类。一般说来，翻译可从5种不同的角度来分类。

(1) 从译出语和译入语的角度来分类，翻译可分为本族语译为外语，外语译为本族语。

(2) 从涉及的语言符号来分类，翻译分为语内翻译(intralingual translation)、语际翻译(interlingual translation)和符际翻译(intersemiotic translation)。语内翻译指同一语言内部进行的翻译，如方言与民族共同语，古语与现代语等。语际翻译指发生在不同语言之间的翻译活动，诸如英汉互译、法英互译等。符际翻译指不同符号之间进行的翻译，此类翻译往往只限于通讯及保密等工作。

(3) 从翻译的手段来分类，翻译可分为口译(interpretation—oral interlingual translation)、笔译(translation—written interlingual translation) 和机器翻译(machine translation)。

(4) 按翻译材料来分，有科技材料的翻译、文学作品的翻译(包括小说、诗歌、戏剧等)、政论作品(包括社会科学论文、报告、演说等)的翻译以及其他应用文(包括新闻报道、电报、文件等)的翻译。

(5) 从翻译的处理方式来分类，翻译可分为全译(full translation)、摘译(partial translation)和编译(translation plus editing)。

不同类型的翻译有着不同的要求，学习时应注意它们的共性和个性。

1.3.2 翻译方法

从历代翻译家们对翻译的原则标准的看法和争论中，我们似乎可以得到这样一个结论：翻译活动本身不是目的，它应该遵循某些原则或标准。从有翻译以来，就有对翻译标准的争论。随着时代的发展和翻译实践的不断丰富，今后这种争论仍然在所难免，翻译标准只能在争论中发展。

1 直译和意译

直译和意译是翻译中最常见的问题，也是最主要的两种翻译方法。直译和意译是翻译史上具有代表性、概括性的两种方法，其目的都是为了忠实地表达原作的思想内容，再现原作的艺术效果。由于人们对直译和意译的理解不同，认识不同，理论界有同时肯定这两种翻译方法的，也有肯定其一方、否定另一方的，或者两方都否定的。

1) 直译和意译的历史渊源

直译与意译是中外翻译界长期争论的一个话题。由于人们看待这个问题的角度不同，这场争论至今尚无定论。在中国，最早始于汉朝的佛经翻译就出现了要求直译与要求意译的两种观点。唐代的佛经翻译达到了鼎盛时期，玄奘是这一时期的杰出代表。他的翻译译笔严谨，多用直译，善参意译，世称“新译”，被梁启超等后人称为直译与意译结合的最好典范。严复是中国翻译史上第一个明确提出翻译理论的人。他在《天演论・译例言》中提出了信、达、雅的翻译理论，对后世有着深远的影响。严复早期的译文偏重意译。同一时期，尤为突出的意译派代表则非林纾莫属。林纾本人不懂外文，翻译全靠别人转述，却翻译了英美等国共计1200万字的183种小说。建国后，傅雷的“神似论”及钱钟书的“化境论”是很有代表性的理论，钱钟书的化境论比神似论更进了一步，两人都是意译的支持者。瞿秋白坚决主张直译，鲁迅在这方面有过之而无不及。

与国内翻译界的争论遥相呼应，直译与意译也是西方翻译界论战的焦点。西方早期的评论家圣杰罗姆(St. Jerome)提倡在翻译文学作品时，应采用意译(圣经是个例外，翻译时应以直译为主)。西塞罗(Marcus Tullius Cicero)不赞成字对字、句对句的逐字逐句翻译。1790年，英国的亚历山大・泰特勒(Alexander Fraser Tytler)在《翻译原理简论》中首次提出了同等效果原则，对后世的翻译家产生了深远的影响。他同时提出了三条翻译法则：①译文应该完全地传达原作的思想；②译文的风格和笔调应和原作属于同一性质；③译文应具有原作的流畅性。他在解释第一条法则时指出，完善的翻译方法介乎两个极端之间，一是仅仅顾及原作的意思和精神，而不问原作的表现形式；一是刻板地拘泥于原作句子的安排、次序和构造。这种观点摆脱了狭隘的直译与意译之争，将二者有机地结合起来。18、19世纪，西方出现了许多翻译名家，各抒己见，论调不一。如诺瓦利斯(Novalis)(1798)，歌德(Goethe)(1813，1814)，洪保德(Humboldt)(1816)，尼采(Nietzsche)

(1882)，叔本华(Schopenhauer)(1851) 等都倾向于直译。20世纪上半叶的评论家，如意大利的科罗莱克(Benedetto Crorec)(1922)，西班牙的加塞特(Ortegary Gasett)(1937)，法国的法勒里(Paul-valery)(1941)等人认为翻译要做到不失原著的韵味是不可能的。本杰明(W. Benjamin)则主张译者用词造句都要模仿原著，亦步亦趋。这些评论家有关译作是要外国化还是本国化，要直译还是意译，以形式为主还是以内容为主的争论都是从文学角度出发的。

20世纪下半叶的西方翻译理论研究将翻译问题纳入语言学的研究领域。众多评论家在现代语言学的结构理论、转换生成理论、功能理论、话语理论以及信息理论的影响下，从各个不同的角度，提出新的翻译理论模式。前苏联的费道罗夫(Federov)(1958, 1968) 认为对于人们的经验，既然一种语言能够表达，那么另一种语言一定也能够表达。前苏联的巴尔胡达罗夫在70年代发表了《语言与翻译》一书中，指出“宁愿意译，不要逐词死译”这一原则在使用时不能太绝对化，采用意译时，一定要掌握好分寸。对于不同体裁的原著，可采用不同的译法，如果翻译文艺作品，完全可以采取意译，如果是翻译公文、法律和外交文件，要严格地逐词、逐句翻译，绝不允许意译。关于等值翻译，巴尔胡达罗夫认为，不管是何种类型和体裁的话语，不管采用哪一种译法，只能实现不同程度的等值翻译，即或多或少地接近“完全等值”，完全的等值翻译只能是理想，是不可能实现的。

直译指翻译时要尽量保持原作的语言形式，包括用词、句子结构、比喻方法等，同时要求语言流畅易懂。直译并非一定是“字对字”，一个不多，一个也不少。

意译则从意义出发，只要求将原文大意表达出来，不注意细节，译文自然流畅即可。意译不注重原作形式，包括句法结构、用词、比喻以及其他修辞手段。但意译并不意味着可以将内容随意删改，或添枝加叶。很多人称直译和意译为传统的翻译方法。

“直译”和“意译”作为实际翻译中具体用到的方法，是可以并存的。但如果把他们当中的任何一种奉为翻译的原则，用来统率翻译实践，显然会出现大的问题。

2) 直译和意译在英汉翻译中的应用

每一个民族语言都有它自己的词汇、句法结构和表达方法。当原文的思想内容与译文的表达形式有矛盾，不宜采用直译法处理时，就应采用意译法。当然意译法不是任意乱译。意译要求译文能正确表达原文的内容，但可以不拘泥于原文的形式。例如：

她怕碰一鼻子灰，话到了嘴边，她又把它吞了下去。

如果我们用直译翻译“碰一鼻子灰”，外国人肯定不能理解它的意思。当我们采用直译来保持原作的想象时，我们也可采用意译做适当的补充，这就使译文能清楚地、准确地传达原作的意思。所以，该句可以译为：She was afraid of being snubbed. So she swallowed the words that came to her lips.再例如：

Do you see any green in my eye?

这句如按原文逐词直译为“你从我的眼睛里看到绿颜色吗？”更是不知所云，所以只能意译：你以为我是好欺骗的吗？再看下面的例子：

What do you think of the man?

你怎么看这个人？

You've stolen my question!

你偷了我的问题！(直译)(×)

我正要问你呢！(意译)(√)

She kept her hands clasped on mine a moment longer than was necessary.

她紧握着我的手，比必要的时间长一点。(直译) (×)

她紧握着我的手，没有马上松开。(意译)(√)

An American girl fell in love with her Chinese classmate，but the young man didn't share her feelings.

一个美国女孩爱上了她的中国同学，但是那个年轻人却和她的感觉不一样。(直译)(×)

一个美国女孩爱上了她的中国同学，可惜她只是一厢情愿。(意译)(√)

更多直译与意译的例子如表1-1所示。

表1-1 直译与意译举例

直译与死译	意译与乱译
原文的结构和汉语的结构是一致的，可完全直译。但如果原文结构与汉语不一致，直译就变成了死译。e.g. In some automated plants，electronic computers control the entire production line. 在某些自动化工厂，电子计算机控制整个生产线。(直译) Manganese has the same effect on the strength of steel as silicon. (manganese 锰 silicon 硅) 锰有同样的影响在强度的钢上像硅。(直译但不符合汉语表达方式=死译) 锰像硅一样会影响钢的强度。(√) Some neologisms(新词)： English translated literally into Chinese : knowledge economy 知识经济 peace-keeping operations 维和运动 digital camera 数码相机 world view 世界观 millennium bug 千年虫 Internet worm 网虫 DINKS (Double income，no kids.) 丁克族(双收入，无子女) GNP (Gross National Product) 国民生产总值	意译指在翻译过程中不拘泥于原文的形式，以表达意义为主。意译强调神似，但不能歪曲原文，否则便是乱译。e.g. To kill two birds with one stone. 直译：一石二鸟。 意译：一举两得，一箭双雕。 Translation Practice： And I do not mistrust the future；I do not fear what is ahead. For our problems are large，but our heart is larger. Our challenges are great，but our will is greater. And if our flaws are endless. God's love is truly boundless. Literal translation： 而我不是不相信未来；我不害怕即将来临的事情。因为我们的问题是大的，但我们的心更大。我们的挑战是大的，但我们的决心更大。如果我们的缺点是没完没了的，上帝的爱是真正的无穷无尽的。

(续表)

直译与死译	意译与乱译
Chinese translated literally into English. one country，two systems 一国两制 with tourism paving the way for economic and trading activities 旅游搭台经贸唱戏 network of personal connections 关系网 practise backdoorism 走后门 leading enterprise 龙头企业 residence houses for low-and-medium wage earners 经济适用房 Be all-round in moral，intellectual，physical and aesthetical development 德、智、体、美全面发展 Development is the absolute principle 发展是硬道理 aid the poor 扶贫	Free translation: 我并非不信任未来；我并不害怕我们面临的问题。我们的问题很多，但我们的心胸更宽广。我们面临的挑战很严峻，但我们的决心更大。如果我们的弊病层出不穷的话，那么上帝的爱更是真正的广袤无边

有些英语习语直译过来不能为汉语读者所理解，甚至可能造成误解，但又没有相应的汉语表达可以套用，这时可采用意译法。也就是说舍去原有喻体，将其基本含义和表达色彩呈现给译文读者。例如：

Every life has its roses and thorns.

每个人的生活中都会有苦有甜。

Every tub must stand on its own bottom.

人要自主必须独立。

Love lives in cottages as well as in courts.

爱情不分高低贵贱。

Every dog has his day.

凡人皆有得意时！

几十年来，在我国翻译界一直存在着关于直译法和意译法的争论。事实上，上面已经谈到，直译和意译都只是在一定条件下所能运用的。两种方法都有其限度，超出了限度，过犹不及，直译就会变成令人不解或不可读的死译或硬译；意译就会变成随意发挥或随意伸缩的胡译、乱译，根本不可能产生完美的译品。

不同的语言各有其特点和形式，在词汇、语法、惯用法、表达方式等方面有相同之处，也有相异之处。所以翻译时就必须采取不同的手段，或意译或直译，量体裁衣，灵活处理。直译和意译的最终目的都是为了忠实表达原作的思想内容和文体风格，殊途同归，互不排斥，互不矛盾。译者必须善于把两者结合起来，用两条腿走路，缺一不可。例如：

Ruth was upsetting the other children，so I showed her the door.

鲁斯一直在扰乱别的孩子，我就把她撵了出去。

前一部分是直译，后一部分是意译。如把后者so I showed her the door 直译为“我把她带到门口”或“我把门指引给她看”，都不能确切表达原意。再如：

This was the last straw. I was very young：the prospect of working under a woman constituted the ultimate indignity.

我再也无法忍受了。我当时很年轻，要我在一个女人手下工作，这对我简直是最大的侮辱。

对第一句话“This was the last straw.”的翻译采用的是意译法，后面的部分则用的是直译法。这是典型的直译与意译并用。

有些长句需要直译与意译相结合，综合处理。例如：

But a broader and more generous，certainly more philosophical，view is held by those scientists who claim that the evidence of a war instinct in men is incomplete and misleading，and that man does have within him the power of abolishing war.

这个句子的主句部分可以意译，从句部分可直译。因此译文为：“科学家的观点更开阔，更富有普遍性和哲理性。他们指出，有关人类战争本能的证据尚不完全，而且容易引起误解，事实上，人类自身具有消除战争的能力。”

It was that population that gave to California a name for getting up astonishing enterprises and rushing them through with a magnificent dash and daring and a recklessness of cost or consequences，which she bears unto this day.

这个句子虽长，但结构不复杂，如果进行直译，其译文将十分逊色，如果进行综合处理，译文将有声有色地传达原文的神韵。因此，该句译为：“那里的人们具有大无畏的开创精神，建立庞大的企业，敢冒风险，势如破竹，坚持到底，不顾及成本，因此为加利福尼亚赢得了声誉。”

一般来说，如果直译能够晓畅达意，则应坚持直译，如果直译不能完全达意则要采取一些补偿措施，做一些必要的添加、删除，甚至采用意译手法。在翻译的过程中，我们要学会灵活机动，哪个方法效果好，就采用哪个方法，不可勉为其难。要摆脱不合理的条条框框，最巧妙、最精确地传达原文内容，决不可随意脱离或替换原文的意思。

2 异化和归化

异化和归化可以被视为直译和意译的概念延伸，但又不完全等同于直译和意译。直译和意译主要是局限于语言层面的价值取向，而异化和归化则是立足于文化大语境下的价值取向，两者之间的差异是显而易见的。

1) 异化和归化翻译策略的提出

美国语言学家、翻译理论家尤金·奈达(Eugene A. Nida)曾说过：就真正成功的翻译而言，译者的双文化能力甚至比双语能力更重要。翻译作为一种文化活动，既是特定政治、经济、社会、文化和历史条件下的产物，也是译者主观的选择。译者所持的人生观、价值观、政治理想、文化态度、文化立场在其对翻译文本、翻译策略的选择上都发挥着非常重要的作用。

"归化""异化"翻译策略的提出可追溯到19世纪初。1813年，德国著名的翻译理论家施莱尔马赫(Friedrich Schleiermacher，1813) 在其《论翻译的方法》一文中对"归化""异化"两种翻译途径进行了阐述，但其只是对两个概念进行一般意义上的区分。1995年，美国著名的解构主义翻译理论家韦努蒂 (Laurence Venuti) 在《译者的隐形》一书中提出了"异化法(domestication)"和"归化法(foreignization)"的概念。尤金·奈达(Eugene Nida)是"归化"策略的推崇者，他对西方翻译标准中的"等值观"进行了全面的阐释，并以语言学理论为基础，对"动态对等"进行了论述，最终提出了"功能对等(functional equivalence)"和"读者反映论(reader's response theory)"的观点。韦努蒂(Laurence Venuti)则是"异化"原则的倡导者，他从解构主义视角提出了"异化"翻译观。

"异化"以源语文化为归宿(source culture oriented)，采取对应于作者所使用的源语表达方式，译文保留源语文化的异域性(foreignness)色彩，保留源语与译语的语言文化差异，译者向源语文化读者靠拢。"归化"则是以目标语文化为归宿(target culture orientied)，使译文顺应译语文化的规范和标准，译者向目标语文化读者靠拢。韦努蒂认为，"归化"策略是"采取民族中心主义的态度，使外语文本符合译入语的文化价值观，把原作者带入译入语文化"；"异化"策略则是"对这些文化价值观的一种民族偏离主义的压力，接受外语文本的语言及文化差异，把读者带入外国情景"。由此可见，译者对"归化""异化"翻译策略的选择，体现了自身的文化立场。韦努蒂(Laurence Venuti，1995)认为，如果在将弱势语言文本翻译成强势语言文本的过程中采用"归化"翻译策略，其结果就是弱势语言文本所包含的"异化"成分被扼杀。这样的译文不仅不能体现异族文化的"异"之所在，反而会误导英美读者，使他们陶醉于本族文化之中不能自拔，不利于文化的传播。所以他确信"将'异化'翻译策略应用于外译英过程中将有利于民主的地缘政治关系，成为对抗种族主义、我族中心主义、文化帝国主义和文化自恋情绪的一种方式"。

2) 异化和归化策略在英汉翻译中的应用

在英汉翻译过程中，对于地域差异、民俗文化差异、历史文化差异、语义联想差异等造成的各种文化差异，译者要秉持"异化为主，归化为辅"的原则，尽量使用"异化"策略，对于无法通过"异化"策略进行翻译的则采取"归化"策略处理。

"异化"翻译策略的优势在于可以更好地促进文化交流，为目标语注入新鲜血液，丰富目标语的语言表达，并为目标语读者了解异域文化创造条件。请看下面的例子：

原文：Unless you've an ace up your sleeve，we are dished.

译文：除非你有锦囊妙计，否则我们输定了。

译文从目的语读者角度出发，套用汉语成语“锦囊妙计”，采取目的语读者所习惯的语言表达方式来翻译原文中的“an ace up one’s sleeve”。这一译法在语义层面上似乎达到了“传真”，却掩盖了源语文化与目标语文化之间客观存在的差异，扭曲了原文所传递的文化信息，导致“文化失真”和“文化误读”。英语表达“an ace up one’s sleeve”原意是指在16世纪的西方，人们的衣服没有口袋，赌徒往往把王牌“A”藏在袖子里作弊。“锦囊妙计”一词出自中国四大名著之一的《三国演义》第五十四回，指诸葛亮给刘备的封在“锦囊”中应对东吴的三条妙计。以上两则成语故事有着截然不同的文化背景和内涵，因而引起的语义联想不同。如果硬要套用汉语成语去翻译，势必误导目标语读者，使其误认为西方也有善出“锦囊妙计”的诸葛亮式的人物。鉴于此，这句话最好还是采取“异化”策略进行翻译：除非你袖中藏有王牌，否则我们输定了。

“异化”翻译策略虽然有很多优点，但其运用也会受两个因素的制约：一是译入语语言文化规范的限度，二是译入语读者接受能力的限度。所以在运用异化翻译策略的时候，既要考虑译入语语言文化规范许可的限度，也要考虑译入语读者所能接受的限度，超出限度就会导致译文晦涩难懂。为了避免这种情况的发生，译者需要进行适当的归化处理。

例如，英语表达“go Dutch”带有浓厚的文化色彩。如果运用异化翻译策略将“Let’s go Dutch”译成“让我们去荷兰人那里吧”，读者就会不知所云。我们先了解一下这一表达的由来：16—17世纪的荷兰是海上商品贸易和早期资源共享主义的发迹之地，荷兰商人终日奔波，具有很强的流动性，请客过后也许请客者与被请者再也不会相遇。为了彼此都不吃亏，各自付费便成为最好的选择，于是便衍生出聚时交流信息、散时各自付费的风俗习惯。又因为荷兰人的特点是精明，凡事都要分清楚，因此出现了与“荷兰人(Dutch)”相关的俗语表达：let’s go Dutch，采用异化翻译策略译为“让我们各付各的(或AA制)”。

出于对读者接受能力的考虑，英国翻译家霍克斯(David Hawkes)将《红楼梦》里刘姥姥的话“谋事在人，成事在天”译成了“Man proposes，God disposes”。这样翻译的结果虽然易于读者理解，但却违背了源语宗教背景和深层文化信息。源语中刘姥姥是佛教徒，在译入语中却变成了基督教徒。出于对这一问题的考虑，杨宪益先生在翻译此书时将该句译为“Man proposes，Heaven disposes”。此外，称呼同样也被赋予了文化色彩。在《红楼梦》中，贾府里的小辈常称贾母为“老祖宗”，杨宪益译为“Old Ancestress”，霍克斯(David Hawkes)则译为“Grannie”。“Grannie”自然是英美人惯用的称呼，特点在于亲热。“Old Ancestress”虽不是正式称呼，但含有敬意，属于中国文化色彩。

汉、英民族属于不同的民族，由于地理位置、生活环境、宗教信仰、风俗习惯及思想表达方式不同，对同一事物的看法在许多情况下是不一致的。如果都采用异化翻译策略，就不能把原文所表达的思想准确地反映出来，从而引起译语读者的误解，导致翻译失败。只好牺牲原文的某些文化特色，根据上下文采用归化翻译策略，以保持原文内容的完整性。例如，对于句子“The man is the black sheep of his family”如果采用异化法译成“这个人是家里的黑羊”便会使人莫名其妙，不知所云。因为汉语民族并不了解西方文化中喻体“黑羊”为魔鬼的化身。如果采用归化翻译策略译为“这个人是家里的害群之马”，喻义就一目了然。翻译英美人难以理解的汉语文化时亦如此。例如把“力壮如牛”翻译成“as strong as a cow”，英美人也会感到难以接受，不如译为“as strong as a horse”。

由于文化差异，英汉两种语言中有些词的形象意义不同，但其文化内涵及交际意义是一样或相似的。为了不使译文较原文逊色，在翻译时可运用替换原喻体的方法，采用归化翻译策略。例如：The spirit is willing，but the flesh is weak(心有余而力不足)，如果采用异化策略译成“精神上愿意，肉体上太弱”，不仅形式上有失精练，意思也不明确，采用了归化翻译策略，使得表达非常精练到位；a lion in the way如果采用异化策略译为“拦路狮”，中国读者将会不知所云，如果运用归化策略，用“虎”替换原喻体“狮子”，翻译为“拦路虎”，其喻义会一目了然。

1.3.3 翻译过程

翻译过程是正确理解原文和创造性地用另一种语言再现原文的过程。一位法国译者说过：“翻译就是理解和使人理解。”翻译的过程就是译者理解原文，并把这种理解恰当地传递给读者的过程。它由三个相互关联的环节组成，即理解、表达和校核。在这一部分，我们将详细讨论在这三个环节里可能遇到的一些问题。

1 理解

理解(comprehension)可分为广义理解和狭义理解。广义理解指对原文作者的个人、原文产生的时代背景、作品的内容以及原文读者对该作品的反应。狭义的理解仅指对原作文本的理解。这种理解主要包括语法分析(grammatical analysis)、语义分析(semantic analysis)、语体分析(stylistic analysis)和语篇分析(text analysis)。理解是翻译成功与否的先决条件和重要步骤，务必正确可靠，杜绝谬误。

理解原文是整个翻译过程的第一步。这是最关键，也是最容易出问题的一步。理解是译文这座大厦的地基。地基没打扎实，大厦迟早是要倒塌的。许多译文里含糊不清、语焉不详的地方，正是译者没有透彻理解原文的地方。大部分的翻译错误都起源于译者的理解错误。没有正确的理解，翻译者传达的就不是原作的意思，翻译活动就从根本上失去了意义。

理解原文并不像一些初习翻译的人和读者想象得那么容易。实际翻译中，在最难料到会出理解问题的地方，却偏偏会出问题。

一位中国学者竟把《红楼梦》中“(王熙凤)自幼假充男儿教养，学名叫作王熙凤”一句译成“Who，as a child，disguised herself as a boy in order to go to school”。把贾母向林黛玉介绍王熙凤时说的话“他是我们这里有名的一个泼辣货”译成“She’s one of those notorious gossips here”。

难怪美国中文学者阿基里斯·方(Achillis Fang)在谈到理解原文之难时指出：“所有关于翻译问题的研究都认为这是理所当然的事，即翻译者已经领会原作的语言和思想。然而我们从经验里懂得：领会并非易事，汉语翻译尤其如此。”

普通读者根据其原有知识水平以及阅读的实际目的，对一个文本的理解可深可浅，可多可少。他毕竟可以绕开一些费解之处，而仍能大体明白作者在说什么。译者就没有这种自由。他必须完全弄明白原作的每个细节，弄明白每个字句在上下文里的确切意思。他必须比任何读者都细心周到，而绝不能马马虎虎，不求甚解，这样才能译起来毫不含糊。例如英语中表示夜间的几个词：evening指晚饭后到睡觉前；night指从日落到日出；small hours指凌晨两三点；early hours则指大清早，比small hours要晚一些。再如：

The secretary and accountant of company was present.

公司的秘书和会计在场(×)。→公司的秘书兼会计在场(√)。

我国出版的汉译英教材里，时常把“郊区”(城市外围的农村地区)译成suburb。其实suburb是指an area of the city where people live，是城市外缘带花园的单幢住宅稀疏分布的住宅区(It can be used to describe a farming area)。有农田的城市周围地区是outskirts。西方人询问一个城市的人口时，并不希望这个数字包括城郊(outskirts)村镇的人口。不过有时候，当上下文中缺少必要的确证材料时，反而需要某种程度的“模糊”，这实际上是一种“精确”。例如：

Crown Prince Fahd headed the Saudi delegation.

沙特阿拉伯代表团的团长是王储法赫德(不知是不是国王的儿子，故不译“皇太子”)。

Three cousins of the French President were also to receive diamonds.

法国总统的三位远亲后来也接受了一些钻石。

从性别说，three cousins有三男、三女、两男一女、一男两女4种可能性。从年龄说，有最大、其次、最小三种排列。从血统说，有堂、表两种可能性。因此，总计就有4×3×2=24种可能性。这还没有包括远房堂表兄妹在内。傅雷在《贝姨》译序中说“一表三千里”，可见cousin所指之广。但法文至少还有一个cousine，英文则只有一个cousin，译起来自然又比法文麻烦一层，所以只好译得模糊一点。

为了达到理解的精确，勤查词典是非常必要的。初习翻译者对自己的外语水平往往估计过高，看到一段话中的词语基本都认识，草草看过一遍，便以为已经理解了原文，可以动手翻译了，殊不知自以为认识的某些词语，也只是同它们泛泛之交，只知其常见义而已；它们在眼前这段话里的意思译者并不清楚。译者用自己所熟知的词义去套某个词语时，如果发现上下文意义不清，就应该意识到词语在此处的确切含义自己可能并不知道，必须去查词典，以便找到适合上下文的、意义畅达的译法。

2 表达

表达是理解后能否保证译文成功的又一关键步骤，是理解的深化和体现。在这一过程中，译者要注意恰到好处地再现原文的思想内容和语体色彩，使译文既忠实于原作又符合译入语的语法和表达习惯。要做到这一点，译者就必须在选词用字、组词成句、组句成篇上下工夫，在技巧运用上下工夫。能直译时尽可直译，不能直译时则可考虑意译，灵活运用翻译技巧。例如：

The winds of November were like summer breezes to him，and his face glowed with the pleasant cold. His cheeks were flushed and his eyes glistened；his vitality was intense，shining out upon others with almost a material warmth.

十一月的寒风，对他就像夏天吹拂的凉风一样。舒适的冷空气使他容光焕发，两颊通红，两眼闪光。他生气勃勃，让别人感到是一团炙手的火。(英语material warmth字面意思是“物质的温暖”，这里具体译作“一团炙手的火”，言明意清，让人一看就懂。)

My dear girls，I am ambitious for you，but not to have you make a dash in the world-marry rich men merely because they are rich，or have splendid houses，which are not homes because love is wanting.

亲爱的姑娘们，我对你们期望很高，可并不是叫你们在世上出人头地——要你们去嫁给富人，仅仅因为他们有钱，有奢华的住房。缺少爱情的话，豪华的住房算不得上家。(英语ambitious既可表示“雄心壮志的”意思，也可表示“野心勃勃的”意思，这里选用褒义词“期望很高”翻译比较妥当。)

It was morning，and the new sun sparkled gold across the ripples of gentle sea.

清晨，初升的太阳照着平静的海面，微波荡漾，闪耀着金色的光芒。(英语the ripples of the gentle sea译成汉语时在结构上作了调整，这样译文念起来意思清楚，行文漂亮。)

The sea was wonderfully calm and now it was rich with all the color of the setting sun. In the sky already a solitary star twinkled.大海平静得出奇，晚霞映照得绚丽多彩，天空已有孤星闪烁。(英语原文两句译成汉语合为一句。)

表达时还应注意避免翻译腔、过分表达和欠表达。所谓翻译腔，就是指译文不符合汉语语法和表达习惯，佶屈聱牙，晦涩难懂。例如：

To appease their thirst its readers drank deeper than before，until they were seized with a kind of delirium.

为了解渴，读者比以前越饮越深，直到陷入了昏迷状态。

这个句子的译文死抠原文形式，死抠字典释义，翻译腔严重，让人难以明白其意思，可改译为：读者为了满足自己的渴望，越读越想读，直到进入了如痴如醉的状态。

所谓过分表达，就是指译文画蛇添足，增加了原文没有的东西；而欠表达则是省略或删节原文的内容。翻译时均应避免这类错误。

3 校核

校核是对理解和表达质量的全面检查，是纠正错误、改进译文的极好时机，切不可认为是多余之举。优秀的译者总是十分重视校核的作用，总是利用这一良机来克服自己可能犯下的错误，初学翻译的人就更应该如此了。

1) 校核的目的

(1) 检查译文是否存在失误、遗漏或不妥；

(2) 检查译文是否自然、精确、简练；

(3) 检查理解和表达是否需进一步深化；

(4) 对译文语言做进一步推敲、落实。

2) 校核注意事项

(1) 校核译文在人名、地名、日期、方位、数字等方面有无错漏；

(2) 校对译文的段、句或重要的词有无错漏；

(3) 修改译文中译错的和不妥的句子、词组和词；

(4) 力求译文没有冷僻罕见的词汇或陈腔滥调，力求译文段落、标点符号正确无误；

(5) 通常必须校核两遍。第一遍着重校核内容，第二遍着重润饰文字；如果时间允许，再把已校核两遍的译文对照原文通读一遍，作最后一次检查、修改，务使所有的问题都得到解决，译文才算是定稿。

1.4 中西方翻译史

“语言是人类最大的财富。”语言在荒渺莫考的原始人类的太古时代就产生了，而且不同的民族在劳动中创造了各自不同的语言。因此从一开始，不同的语言便分属于不同的民族。

语际交际基本上与语言的产生是同时发生的。早先的语际交际是原始性的。经过悠悠岁月之后，随着语言的成熟，大约在氏族合并为部落及其后部落合并为部族的时期，语际开始了真正意义的互相接触与交融，并从此开始了语言的分化与统一的过程。只要发生语言的交流，这种交流自始至终一定具有跨民族跨文化交流的性质。

翻译活动应该是与语际交流的发生相伴而生的。不过，早期的翻译活动是相当原始的。真正意义的语际翻译的出现，大约是在原始社会末期及奴隶社会时期。由于生产力的发展，商业及文化交流的需要及连绵不断的部族战争，正式开始了人类早期的翻译活动。中国与西方见诸文字记载的严格意义上的翻译活动均发生在大约公元前二至三世纪，也就是说，人类有史可考的正式译事至少已有两千多年的历史了。

人类的伟大在于其思维能力和对自然规律的不懈探索。实践必然产生理论，而理论的产生也必然是在实践的基础上。人类在开始翻译实践的时候，就开始了对翻译理论的探讨。因此，翻译活动从一开始发生便孕育着译学的诞生。译论的兴衰发展基本上是随着翻译活动的兴衰发展而同步进行的。

1.4.1 中国翻译史

翻译活动在我国可谓源远流长。据史书记载，早在四千多年前的夏朝，我国各部族之间就有了语言的交流。不过当时的翻译活动是以沟通言语为主，即我们现在所谓的口译。我国翻译活动大致经历了四个不同的发展时期，即古代、近代 、现代和当代。

古代——起于先秦时有关翻译的零星论述，至清朝乾隆初年《翻清说》为止。这一时期包括两次翻译高潮，即东汉至宋代的佛经翻译和明清的宗教、科技翻译。

中国的翻译活动可以追溯到春秋战国时期。当时的诸侯国家相互之间交往就出现了翻译，当然这种翻译还谈不上是语际翻译。中国真正称得上语际翻译的活动应该始于西汉的哀帝时期的佛经翻译。西汉哀帝元寿元年(公元前2年)贵霜帝国大月氏王遣使者伊存来中国口授佛经，博士弟子秦景宪协助，得以记录伊存的《浮图经》。从东汉开始到唐宋时期，历经了萌芽、发展再到鼎盛的过程，历时一千多年。笔译佛经始于东汉桓帝建和二年(公元148年)，波斯帝国(伊朗)安清(安世高)来到中国，翻译了30部40卷佛经，其中最著名的是《安般守意经》。他所译的经文变而不滑，质朴而不粗俗，因而被称为直译的鼻祖。此后月氏国(我国古代西部民族名)的娄迦谶(又称支娄迦谶)来中国，译了十多部佛经。支娄迦谶译笔生硬，基本上是字对字、句对句地翻译，中国读者不易看懂。中国翻译界现在的直译和意译之争大概就是从这个时候开始的。他和他的弟子支亮及支亮的弟子支谦号称“三支”。月氏派另有一翻译家叫竺法护，此人共译佛经175部。上述翻译佛经活动为民间译事。

十六国时期，前秦国王苻坚热心提倡佛教，并将其奉为国教。他请释道安来主持，成立了专门的译经机构“译场”。至此，翻译事业成为有组织的活动。

隋代至唐代是我国佛经翻译事业发展的鼎盛时期。

从隋代到唐代，这段时间是我国翻译事业高度发达时期。隋代历史较短，译者和译作都很少。比较有名的翻译家有释彦琮。他是译经史上第一位中国僧人。一生翻译了23部100余卷佛经。唐代到了顶峰，造就了包括古代翻译巨星玄奘在内的一大批著名译者。其中鸠摩罗什、真谛、玄奘一直被视为我国佛学三大翻译家，号称华夏三大翻译家。鸠摩罗什共译了《金刚经》《法华经》等39部，313卷。译著文字优美、畅达，忠实地再现了原著的道理，具有“天然西域之情趣”。鸠摩罗什开了意译的先河，译文妙趣盎然，为我国翻译文学奠定了基础。他还进一步完善了译场，原来的译场只有“口授、传言、笔授”三个环节，他增加了“校对”这一环节。译完作品之后写上译者的名字也是从他开始的。梁启超评价他所译经文为“秦梵两娴，诵写自在，信而后达，达而后雅”。

南北朝时期，应梁武王之聘，一个名叫真谛的印度佛教学者来到中国，译了49部经书，其中尤以《摄大乘论》的翻译，对中国佛教思想有较大影响。

玄奘(玄奘本姓陈，法号“三藏法师”，河南人，因出身贫苦，13岁出家)在唐太宗贞观二年(公元628年)从长安出发去印度取经，经16国、历时4年到达印度。留学印度17年，成为当地最著名的外籍高僧。他曾在印度连续做了18天的道场，从而名震印度。后返回长安，取回佛经六百五十七部，于是便在大慈恩寺内领导几千弟子从事佛经翻译。共译出75部，1335卷经文。他不但把佛经从梵文译成汉文，而且把老子的部分著作译成梵文，成为第一个把汉文著作介绍到国外的中国人。玄奘翻译的特点是直译和意译相结合，他明确地提出翻译的标准“既需求真，又需喻俗”，意思就是译文要“忠实准确，通俗易懂”。50年代有人对照了原文，发现那时就运用了补充法、省略法和假借法等翻译技巧，故玄奘被称为“空前绝后之伟人”。同时玄奘还完善了译场，翻译的职司多至11种：译主(为全场主脑)；证义(译主的助手)；证文(看是否读错)；度语(口译)；笔授(记录下梵文译成汉文)；缀文(整理)；参译(校对)；刊定(去掉重复)；润文(从修辞上加以润饰)；梵呗(对照原文音调，看译文是否朗朗上口)；监护大使(最后审定)。

到了明代万历年间直至清朝“新学”时期，我国出现了以徐光启、林纾、严复等为代表的翻译家，介绍了西欧各国的科学、文学和哲学。

近代——起于鸦片战争止于“五四”运动。“五四”是我国近代翻译史的分水岭。“五四”以前，最显著的表现是以严复、林纾等人为代表，翻译了一系列西方资产阶级学术名著和文学作品。“五四”以后，我国翻译事业开创了一个新的历史时期，开始介绍马列主义经典著作和无产阶级文学作品，翻译的主要内容包括洋务派和维新派人士的理论。

徐光启和意大利人利玛窦合作，翻译了欧几里得的《几何原本》《测量法义》等。

清朝林纾和他的合作者以口述笔译的形式译了一百六十多部文学作品，其中最著名的有《巴黎茶花女遗事》《黑奴吁天录》《块肉余生述》《王子复仇记》等。清末翻译界最重要的代表人物是资产阶级启蒙思想家、翻译家严复，他常借西方著名资产阶级思想家的著作表达自己的思想。

他的贡献不仅在于翻译实践，更重要的是他根据我国古代翻译佛经的经验，结合自己的翻译实践，在《天演论》卷首的《译例言》中提出了“信，达，雅”(faithfulness, expressiveness and elegance)的翻译标准：信——忠实、达——通顺、雅——文采(涉及风格、文体、修辞等)。

现代——从五四运动到1949年新中国成立。“五四”运动以后，中国译坛又陆续涌现出一大批翻译实践和翻译理论大家，其中有很多都是著名的文学家，如鲁迅、胡适、林语堂、茅盾、郭沫若、瞿秋白、朱生豪、朱光潜等。这个时期翻译理论开始受到重视并有了长足的发展。

鲁迅和瞿秋白是“五四”时期翻译界的杰出代表。鲁迅译过许多俄国和前苏联的优秀作品。

鲁迅倾向于直译，他提出了“宁信而不顺”的原则。鲁迅也提出：凡是翻译，必须兼顾着两面，一当然力求其易解，一则保存着原作的丰姿。

当代——从建国后至今。一九四九年，随着新中国的成立，翻译事业也得到了解放。从那时起，在党的领导下，翻译工作一直是社会主义新文化的一个重要组成部分，迅速发展，取得了巨大成绩，在翻译理论方面也日益充实完善。

这一时期具有代表性的翻译理论著作和译作不仅来自老一辈翻译家和文学家，还包括港澳台三地的翻译者。董秋斯发表了《论翻译理论建设》一文后，中国译论开始了有目的地建立体系，进行“转型”。期间傅雷提出“传神”、钱钟书提出“化境”，这又为传统翻译理论增添了光辉的一页。文革期间，翻译工作基本停止。改革开放后，译界长期徘徊于原有的认识水平上。80年代后半期，谭载喜等人“必须建立翻译学”的呼声日益高涨。到了1990年，刘宓庆出版了《现代翻译理论》，译界公认此书为现代翻译理论体系建立的标志，传统译论就此圆满地画上了句号，取而代之的是科学的、成体系的现代翻译理论。

翻译事业进入了新时期。翻译工作成了多方位、多层次的交际媒体。翻译规模、质量进一步提高，题材扩大，形式繁多。口译(含同声传译)和笔译并驾齐驱，并出现了机器翻译。

这一时期的主要代表人物有梁实秋、吕叔湘、张谷若、季羡林、钱钟书、杨绛、刘重德、杨宪益、许渊冲、罗新璋、刘士聪、刘宓庆、谭载喜等。

1.4.2 西方翻译史

1 西方翻译实践史

在西方，翻译实践活动比翻译理论开始得更早。在历史上表现为六次高潮。

第一次翻译活动高潮始于公元前3世纪中叶。罗马文学三大鼻祖之一的安德罗尼柯，于公元前3世纪翻译的拉丁文版《奥德赛》被视为西方翻译史上最早的译作，其后的一些大文学家们也都开始尝试用拉丁语翻译或改写希腊戏剧作品，从而掀起了西方历史上第一次翻译活动高潮。这一阶段的翻译活动将古希腊文学介绍到罗马，促进了罗马文学的诞生和发展。

第二次高潮出现在罗马帝国后期。此时圣·哲罗姆翻译的《通俗拉丁文本圣经》成为定本，标志着《圣经》翻译取得了与世俗文学翻译同等重要的地位。

第三次高潮出现在11—12世纪。此时，西方世界出现了大规模的翻译活动。西方翻译家把大批阿拉伯语作品译成拉丁语，在翻译史上留下了重要的一页。

第四次高潮发生在文艺复兴时代晚期。这时候，除了宗教之外，翻译活动已经深入思想、政治、文化等各个方面，同时也涌现出一批优秀的翻译家和译作。其中英王詹姆士一世1611年命人翻译的英文钦定本《圣经》则标志着英国翻译的一次飞跃。这部译著至今仍被奉为英语语言的经典之作，对英语语言和英国文学的发展产生了巨大的影响。

第五次高潮是在17—20世纪。这一时期的翻译比文艺复兴时期稍为逊色，但仍有大批西方文学名著被翻译出来，此时东方的一些优秀文学作品也开始被译成各国文字。

第六次高潮开始于二战时期，一直延续至今。二战以来，世界经济获得了巨大的发展，科技领域也取得了前所未有的成果，翻译的范围随之大大扩展，科技和商业翻译日趋成熟。各种国内、国际翻译协会和团体的组建，为集中翻译力量多出翻译精品打下坚实的基础。更重要的是，随着计算机的出现，人们对机器翻译的研究也已正式提上议事日程。虽然目前计算机翻译的质量远远不如人工翻译，但其速度却是人类无法比拟的，这无疑对人工翻译提出了严峻的挑战。在未来的世纪里计算机到底能不能代替人脑还是个谜。

2 西方翻译理论史

如果将符号学计算在内，西方翻译理论研究始于公元200年左右的盖伦；若只将有关翻译的论述视为西方译论之始，那么从公元前1世纪的西赛罗就开始了。

——刘宓庆

西方最早的翻译理论家是罗马帝国时期的著名哲学家西赛罗(Cicero)。公元前55年，他首次提出整体意义应重于单个词的意义的观点，并指出了修辞在翻译中的重要作用。

从西赛罗之后，西方翻译界便围绕着相关问题不断地发展完善。公元400年基督教学者圣·哲罗姆(St. Jerome)也曾发表过重要的翻译理论论文，提出了“文学用意译，《圣经》用直译”的观点。1530年马丁·路德(Luther)提出了必须采用民众语言使译文通俗自然的重要观点。文艺复兴时期，但丁提出了“文学不可译”论；多雷提出了所谓的“翻译五原则”，即译者必须理解原作内容，必须通晓两种语言，避免逐字对译，采取通俗形式和讲究译作风格。

17－19世纪，巴托(Charles Batteux)、德莱顿(John Dryden)和泰特勒(Alexander Fraser Tytler)等理论家也先后提出了自己的观点，而其中最著名、对中国和世界译界影响最大的要数泰特勒。1790年，英国的泰特勒(Alexander Fraser Tytler)发表了世界翻译史上影响深远的专著《论翻译的原则》。在这部书中他提出了著名的翻译三原则，即：“译文应完全复写出原作的思想；译文的风格和笔调应与原作相同；译文应和原文同样流畅自然。”他认为好的翻译应该“能够把原作的长处完全地移注到另一种语言中，使译入语国家的人能够清楚地领悟、强烈地感受，就像源语国家的人所领悟和感受的一样”。奈达(Engene A Nida)认为，在某种意义上可以说泰特勒(Alexander Fraser Tytler)的这部著作标志着西方翻译史上一个新时期的开端。

在20世纪里，出现了诸如费道罗夫(Federov)、雅可布逊(Roman Jakobson)、卡特福德(Catford)、奈达(Engene A Nida)、纽马克(Peter Newmark)、穆南(Georges Mounin)、威尔斯(Wells)、斯坦纳(George Steiner)、图里(Gideon Toury)等一大批杰出的理论家和实践家。

50年代我国建国初期，费道罗夫(Federov)的《翻译理论概要》一书传入中国，这部著作从语言学角度对翻译理论进行了分析研究，其核心内容就是“等值论”。

“有两项原则，对于一切翻译工作者来说都是共同的：①翻译的目的是尽量确切地使不懂原文的读者(或听者)了解原作或讲话的内容；②翻译就是用一种语言把另一种语言在内容与形式不可分割的统一中业已表达出来的东西准确而完全地表达出来。”在接下来的论述中，费道罗夫(Federov)讨论了“可译性”和“等值性”问题。他认为“实践本身已经证明可译性原则是现实的”，但同时他又指出了两种使可译性原则受到挑战的情况：“在原文相当明显地违背某一民族全民语言准则而具有该语言的地方特色或狭隘的游民集团用语时，可译性的原则就受到一定的限制。”所谓“确切性”，其核心就是“确切”地传达原文的意思，并且在不违背原文的基础上可以在必要时对译文进行必要的调整。

奈达(Engene A Nida)博士(美)是一位以翻译《圣经》而著称的伟大的翻译实践家。奈达(Engene A Nida)的一个重要贡献是纠正了以往有人认为语言有先进和落后之分的错误观点，从而确立了“可译性”原则。20世纪六七十年代奈达(Engene A Nida)提出了著名的“动态对等”，即“功能对等”理论，强调译文与原文在内容上的一致和形式上的一致必须同时兼顾，但在5种情况(这5种情况是：直译会导致意义上的错误时；引入的外来语形成语义空白，且读者有可能自己填入错误的意义时；形式对等引起严重的意义晦涩时；形式对等引起作者原意所没有的歧义时；形式对等违反译入语的语法或文体规范时)下必须改变形式，优先照顾内容的一致性。

英国著名翻译理论家、英国语言学会会长纽马克(Peter Newmark)的主要观点是“文本中心论”。纽马克(Peter Newmark)把要翻译的对象看成文本，并根据语言的功能把文本分为表达型、信息型和召唤型三大类。表达型包括严肃的文学作品、声明和信件等；信息型包括书籍、报告、论文、备忘录等；召唤型包括各种宣传品、说明书和通俗小说等。他认为不同的文本应该用不同的翻译方法(纽马克(Peter Newmark)把翻译方法分为语义翻译和交际翻译两种。前者强调忠实于原作“原作者”；后者强调忠实于译作“读者”)，不同的评价标准，不同的“等效”要求。

对现、当代西方翻译理论的分类，现在较为流行的一个做法是按翻译研究的基本途径和方法或思想流派的基本特色，将西方译论划分为翻译的文艺学理论、语言学理论、交际学理论、社会符号学理论或翻译的语言学派、翻译科学派、翻译研究派、翻译文化派、翻译目的派、翻译功能派、翻译解构派、多元系统派等。

第2章

英汉语言对比与翻译

吕叔湘先生曾经指出：“只有比较才能看出各种语文表现法的共同之点和特异之点。拿外语跟汉语进行比较，可以启发我们注意被我们忽略了的现象。”

汉语和英语的对比研究，始于100年多前的《马氏文通》，是我国第一部汉语语法书，是在比较和模仿拉丁文法的基础上写成的。

世界上每一种语言都有自己的语法，否则，人们就不能进行翻译实践和翻译理论的研究。而通过分析和对比英汉两种语言，译员必将更加深刻地体会到译事之艰辛。

2.1 英汉语言宏观对比与翻译

2.1.1 综合语与分析语

英汉语言属于不同的语系：

英语属于印欧语系(Indo-European Family，including English，Portuguese，French，German，etc)。

汉语属于汉藏语系(Sino-Tibetan Family，Including Chinese，Siamese，Burmese，etc)。

汉语是世界上最古老语言之一，英语是世界上使用最广的语言之一。

英语是一种拼音(alphabetic)文字，单词有重音、次重音等，句子可以有不同的语调(intonation)；

汉语是一种表意(ideographic)文字，音节有四种声调(tone)变化，语调也很丰富。

1 综合语

所谓综合型语言，是指这种语言主要通过本身的形态变化来表达语法意义。

A synthetic language is characterized by frequent and systematic use of inflected forms to express grammatical relationships.

2 分析语

所谓分析型语言，是指这种语言中的句法关系主要不是通过词本身的形态来表达，而是通过虚词、词序等手段来表示。

An analytic language is characterized by a relatively frequent use of function words(虚词)，auxiliary verbs，and changes in word order to express syntactic relations，rather than of inflected form.

3 形态变化

英语形态变化，即词的形式变化，主要包括构词形态和构形形态。

1) 构词形态

构词形态即：起构词作用的词缀变化(affixation)，包括大量的前缀(prefix)和后缀(suffix)。

英语通过词形变化，改变词性，用这些词灵活组句，可以表达一个几乎相同的意思；汉语则不能。

例如，汉语语句“他前进的速度令人诧异！”在英语中对应表达多达10种：

(1) He moved astonishingly rapidly.

(2) He moved with astonishing rapidity.

(3) His movements were astonishingly rapid.

(4) His rapid movements astonished us.

(5) His movements astonished us by their rapidity.

(6) The rapidity of his movements was astonishing.

(7) The rapidity with which he moved astonished us.

(8) He astonished us by moving rapidly.

(9) He astonished us by his rapid movements.

(10) He astonished us by the rapidity of his movements.

2) 构形形态

构形形态即表达语法意义的词形变化。

英语的动词、助动词和情态动词常常结合起来，运用其形态变化，标示动词的时态、语态和语气。

现代英语的形态变化主要包括动词的变化(conjugation)和名词、代词、形容词及副词的变化，以及上述的词缀变化。

这些变化有：性(gender)、数(number)、格(case)、时(tense)、体(aspect)、语态(voice)、语气(mood)、比较级(degree of comparison)、人称(person)和词性(parts of speech)等。

有了这些变化，一个词可以表达几种语法意义。例如：

I *gave* him a book. 我给他一本书。

He has *given* me two books.他已给我两本书。

His father often *gives* him books.他爸爸常常给他一些书。

4 汉语词性与词序

在汉语中，如果孤零零来看，“学习”“困难”“危险”这些词，很难判断是名词，还是动词，或是形容词。但在下列短语中，我们不难看出其词性：

“政治学习”(the study of politics)；“学习政治”(to study politics)；

“克服困难”(to overcome difficulties)；“困难问题”(a difficult problem)；

“脱离危险”(to get out of danger)；“非常危险”(exceedingly dangerous)。

可见汉语词性往往要通过它在句子中的词序或位置加以判别。可以说词序在汉语里是重要的语法手段。

5 汉语词序与意义

汉语的词序会影响句子的意义，试比较表2-1中的几组句子。

表2-1　句子比较

一吨煤用不了一个月	一个月用不了一吨煤
三天读一本书	一本书读三天
他昨天坐车到郊外	他昨天到郊外坐车
一会儿再说	再说一会儿

6 汉语词尾变化

汉语也有一些词尾变化。如词尾“X子”可以指人：孩子、瞎子、胖子；也可以指物：箱子、刷子、椅子；还可以指时间，日子等。类似的还有“X儿”“X员”“X们”“X者”“X家”“X了”“X着”“X过”等。但汉语词形变化比较少，所以说汉语是以分析型为主的语言。

汉语还被认为是粘着型(agglutinative)语言，词的组合依靠词素的粘着。如光(+明)—光明(+正大)—光明正大；打(+击)—打击—(+犯罪+分子)—打击犯罪分子。

7 英语趋向分析型

现代英语中，名词已失去了若干“性”的形态变化；形容词也失掉了与所修饰的名词之间的性、格、时等方面的一致形式，因此，形容词与名词的搭配就不要求性、数、格方面一致了，如，goldfish(金鱼)，history teacher(历史教员)；同时句子的词序也逐渐地固定下来，与汉语的句子的词序也基本相似：主、谓、宾，如“We drink water.”(我们喝水。)。

其分析型特征也体现在词序和助词(auxiliary)的组句功能上。如：

“He works well.”是正确句子，不能颠倒词序将其变为“Works he well”，但可以改变词序变为“Well he works.”以突出“well”。

又如：“Does he work hard?”一定得将does置于句首成为一般疑问句，若改变词序使其为“He does work hard.”则改变了该句的功能，变为陈述句，强调“work hard”。

所以我们说现代英语是正在不断由综合型语言向分析型语言发展的语言。

综合练习

请翻译以下几个词组与句子，注意英汉语言的综合与分析

1. two cultures taken as a whole

2. two cultures taken as wholes

3. They loved each other and there is no love left between them.

4. In every game, they were bested by the visitors.

5. Few follow the advice of Isabella Beeton, the guru of British cooks in the 19th century, who decreed in an early edition of her book that "a good meal, if enjoyed and digested, gives the support necessary for the morning's work."

参考译文

1. 将两种文化视为一体

2. 将两种文化各自视为一个整体

3. 他们过去是相爱的，但现在已没有什么感情可言了。

4. 每场比赛他们都败在客队的手下。

5. 19世纪英国烹饪大师伊莎贝拉·比顿曾在其著作的一个早期版本里说过："享用一顿美餐，能使整个上午工作精力充沛。"这番高见，现在很少有人领教了。

小结

本节从语言形态学分类讨论汉英两种语义的不同，主要关注的是汉语与英语在表达语法意义时的不同倾向：无论是名词的数、动词的时态、语态，汉语均需用词汇的手段来表达，而英语只需词汇自身的形态变化即可。

汉英翻译即用目的语的形态变化来表示分析型汉语的语法意义。在这一过程中尤其应该注意的是如何选择动词的适当形态表达汉语中某些词汇包含的意义。

2.1.2 形合与意合

英语句法结构重形(hypotaxis)，句中各成分的相互结合常用适当的连接词语，以表示其结构关系。

汉语句法结构重意(parataxis)，句中各成分的相互结合多依靠语义的贯通，语境的映衬，少用或不用连接词语。

汉语与英语对比如表2-2所示。

表2-2 汉语与英语对比

汉语	英语
汉语是表意文字，属分析型语言。因为汉字起源于象形文字，文字的图形表示某种意义，汉语是以意念逻辑排列为主的语言，所以汉语的句法结构重意合。汉语重意合是指句子各成分的相互结合多依靠语义的贯通、语境的映衬和词序的排列，往往不用连接词语，逻辑关系靠语序体现	英语是拼音文字，属综合型语言，二十六个字母是基本的文字表达符号，句子的表达靠符号按一定的语法逻辑关系排列组合，所以说英语是一种重形式逻辑的语言，英语的句法结构重形合。英语重形合是指句中各成分的相互结合常用适当的连接词语，体现其逻辑关系，句子显得严密紧凑
意合法(parataxis)：就是一个复句所包含的分句(并列分句或主从分句)或短语等，顺次排列，分句与分句之间，或短语与短语之间，在意思上有联系，但不用关联词。 意合(形散)强调内容和表意的完整性，常靠语意的逻辑将句子串起，连词介词都少于英语。注重以神统形	形合法(hypotaxis)：就是在分句与分句之间或短语与短语之间，要有关联词把关系明确表达出来。 形合长句多，强调结构的完整性和形态的严谨性，结构严密紧凑，主次分明，依靠代词、介词、连词建立骨架并将句子串起来

试比较以下的英汉句子。

(1) *Even if* I were to be beaten to death，I will not tell.

打死我也不说。(汉译后省略了连接词*Even if*)

(2) Modesty helps one go forward，*whereas* conceit makes one lag behind.

谦虚使人进步，骄傲使人落后。(汉译后省略了连词*whereas*)

(3) We will not attack *unless* we are attacked.

人不犯我，我不犯人。(汉译后省略了连词*unless*)

(4) 拿近点，我好看得清楚。

Bring it nearer *so that* I may see it better. (英译后增补了连接词*so that*)。

(5) 发展体育运动，增强人民体质。

Promote physical culture *and* build up the people’s health. (英译后增补了连接词*and*)

英语中也存在一些意合句子，但主要是古英语或中古英语遗留下来的谚语成语，例如：

Man proposes，God disposes.

No pains，no gains.

Easy come，easy go.

Out of sight，out of mind.

First come，first served.

Like father，like son.

Nothing venture，nothing gain.

英译汉时，往往要先分析句子的结构、形式，才能确定句子的功能、意义；汉译英时，往往要先分析句子的功能、意义，才能确定句子的结构、形式。

综合练习

请翻译以下几个句子，注意英汉语言的形合与意合

1. As the weather was fine，we decided to climb the mountain.

2. My sister was expecting me，so I had to go now.

3. A body in motion remains in motion at a constant speed in a straight line unless acted upon by an external force.

4. We knew spring was coming as we had seen a robin.

5. But if you have special abilities，training，or experience in a certain skill，then you can have reason to be confident in your special ability and know what you're worth，whether it's cooking，farming，painting，financial adviser，or whatever you do well.

6. 中国是一个有五千年文明历史的国家，从历史文化来了解和认识中国，是一个重要的视角。

7. 我常见许多青年的朋友，聪明用功，成绩优异，而语文程度不足以达意，甚至写一封信亦难得通顺，问其故则曰其兴趣不在语文方面。

8.《天净沙·秋思》马致远

枯藤老树昏鸦，
小桥流水人家，
古道西风瘦马，
夕阳西下，
断肠人在天涯。

参考译文

1. 天气很好，我们决定去爬山。

2. 我妹妹在等我，我得走了。

3. 没有外力的作用，运动的物体就连续做匀速直线运动。

4. 我们看见了一只知更鸟，知道春天快要到了。

5. 但是，如果您的确有真本事、训练有素或有一技之长，不论是烹饪、农业种植、画画、金融顾问，还是其他什么你擅长的本事，你都有理由相信自己的特长和价值。

6. China is a country with 5000 years of civilization. Therefore，it is important to approach China from a historical and cultural perspective.

7. I have come across a great many young friends who are bright and diligent and have done exceedingly well in their studies，but are rather weak in Chinese. They can not even write a letter in correct Chinese. When asked why，they said they were not interested in the

Chinese language.

8. Crows hovering over rugged old trees wreathed with rotten vine—the day is about done.

Yonder is a tiny bridge over a sparkling stream, and on the far bank, a pretty little village.

But the traveler has to go on down this ancient road,

the west wind moaning, his bony horse groaning, trudging towards the sinking sun, farther and farther away from home.(翁显良译)

Over old trees wreathed with rotten vines fly evening crows;

Under a small bridge near a cottage a stream flows;

On ancient road in the west wind a lean horse goes.

Westward declines the sun;

Far, far from home is the heartbroken one.(许渊冲译)

小结

汉语重意合，连接成分“尽在不言中”，句群组合讲求流洒铺排，疏放迭进。英语重形合，具有实际意义的形合连接成分一般不能省略，句群组合讲求环环相扣，严密紧凑。因此汉英翻译的过程就是一个从“形散神聚”的源语析出条理，然后用“以形驭意”的目的语使诸般条理各就各位的过程。

2.1.3 主语与主题

中国传统哲学主张“天人合一”“万物与我为一”，反映在语言上就是施事主体可以蕴含在行为事件的主观表现中。正如王力所说：“就句子结构而论，西洋语言是法治的，中国语言是人治的。法治的不管主语用得着用不着，总要呆板地求句子形式的一律，人治的用得着就用，用不着就不用，只要能使人听懂说话人的意思，就算了。”因此在句子构造中，汉语并不把主语看成必要的成分。正因为汉语缺乏主语或主语不明显，语言学家从语言类型学的角度出发，认为汉语是主题显著(topic-prominent)的语言。而英语是“注重主语的语言”(subject-prominent language)。例如：

I worked very hard on this book.

这本书我花了很多心血。

This is the first time in my life that I've experienced the masses voting on rewards for cadres.

群众投票给干部发奖，这是我有生以来经历的第一次。

He isn't interested in things like watching TV, listening to songs, or dancing.

看电视、唱歌、跳舞这类活动他都不感兴趣。

综合练习

请翻译以下句子

1. I would not believe what he said.
2. I did not remember a single point discussed at the meeting.
3. I know Mr. Zhang.
4. He is the best singer of English songs.
5. 他会干这种事我不相信。
6. 桌子上他放了一本书。
7. 昨天的事多亏你帮忙。
8. 他的学识我羡慕，他的为人我鄙视。

参考译文

1. 他的话，我可不信。
2. 会上讲了什么，我一点没记住。
3. 张先生我认识。
4. 唱英文歌，他是最棒的。
5. I don't believe (that) he should have done such things.
6. He put a book on the desk.
7. I own you a lot for your help yesterday.
8. I admire his learning，but I despise his character.

小结

英语的主谓：支配与被支配，具有明确的形式结构特征。汉语的“话题+说明”：陈述与被陈述、说明与被说明，语义上结合的汉语是主题显著(topic-prominent)的语言，建构在意念主轴(thought-pivot)上。英语是主语显著(subject-prominent)的语言。英语句子建构在主谓主轴(subject-predicate-pivot)上，主语和谓语之间存在一种形式上的一致关系。

2.1.4 表态与叙事

如果一个句子里既有叙事的部分，又有表态的部分，汉语的表达习惯往往是叙事在前，表态在后。在英语里则往往相反，表态在前，叙事在后。例如：

We believe that it is right and necessary that people with different political and social systems should live side by side—not just in a passive way but as active friends.

我们认为生活在不同政治制度下的各国人民应该共处，不仅仅是消极共处，而是要积极地友好相处，这是正确而必要的。

The visit gives me the opportunity which I have long sought，to see for myself the achievements of the Chinese people.

这次访问使我有机会亲眼看一看中国人民取得的成就，这是我向往已久的。

I am hearted by the assurance which your Government has repeatedly given that the arrangements for Hong Kong contained in the Agreement are not measures of expediency.

贵国政府一再保证，协议中有关香港的安排不是权宜之计，这种保证使我深受鼓舞。

2.1.5 树状与竹状

西文句中名物字，多随举随释，如中文之旁支，后乃遥接前文，足意成句。

——严复

英语句子“多随举随释”，枝杈蔓生，呈树状结构，分叉处有介词，关系代词连接。而汉语按时间顺序或逻辑顺序逐层展开，节节延伸，犹如竹子。

英语的词组与词组、句子与句子之间结构关系和逻辑联系必须交代得十分清楚。英语的关系词(包括介词、关系代词、关系副词、连接词等)十分丰富，英语正是靠这些关系词的过渡和连接，从形态上来维系句内和句间的各种关系的。因此英语句子结构呈树状，往往有一主干(复合句中的主句或简单句中的某主要成分)，主干上枝蔓横生：句子成分随时可加以修饰，而修饰语中的某成分又可被别的成分修饰。由此往往形成长句。

英语句子，以主语和谓语动词为主干，借助关系词进行空间搭架，把各个子句有机地结合起来，构成葡萄串似的句子，主干可能很短，却硕果累累。

汉语句子，一般是按思维程序的先后顺序，事情发生的前后或逻辑顺序，将内容在说明部分逐项交代出来，犹如竹竿，一节连一节，又如行云流水。

英语：树状，重词形与句法。汉语：竹状，重直觉，强调意识流。

例如：In Africa I met a boy，who was crying as if his heart would break and said，when I spoke to him，that he was hungry because he had had no food for two days.

在非洲，我遇到了一个男孩，他哭得伤心极了，我问他时，他说他饿了，两天没有吃饭了。

It is a curious fact，of which I can think of no satisfactory explanation，that enthusiasm for country life and love of natural scenery are strongest and most widely diffused precisely in those European countries which have the worst climate and where the search for the picturesque involves the greatest discomfort.

这些欧洲国家，天气最为恶劣，那里的人们要费上一番辛苦才能寻到优美的景致。

奇怪，他们恰好最热衷于乡村生活，也最喜爱天然风景，这种情形极为普遍。这是实情，可我怎么也找不出令人满意的解释来。

综合练习

请翻译以下两个句子，特别注意句子的主干和连接部分的翻译

1. The moon is so far from the earth that even if huge trees were growing on the mountains and elephants were walking about, we could not see them through the most powerful telescopes which have been invented.

2. Upon his death in 1826, Jefferson was buried under a stone which described him as he had wished to be remembered as the author of the Declaration on Independence and the Virginia Statute for Religious Freedom and the father of the University of Virginia.

参考译文

1. 月球离地球非常遥远，即使那边山上长着大树，有大象在跑来跑去，我们用已经发明的最高倍率的望远镜也不能看到它们。

2. 1826年杰斐逊逝世。按他生前遗愿，在他墓地的石碑上刻着：独立宣言和弗吉尼亚洲信教自由法令的作者，弗吉尼亚大学创建人之墓。

2.1.6 静态与动态

英语有一种少用(谓语)动词或用其他手段表示动作意义的自然倾向；而汉语则有一种多用动词的固有习惯。英语每个句子中只能使用一个限定式动词(finite verb)，唯一例外形式是并列句动词谓语；而汉语中却存在着连动式和兼语式，以及紧缩句，连动式如“他到了火车站发现火车已经开走了”，紧缩句如“我们下雨也去”，有的句子几乎全句都是动词，如“打得赢就打，打不赢就走，不怕没办法”。

汉语为数不多的介词，大都是从古代汉语动词演变而来的，有些还具备动词的一般特点，兼属于介词和动词两类。“汉语中的绝大多数的介词，应该划归动词的范畴，只是入句时，表现了相当于英语介词的作用。”

由此可见，英语是“静态”的语言，而汉语则是“动态”的语言。“英语的静态修辞实质是名词优势和介词优势，而介词优势又是名词优势的必然结果。因为名词与名词之间要借助介词来联结。”

因此，在英译汉时常常要变“静”为“动”，摆脱名词化的框架和大量介词的干扰，突出原文的动态色彩。例如：

The doctor's extremely quick arrival and uncommonly careful examination of the patient brought about his very speedy recovery.

医生迅速到达，并非常仔细地检查了病人，因此病人很快就康复了。

There is a crying need for a remedy.

现在急需提出新的补救方法。

Two dials got me through to the switchboard.

我拨了两次才接通了总机。

There was a mumbled conversation in the background. Then a man's voice came on the phone.

电话里有人在叽里咕噜地交谈，过了一会，一个男人给了我回话。

综合练习

一、翻译下列标识语

1. Admittance Free
2. Out of Bounds
3. No Admittance Except on Business
4. Danger ahead!

参考译文

1. 免票入场
2. 游客止步
3. 闲人免进
4. 高压(电)，危险！/前方危险！

二、翻译以下几个句子，看怎样变原文的“静”为译文的“动”

1. Party officials worked long hour on meagre food，in old caves，by dim lamps.
2. What film will be on this evening?
3. He walked around the house with a gun.
4. A study of that letter leaves us in no doubt as to the motives behind it.
5. The very first sight of her made him fall in love with her.
6. He is a good eater and a good sleeper.
7. You must be a very bad learner；or else you must be going to a very bad teacher.
8. The computer is a far more careful and industrious inspector than human beings.

参考译文

1. 党的干部吃着粗茶淡饭，住着寒冷的窑洞点着昏暗的油灯，长时间地工作。

2. 今晚放映什么影片?

3. 他拿着枪，绕着屋子走。

4. 研究一下那封信，就使我们毫不怀疑该信是别有用心的。

5. 他对她一见钟情。

6. 他能吃又能睡。

7. 你一定很不善于学习，要不然就是教你的人很不会教。

8. 计算机比人检查得更细心、更勤快。

三、翻译下列句子，看怎样变原文的“动”为译文的“静”

1. 他通晓多种不常使用的外国语，这使我们大家感到惊讶。

2. 我先是诧异，接着是很不安，似乎这话与我有关系。

3. 他想远走高飞，免得心烦。

参考译文

1. His familiarity with many rarely used languages surprised us all.

2. My initial astonishment gave way to a deep uneasiness；I felt that this had something to do with me.

3. He sought the distraction of distance.

小结

汉语动词无形态变化，使用方便，且重于动态描写，所以汉语中动词用得多。在英语句子中，动词受形态变化的约束，通常只有一个谓语动词，把含有一个以上动词的汉语句子译成英语时，应将主要动词译成谓语，其他次要动词用目的语的名词、介词和形容词来传达，使译文更加符合目的语的表达习惯。

2.2　英汉语言微观对比与翻译

2.2.1　英汉词汇对比

吕叔湘先生曾经说过：对于中国学生最有用的帮助是让他们认识英语和汉语的区

别。英语、汉语分属不同的语言系统，它们的词类有一定的共性，也存在很多的差异。

1 英语词汇若干特点

1) 词源不同

例如：临危不惧

brave：源自意大利语

bold：古英语

courageous：古法语

valorous，valiant：源自拉丁语

2) 词义轻重不同

例如表示“打破、破坏”的英语词语：

break：最通用的词语，意思是经打击或施压而破碎。

crack：出现了裂缝，但还没有变成碎片。

crush：从外面用力往内或从上往下压而致碎。

demolish：破坏或铲平(如土堆、建筑物、城堡等)。

destroy：完全摧毁，使之无法复原。

shatter：突然使一物体粉碎。

smash：由于突如其来的一阵暴力带一声响而彻底粉碎。

又如表示“闪光”的词：

shine：照耀，指光的稳定发射。

glitter：闪光、闪烁，指光的不稳定发射。

glare：耀眼，表示光的最强度。

sparkle：闪耀，指发出微细的光度。

3) 词义范围大小和侧重不同

例如agriculture、farming、cultivation、agronomy都表示农业，但4个词语的侧重点不同：

agriculture：指农业科学、农业技术、整个农业生产过程，所包含的范围最广；

farming：指农业的实践；

cultivation：指农作物的栽培过程；

agronomy：农学，指把科学原理运用到农业耕作的实践。

表示“国家”的英语单词：

country：表示国家的地理范畴；

nation：体现在共同的地域和政府下的全民概念；

land：给人以国土或家园之感；

state：指国家的政治实体；

power：表示国家的实力。

4) 形容对象和强调的内容不同

empty：用来修饰 house、room、cup、box、stomach、head、words 等词语，表示空的，一无所有；

vacant：可用来修饰position、room、house、seat等词语，表示没有人占用的，空缺的；

hollow：可与 tree、voice、sound、cheeks 等词连用，表示空洞的，虚的，不实的，下陷的；

blank：可以用来修饰look、mind、page、check等，表示空白的，无表情的，无思想的。

所以汉译英时，“说”这个词在不同上下文中可分别译成：speak、tell、say、express、mention、persuade 等。例如：

他说英语。

He speaks English.

他说谎。

He's telling a lie.

他说他很忙。

He says he is busy.

我说不好。

I'm unable to express.

这可说不得。

It must not be mentioned.

别胡说八道！

Be reasonable!

2 英汉词汇差别

英汉词汇之间有着很大的差别，这种差别首先表现在词义上。英国语言学家杰弗里・利奇(Geoffrey Leech)在他的《语义学》(*Semantics*)(1987) 中把最广义的意义划分为以下7 种不同的类型。

概念意义(外延意义)(denotative meaning)：逻辑的，认知的，或外延的内容联想意义；

内涵意义(connotative meaning)：通过语言所指所传达的意义；

风格意义(stylistic meaning)：所传达的关于语言使用的社会环境的意义；

感情意义(affective meaning)：所传达的关于说话人或作者感情、态度方面的意义；

联想意义(reflective meaning)：通过联想同一表达式的其他意思所传达的意义；

搭配意义(collocative meaning)：通过联想词语的常用搭配而传达的意义；

主题意义(thematic meaning)：通过由顺序和重音组织信息的方式所传达的意义。

1) 英汉词语的意义不对应

(1) 外延意义不对应。

红茶 black tea；红糖 brown sugar；浓汤thick soup(而不是strong soup)；

白酒 spirits/liquor (不是white wine白葡萄酒)；

红眼 pink eye (to be green-eyed) (不是red eye)。

(2) 内涵意义不对应。

只要我们坚持改革开放政策，就一定能把我国建设成为强大的社会主义国家。

[译文] So long as we stick to the reform and opening-up policy，we will be able to turn / transform China into a powerful socialist country.

[分析]初学翻译的人很可能把“把我国建设成为……”译成“to build China into...”，这违背了英语惯用法。

(3) 联想意义不对应。

有一次，译员用英语通知一位外国专家参加一个会议，其中有一句话是“You had better attend the meeting on time.” (您最好及时参加这个会。)英语的语法是毫无问题的。但外国专家听后十分不悦，原来“had better do sth.”只能用于上级对下级，老师对学生，老一辈对下辈，同等地位或年龄的人之间。

(4) 搭配意义不对应。

当前最重要的任务是发展国民经济，提高人民生活水平。

[译文] Our primary task at present is to develop national economy and improve the standards of living.

[分析]“提高人民生活水平”译为“to improve (better) the lives of the people / to improve (uplift) the quality of the lives of the people / to improve the texture of the lives of the people / to improve (raise) standards of living”，都是符合英语惯用法的。如译成“to raise the level of the lives of the people”则成了中国式英语。

(5) 情感意义不对应。

过去我们在对外宣传中，一直把“宣传”译为 “propaganda”(贬义的成分为多，使人易与吹牛、说谎、怀有政治目的等负面含义联系起来)，现在多使用“publicity”等中性词；“精神文明”被译为“ritual civilization”，在外国人的心目中含有宗教色彩，现在改为“ethical and cultural progress”以及其他译法。

2) 英汉词语的语义错位

英汉语之间上义词和下义词之间不对称。如图2-1所示。

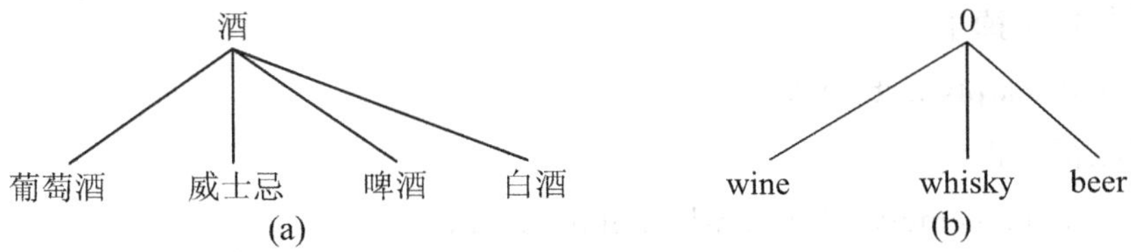

图2-1　英汉词语的语义错位举例

3) 英汉词语语义的宽窄不同

汉语有些词含义较英语宽，如：

山hill，mountain；借lend，borrow；拿 take，bring，fetch；叫 cry，shout，call；笑smile，laugh；鼠mouse，rat；羊 sheep，goat。

英语中有些词含义比汉语宽，如：

wear穿、戴；river 江、河；marriage 娶、嫁；net 网、帐子；gun 枪、炮。

尤以称呼语为典型：

brother 兄弟、同胞、同业、社友、会友；

brother-in-law 姻兄、姻弟、内兄、内弟、姐夫、妹夫、大伯、小叔；

uncle 伯父、叔父、舅父、姑父、姨父；

sister 姐、妹、姑、姨、嫂；

aunt 伯母、大妈、婶娘、叔母、姨母、姑母、舅母、姑妈、阿姨。

4) 英汉词语的搭配能力不同

用名词作定语修饰词，反映了当代英语简约的总趋势，但这类搭配译成汉语时，要作必要的调整，常常需要增补汉语动词。请看下例。

parent ticket **发给**家长的入场券；

shoe habit **穿**鞋的习惯；

wheat farmers **种**小麦的农民；

street sense **在**街上**辨方向**的能力；

life work **为之奋斗**了一生的工作；

smog fighters **清除**烟尘的工作人员；

community gossips **在**邻里间**流传**的风言风语；

age group **按**年龄**划分**的人群。

英语和汉语在词的搭配能力方面有所差异。如英语某些动词的搭配能力很强，以动词“fall”为例，它在不同的语境之下就有多种搭配能力，在译成中文时需要选择不同的词汇，以符合汉语表达习惯，如：

Don’t walk along the top of the wall; you might fall.

别在墙顶上行走，你会**摔**下来的。

The ripe fruit fell from the tree.

熟了的果子从树上**掉**了下来。

Interest rates fell sharply last week.

上周利率**下跌**很厉害。

A prayer was said in memory of those who fell in the war.

举行祷告是为了纪念战争中的**阵亡**将士。

She fell asleep.

她**入**睡了。

The city fell to the enemy.

这座城市**沦陷**了。

Her face fell when I told her the news.

当我告诉她这个消息时，她突然**沉下**脸来。

2.2.2 英汉句法对比

汉语和英语都经历过漫长的发展，都处于高度完善的状态，词汇分类非常相似，语句结构在表面上也大致相同，从表面上看许多英语语言学理论应该适用于汉语语法学的学科建设，特别是汉语语句的解析是完全可以套用英语的句法解析模式的。但事实上却并非如此，汉语语法化不应受英语语言学理论过多的影响，因为汉语与英语相比在构词造句方面具有许多本质上的差异。

1 英汉定语位置对比

汉语里定语的位置一般放在名词之前，即使几个定语连用或使用很长的词组作定语，也都要放在前面。英语里单词作定语时，通常放在名词之前(特殊情况下置于名词之后)，短语和从句作定语时总是放在名词之后。所以，英语是孔雀型语言，末端开放(right-extending，heavy-tailed like a peacock)。汉语是狮子型语言，首端开放(left-extending，heavy-headed like a lion)。

汉语重前饰，句子的语序一般以思维程序展开，而中国人的思维方式多是先考虑事物的环境和外围因素，再考虑具体事物和中心事件。反映到句式上，就是状语总放在谓语或句子主体的前边，定语无论长短，都要置于中心词之前。这样就使得单句的状语部分长，主谓部分短；主语部分长，谓语部分短；修饰成分长，中心词短，整体上形成头大尾小的狮子头形状。

英语重后饰，定语成分除单词外，多数都要置于中心词之后。英语重视末端重量，凡较长的词语及累赘的成分均须后移至句末。有时必须使用形式主语来避免句子的头重脚轻。由此造成句子结构头小尾大，像一只开屏的孔雀。

例如：

我们得到的大部分消息是通过那个渠道获得的。

Most of the information we have got is through that channel.

树

一棵树

一棵大树

一棵枝繁叶茂的大树

花园里一棵枝繁叶茂的大树

李家花园一棵枝繁叶茂的大树

同里镇李家花园一棵枝繁叶茂的大树

对。

不对。

他不对。

我认为他不对。

我告诉过你我认为他不对。

我明明告诉过你我认为他不对。

我开会时明明告诉过你我认为他不对。

我昨天开会时明明告诉过你我认为他不对。

This is the cat.

This is the cat that killed the rat.

This is the cat that killed the rat that ate the malt.

This is the cat that killed the rat that ate the malt that lay in the house.

This is the cat that killed the rat that ate the malt that lay in the house that was built by Jack.

He is reading.

He is reading a book.

He is reading a book written by Mark Twain.

He is reading a book written by Mark Twain in the reading-room.

He is reading a book written by Mark Twain in the reading-room on the second floor of our library.

某些外来语和固定词组中，形容词作定语，常放在所修饰词的后面，例如：

consul general 总领事

secretary general 秘书长
director-general 总干事
president-elect 当选总统
heir apparent 有确定继承权的人
court martial 军事法庭
matters political 政治上的问题
a position unique 独一无二的地位
things foreign 外国事物

2 英汉状语位置对比

如果出现一系列包含时间、地点和方式的状语，汉语的习惯是：时间，地点，方式；英语的语序是：方式，地点，时间。且时间(地点状语)之间的排列：在英语中是由小到大，而在汉语中正好相反。

Ba Jin was born into a big landlord family in Sichuan Province in China，1904.

巴金1904年出生在中国四川省的一个大地主家庭。

The news briefing was held in Room 301 at about nine o'clock yesterday morning.

新闻发布会是昨天上午大约九点在301会议室召开的。

The conference delegates discussed Premier Wen's report animatedly in the meeting room yesterday morning.

会议代表昨天上午在会议室热烈地讨论了温总理的报告。

3 英汉某些固定短语词序对比

冷热hot and cold
左右right and left
水陆land and water
强弱weak and strong
沉浮ups and downs
新旧old and new
悲欢joy and sorrow
贫富rich and poor
好坏bad and good
迟早sooner or later
田径track and field
视听audio-visual

新郎新娘bride and bridegroom

无论晴雨rain or shine

男女老少men and women，young and old

钢铁工业the iron and steel industry

救死扶伤heal the wounded，rescue the dying

来来回回 back and forth

东南西北north，south，east and west

4 英汉句子重心对比

在复合句子中，英语的主句为主要部分，一般放在句首，即重心在前。而汉语则一般按照逻辑和时间顺序，将主要部分放在句尾，形成后重心。例如：

Nothing has happened since we parted.

自我们别后没发生什么事情。

He has to stay at home because he is ill.

他病了只得待在家里。

He cannot be operated upon as he is very weak.

他身体很弱不能动手术。

Tragedies can be written in literature since there is tragedy in life.

生活中既有悲剧，文学作品就可以写悲剧。

The people of a small country can certainly defeat aggression by a big country，if only they dare to rise in struggle，dare to take up arms and grasp in their own hands the destiny of their own country.

小国人民只要敢于起来斗争，敢于拿起武器并掌握自己国家的命运，就一定能打败大国的侵略。

5 英汉语态对比

在英文文章中被动语态用得较多，汉语中被动语态用得少。在汉语中，有不少具有被动的概念可以用主动形式来表达。

Individualized tuition and assessment are carried on to help the students.

继续实施个性化收费和评估以帮助学生。

The happy man cannot be harried.

吉人自有天相。

A new instant Nespray has been put into the market in HongKong.

新配方雀巢即溶奶粉在港上市。

6 英语多代词，汉语多名词

英语为了避免表达上的重复，多用代词；而汉语结构相对松散，句子相对较短，一般不使用太多的代词。

He hated failure; he had conquered it all his life, risen above it, and despised it on others.

他憎恶失败；他一生曾战胜失败，超越失败，并且藐视别人的失败。

There will be television chat shows hosted by robots, and cars with pollution monitors that will disable them when they offend.

届时，将出现由机器人主持的电视访谈节目及装有污染监测器的汽车，一旦这些汽车污染超标，检测器就会使其停止行驶。

7 英语多省略，汉语多补充

英语一方面十分注重句子的结构，另一方面又喜欢使用省略。英语省略的类型有很多：名词的省略，动词的省略，句法方面的省略，情景方面的省略。而汉语往往补充这些省略了的内容。

Ambition is the mother of destruction as well as of evil.

野心不仅是罪恶的根源，同时也是毁灭的根源。

Reading exercises one's eyes; speaking one's tongue; while writing, one's mind.

阅读训练人的眼睛，说话训练人的口齿，写作训练人的思维。

8 英语多长句、从句，汉语多短句、分句

英语句子中只能有一个谓语动词，动词是句子的轴心与核心，然后借用名词来表达。在主干上附加层层修饰成分，成葡萄状，多长句、从句；而汉语多短句，分句。

In the doorway lay at least twelve umbrellas of all sizes and colors.

门口放着一堆雨伞，少说有十二把，五颜六色，大小不一。

Can you answer a question which I want to ask and which is puzzling me?

我有一个问题弄不懂，想请教你，你能回答吗？

由此得出翻译时应注意以下事项。

注意连词，特别是相关的连词，一方面注意逻辑关系，一方面注意翻译时的灵活性。

注意代词，尤其是关系代词，明确它的先行词所指代的部分，分析代词在定语从句中所起的作用。

注意省略部分，因为省略是长句中常见的现象。译者要把省略部分适当补充出来。

注意使用切分法把英语长句切分成短句。

注意语态的转换。

第3章

英汉文化对比与翻译

有一则趣谈：一所国际公寓发生火灾，里面住有犹太人、法国人、美国人和中国人。犹太人急急忙忙先搬出的是他的保险箱，法国人先拖出的是他的情人，美国人则先抱出他的妻子，而中国人先背出的则是他的老母亲。

这一趣谈反映了一个事实：不同的民族有着自己区别于其他民族的特殊的文化心理素质、思维方式、价值尺度、道德规范和情感取向。

3.1 英汉文化对比

3.1.1 文化的定义

文化(拉丁语：cultura；英语：culture；德语：Kultur)是指人类活动的模式以及给予这些模式重要性的符号化结构。

英国著名人类学家爱德华·伯内特·泰(Edward Burnett Tylor，公元1832－1917年)在《原始文化》(1871年，*Primitive Culture*)中这样定义文化："所谓文化和文明乃是包括知识、信仰、艺术、道德、法律、习俗，以及包括作为社会成员的个人而获得的其他任何能力、习惯在内的一种综合体。"

20世纪美国文化学家克鲁伯和克拉克洪(Alfred Kroeber & Clyde Kluckhohn)在《文化：概念和定义的批判性回顾》一书中认为：文化是包括各种外显或内隐的行为模式，通过符号的运用使人们习得并传授，并构成了人类群体的显著成就。文化的基本核心是历史上经过选择的价值体系。文化既是人类活动的产物，又是限制人类进一步活动的因素。

《现代汉语词典》："人类在社会历史发展过程中所创造的物质财富和精神财富的总和，特别指精神财富，如文学、艺术、教育、科学等。"

《中国大百科全书——社会学》："广义的文化是指人类创造的一切物质产品和精神产品的总和。狭义的文化专指语言、文学、艺术及一切意识形态在内的精神产品。"

文化是指人类社会历史实践过程中所创造的物质财富、精神财富和相应的创造才能的总和。文化包括物质文化与精神文化，物质文化是指文化中看得见、摸得着的那部分，因此被称为硬文化。相对来说，精神文化就是软文化，而软文化则是文化的深层结构。美国著名翻译理论家奈达(Engene A Nida)将语言文化特性分为五类：

Ecological Culture 生态文化

Material Culture 物质文化

Social Culture 社会文化

Religious Culture 宗教文化

Linguistic Culture 语言文化

语言是记录人类历史及表达人类生活和思想的工具，每一种语言都有其深远的历史背景和文化内涵。因此，语言是文化的载体，它反映一个民族的特征，语言的发展常常折射文化的变迁。而翻译是在译语中用切近而又最自然的对等语再现原语的信息，它不仅涉及两种语言，而且涉及两种社会文化。翻译是通过语言机制的转换连接或沟通自身文化和异国文化的桥梁，翻译是具有不同语言文化背景的人相互交际、交流思想、达到相互了解的媒介。

3.1.2 中西方文化差异

东西方民族各自具有独特的文化背景和社会心理结构，生产活动方式和发展水平不同，反映在思维、认识方式和风格上就存在着很大的差异。

1 启蒙教育的认知方式不同

西方民族思维方式以逻辑分析为主要特征，而以中国为代表的东方民族思维方式则以直观综合为基本特征。中西方不同的认识方式深深影响了本民族理论思维和科学文化沿着不同的路向前发展。

西方重理性，思辨，中方重经验，直觉。希腊哲学是西方哲学的源头，古希腊对自然有着浓厚的兴趣，他们关心世界本源，主客体关系，事物如何发展变化等。虽然他们在简单仪器下的观察和实践缺乏逻辑连贯性，理性的方式并不系统，但人们的这种直接观察总是弥漫着理性思维的色彩，抽象思辨是西方思维的特征。而作为东方民族典型代表的中国传统思维方式，则以直觉和经验为特征。中国古代科学和哲学的各种概念是靠向内思维得到的，是对各种经验现象进行总结而提出的。与西方向外思维逻辑演绎所得到的不同，中国传统思维的理解只能意会而难以言传，如对中医医理和气功的理解，又如对一幅书法作品、一幅国画的欣赏，只能向内领会，才能领略作品的神韵。

2 中国人注重伦理(ethics)，英美人注重认知(cognition)

儒家思想是对中国社会影响最广泛的思想之一。儒家思想关心的是人道，而非天道，是人生之理，而非自然之性。而在海洋型地理环境中发展起来的英美人对天文地理的浓厚兴趣，使他们形成了探求自然的奥秘、向自然索取的认知传统。

重伦理思想观念的体现之一是重宗族和宗族关系，重辈分尊卑，汉语中亲属称谓特别复杂，英语的亲属称谓比较笼统。如："张明和李丹是表亲。张明的母亲是李丹的姑母，李丹的母亲是张明的舅母。"译为："Zhang Ming and Li Dan are cousins. Zhang Ming's mother is Li Dan's aunt who is the sister of Li Dan's father，while Li Dan's mother is Zhang Ming's aunt who is the wife of Zhang Ming's mother's brother."。语义是清楚的，反

映的关系也清楚，英美人得颇费一番思考才能弄清中国人一看就明白的关系。按英美人的习惯，姑母也好，舅母也好，都称aunt，若要区别，不妨冠以名字。若张明的母亲叫李维明，李丹的母亲叫王明兰，就称Aunt Weiming和Aunt Minglan。但这不符合中国人重宗族关系的习惯。

中国人的伦理精神重视“群己合一”，突出“群体”的人格，倡导集体主义，较轻视个体的人格；而英美人注重个体的人格，倡导个人主义。正因为如此，“个人主义”译为“individualism”是不准确的。因为“个人主义”在汉文化中意为“一切从个人出发，把个人利益放在集体利益之上，只顾自己，不顾别人的错误思想。个人主义是生产资料私有制的产物，是资产阶级世界观的核心，它的表现形式是多方面的，如个人英雄主义、自由主义、本位主义等”。(《现代汉语词典》)而individualism的释义为：①feeling or behaviour of a person who likes to do things his / her own way, regardless of what other people do(不管别人怎样做)只按个人方法行事的感觉或行为；我行我素；②theory that favours free action and complete liberty of belief for each individual person(contrasted with the theory that favours the supremacy of the state个人主义。可以看出“个人主义”在汉语中是贬义词，而individualism在英语中是中性词，其确切意义是“个体主义”。

3 西方的细节分析与中方的整体综合

西方文化结构以细节分析居优，东方文化结构则以整体综合见长。如：在姓氏排列中，中国姓氏先是宗姓、辈分，其次才是自己的名字，突出的是氏族整体。西方国家则先是自己的名字，再是父名，然后才是族姓，突出的是自己。又如：在时间、地址的书写表达顺序上，中国人习惯以年、月、日，从大到小依次为序，地址则是按省、市、县到门牌号码排序，突出的是从整体到个别的析出关系，西方人则与中国人的顺序表达恰好相反，突出的是个别到整体的合成关系。可见在中华民族的精神文化和意识结构中，从整体出发的综合观占突出地位，而这种整体综合观在考察事物时，通常忽略细节和成分分析，往往提供的是关于对象模糊整体的图景。

4 中西方价值观与人生追求的不同

中西方价值观与人生追求的不同表现在社会生活的各个层面。

(1) 中西方人生价值取向不同。儒家给中国人提供的价值观念，在封建专制制度的支持下，逐步转变为一种根深蒂固的人生信念。作为2000余年来中国文化精神支柱的这种人生信念，认为人生的价值就是在现世的作为之中，一个人在社会越有作为，他的生命就越有意义。在专制社会中权力就是一切，因此，人的作为最大者莫过于实现从政的抱负。齐家治国平天下的宏伟理想主导着千百万中国文人的一生。受这种一元化的人生价值观的影响，多数人不愿研究自然科学，致使科学被困于萌芽状态。另外，人的智慧才能都集中到了政治权术上，创造了一个世界上独一无二的变幻莫测而实质又超稳固的政治、文化模式。在这种特殊的模式中，产生了中国独有的历史现象：当官不成，求当圣人；报国不得则退做隐士，或吟诗饮酒自得其乐，于是道教、佛教随之兴起。贪生的自去修道，厌世的不妨念佛。而西方文化中人生价值观呈多元化，从政也是人生价值的实现，经商也被认为相当有价值。西方人眼中最好的职业莫过于律师、医生。

(2) 西方的个人本位和中国的家族本位。近代西方人文主义是在神学背景上产生的，原罪观念在西方根深蒂固。因此，西方人的道德指向是个人对自己负责，通过个人奋斗向上帝赎罪，由此引申出一条基督教义，即“上帝面前人人平等”。当上帝被否定了时西方又产生了社会原子观念：个人就是原子，不依靠任何人而存在，个人权利任何人不得侵犯，信奉个人本位，自我中心。这种个人本位的思想影响了生活的各个方面，亲人间界线划分明确，老少聚餐，各自付款，对孩子也非常尊重，进孩子房间首先要问：“我能进来吗？”以子女脱离父母独立生活奋斗为荣，乐于谈论个人一己之见。而中国以家族为本位。家在中国人心目中是生活的宇宙，是一个生活的港湾，具有至高无上的凝结力。脱离家便是“游子”，强调“父母在，不远游”。家庭中有长幼关系，夫妻关系，要各安其分，各尽义务，即“尽伦”！孟子认为：圣人是“人伦之民”，伦的核心是“绝对服从”，幼服长，妻服夫。使家变得如此重要的原因之一就是“孝”，“百善孝为先”，“孝道”是中国的国本，国粹，中国自古就有孝的文化，有以孝治天下之说。家与孝原本有伟大的理性意义，但由于过分强调，终成了一种过分的家族意识，而忽略了个人自由的发展，“存天理，灭人欲”，以个人向群体负责为人生宗旨。

(3) 西方讲功利，时效，中方讲伦理，道德。西方文化由于自然科学的发展，因此比较重功利和实效，善于算经济账。例如：在一个大公司，如果每人节约几秒，加起来可节约几个人的时间，可少雇几个职员，减少多少开支。又如：一个人在写字，圆珠笔的笔尖向外放还是向内放比较节约拿笔写字的时间，怎么放的状态最有效等。中国文化由于长期处于封建的农业社会，自然科学不发达，着重于人伦关系的调节。礼义规范高于一切，“义”“利”之辩的结果使价值观念产生偏差，提倡人为了符合某种礼义规范应该牺牲自己的利益，“重义轻利”被视为高风亮节，品格高尚。

3.2 英汉文化差异对翻译的影响

翻译活动自产生开始，便与各民族之间的文化交流结合在了一起。就其具体操作形式而言，翻译活动被视为不同语言之间的转换活动，而就其实质而言，翻译又被理解为一项跨文化交流活动。王佐良先生曾经说过："翻译的最大困难是两种文化的不同。"因此，解决好翻译中文化差异的问题是保证译作成功的关键。

3.2.1 英汉文化差异导致词汇空缺现象

词汇空缺是指原语词汇所载的文化信息在译语中没有其"对等语"或"对应语"。有些词在一种语言里存在，而在另一种语言里没有对等的词。目前存在以下三种词汇空缺的定义：一指各自文化中特有的词汇；二指源语中存在某种为异族文化所不明白、莫名其妙的、易于误解的东西，造成异族文化的空白；三指负有特殊文化色彩的词和表达方式。语言之间的词汇空缺是一种自然现象，存在两种情况：一种是物质生活方面的词汇空缺，另一种是文化方面的词汇空缺。前者指一个民族物质生活中表示特有事物的词语在异族语言中没有与其概念相同的对应语，但进入异族生活后通过音译、意译等手段在异族语言中找到对等语，成为该语言的借词。我们知道语言常常是客观世界的反映，是一种社会现象。人们生活在什么样的环境里，就会产生什么样的语言。如果某一事物在人们所生活的客观环境中不存在，那么语言就可能出现空缺。例如，"salad"这种凉拌菜源于法国，英国原先没有这道菜，语言中也不存在这个词，因此只好从法语中原封不动地"移植"过来，中国人通过将其音译为"沙拉"引入汉语词汇中。再如，英语从汉语中借去了ginseng、mahjong、kowtow等词；汉语又从英语中借来了俱乐部、坦克、维他命、咖啡、因特网、模特儿、沙发等词语。文化方面的词汇空缺主要是指某些具有民族文化色彩的词语或语义无法在另一种民族的语言中找到对应的表达。中国是重视人际关系和亲属关系的国家，表示亲属关系的词大约有33个，比英美国家多很多。很多词无法在英语中找到对应的表达。

汉民族自古以来价值观的核心是天人合一，强调人与自然的和谐，在人与人的关系上重集体主义，轻个人主义。而以英美为代表的西方强调自由，平等。语言是文化的载体。美国不同阶段的经济文化变化都反映在语言中。随着时代变化，新的词语不断应运而生。继一次大战后的"迷惘的一代"(Lost Generation)和二次大战后的"垮掉的一代"(Beat Generation)，又出现了"Baby Boomers""Yuppies""Dinks""Sandwich Generation""Couch Potato""Mall Rats"等等。

英语中"American Dream""Aunt Jemima""Yuppies"等这些文化空缺词汇在汉语中都没有一一对应的汉语词汇。Yuppies(雅皮士)，属于中上阶层的年轻专业人士(young urban professionals)。在第二次世界大战期间，美国大约有一千三百万人服役，其中许多人都没有结婚。在战后，他们纷纷组建家庭，生儿育女，因此在1946年至1964年这18年间，美国人口急剧增长，新生儿的人数共有七千八百万。不久美国人就称这一代为"Baby Boomers"。这些"Baby Boomers"一改其父母对战争的"狂热"，对生活采取务实的态度。他们要弥补战争给父母所造成的损失，他们勤奋工作，少生孩子。他们中的许多人都获得了成功，他们有抱负，受过高等教育，生活在城市，有专业性的工作，收入颇丰，生活很富裕。美国又将这些成功者命名为“Yuppies”，前三个字母是“young urban professionals”缩略。对“Yuppies”中那些不要孩子的人，美国人又将他们称为“Dinks”，它是“Double Income，No Kids”的缩写。其实，“Baby Boomers”并不都是富有的“Yuppies”，有的夫妇不仅有孩子而且有老人要抚养，这样另一个名字又产生了，那便是“Sandwich Generation” (三明治世代)——同时扶养与照顾父母和子女的人，意味着这些人像三明治中的肉一样夹在老人和孩子之间，负担很重。美国的电视业发展迅速，几乎所有人都能看到有线电视节目，家庭影剧院的出现更是让许多人沉迷于电视，这种一有时间就坐在沙发上看电视的人被称为“Couch Potato”，所以又称为“电视迷”。它不禁使人们想到悠然坐在沙发里一声不吭，一动不动，像土豆似的人。随着商业的发展繁荣，大的购物中心(shopping mall)不断涌现。逛购物中心成了一种乐趣，尤其是年轻人，他们即使不购物也在中心钻来钻去，像老鼠一样，美国人将他们戏称为“Mall Rats”(购物狂)。

产生于美国60年代的“Hippie”，由于它是美国文化的独特产物，在汉语中无法找到与之相对等的词语，曾音译为“希比士”或“希比派”，现定译为“嬉皮士”。这个译名虽然比前两个译名要好些，但仍然无法确切表达Hippie的词义内涵，且有可能造成误解。Hippie指的是美国社会中一类特殊的人群，他们虽然对当时的社会现实不满，生活方式与众不同，头蓄披肩长发，身着奇装异服，沉迷于酗酒吸毒，但他们并非都是“嬉皮笑脸”之人，其中不少对社会问题持有严肃的态度。

还有一些民族文化内涵特别丰富的词语，在翻译时也必须采用释义或注释等方法，说明该词的语用含义，才能使译语读者了解原语独特的文化现象。如：钱先生周岁时“抓周”，抓了一本书，因此得名“钟书”。(舒展文，《钱钟书与杨绛》)When Qian was just one year old，he was told by his parents to choose one thing among many others. He picked up a book of all things. Thereupon， his father very gladly gave him the name: Zhongshu(= book lover)。“抓周”是古时风俗，小儿周岁时陈列各种玩物和生活用具，任他抓取，来预测他的志向和兴趣，也近似占卜他的命运。这是中国人独有的民风习俗，蕴含着“生死在天，富贵由命”的儒家中庸思想观念。在西方根本无此风俗，因此英语中也无与“抓周”相对应的词语。翻译时只能采用释义的方法，用一个长句来解释汉语“抓周”的语用含义，以使英语读者能理解“抓周”的文化内涵。

世界各族虽处于大体相同的生存环境中，却往往有自己独特的社会生活状况，有自己独特的人情风俗，这也导致了巨大的文化空缺。中国人把娶媳妇、贺生日称为“红喜”，把老人过世称为“白喜”。对于没有接触过我国文化的欧美人来说，把娶媳妇说成“红喜”并不费解，英语就把喜庆日称为“Red-letter day”。但把上年纪人的去世也当成一大“喜事”，这就令他们奇怪了。因此，与欧美文化相比把死人称作“白喜”是我国文化的个性。

缔结婚姻，中国人希望是“门当户对”“郎才女貌”，英语中则有“marriage of true minds (真诚的结合)”。结婚时，中国人要选择“良辰吉日”，再“拜天地”，“进入洞房”。英美人则来到教堂，举行“a white wedding”，再去度“honey moon(蜜月)”。文化空缺是一种客观存在的事实，这是由两种文化的特性所决定的。本民族语交际的双方以为是不言而喻的文化信息，对于另一语言文化的读者来说则往往会不知所云，文化空缺的存在为翻译带来了困难，使文化内涵词的翻译更加充满挑战。

汉语中的某些文化内涵词在英语中找不到对应词，即属于完全空缺现象的，宜采用音译或音译加注方法。例如：

功夫：kongfu

叩头：kowtow

炕：kang

太极：Taichi

风水：fengshui

围棋：weiqi

饺子：jiaozi

粽子：zongzi

在中国历史进程和社会发展中，特别是改革开放以来特有的事物宜通过借译或语义再生译成中国英语。如：

纸老虎：paper tiger

八股文：eight legged essay

毛泽东思想：Mao Tsetung Thought

四个现代化：four modernizations

思想改造：ideological remolding

改革开放：reform and opening up

一国两制：one country，two systems

源自中国古代文学、哲学思想或佛教文化的特有的事物也宜通过借译或语义再生译成中国英语。如：

儒释道：Confucianism，Buddhism，Taoism

三纲五常：three cardinals and five permanent virtues

四书五经：the Four Books and the Five Classics

论语：the Analects

易经：the Book of Changes

3.2.2 英汉文化差异导致语义联想差异

朱光潜先生曾在其著作《谈文学》中的《谈翻译》一文中提到：英语中的fire、sea、Roland、castle、rose在英汉两个民族中所引起的联想有很大区别。它们对于英国人意义较为丰富。同理，中文中“风”“月”“江”“湖”“梅”“菊”“燕”“碑”“笛”“僧”“隐逸”“礼”“阴阳”之类字词，对于我们中国人所引起的联想和情趣也绝不是西方人所能完全了解的。

作为人类认识世界的重要领域之一，色彩不但被赋予了物理属性，同时也反映出各民族独特的文化特征，因此成为语言文化及翻译领域很重要的研究课题。地理环境、宗教信仰、风俗习惯、民族心理、思维方式等方面的差异导致各民族对各种颜色所产生的联想意义也不尽相同。比利时人最忌蓝色，认为蓝色是不吉利的凶兆；土耳其人绝对禁止用花色物品布置房间和客厅，他们认为花色是凶兆；日本人忌绿色，而印度人却喜爱绿色。“yellow”在英语中除了是一个表示颜色的名词外，在美国俚语中含有胆小卑怯之意，如a yellow dog(卑鄙的人)，a yellow livered(胆小鬼)。而在汉语中，黄色在封建社会中是法定的尊色，有崇高、尊严、辉煌的意思，如“黄袍”“黄屋”“黄榜”等。现代汉语中，黄色又被赋予了不同的文化内涵，有“失败”(如“买卖黄了”)和“污秽”“下流”(如“黄色书刊”“扫黄打非”)的意思。例如，在翻译中国四大名著之一《红楼梦》时，英国翻译家霍克思(David Hawkes)认为对汉语民族而言，红色表示喜庆、吉祥、幸福，但在讲英语国家人的心目中，红色意味着流血、暴力或危险，而金黄色和绿色则与汉语中的红色具有类似的联想意义。因此，他在翻译涉及红色的词语时做了一定的变通处理。在进行英汉汉英互译时，有时可以完全对应，有时却大相径庭。例如：

红旗：red flag

红糖：brown sugar

红茶：black tea

红榜：honor roll

红豆：love pea

在英汉两种语言中有很多动物名词字面意义一样，但其联想意义有很大差别。如英汉两个民族对于“龙”的联想迥然不同。中华民族受图腾文化的影响，对“龙”“凤”非现实动物倍加尊崇，赋予“龙”高贵、尊严的内涵，代表皇权、吉祥等积极意义；把“凤”比喻成美好、才智的象征。古代帝王被尊为“真龙天子”，穿的是“龙袍”，我们自己是“龙的传人”。人们用“龙凤呈祥”“夫龙妻凤”来祝福一对新人。“龙”是中华民族的象征。而在西方文化中“龙”被看作凶恶狠毒的象征，是能喷烟吐火的怪物。《圣经》中把与上帝作对的恶魔撒旦称为“the great dragon”。一些圣徒如圣麦克尔、圣乔治等都因杀死“dragon”而被视为英雄。因此把“亚洲四小龙”译为“Four Asian Dragons”就不妥。若译为“Four Asian Tigers”，就不失为一种较好的文化信息的对等，因为“tiger”(老虎)在西方人心中是一种较强悍的动物，至少不会使人联想到某种可怕的动物。另一种情况就是对于同一种概念或理念，汉英民族用不同的动物作比。例如比喻一个人力气大，汉语的表达为“力大如牛”，英语则是“as strong as a horse”(力大如马)，原因在于中国农业自古以来以牛耕为主，英国古代主要靠马耕。还有很多联想意义不同的词语，例如：

月亮(团圆)——moon(虚幻)

牧童(悠闲)——cowboy(冒险)

农民(忠厚朴实)——peasant(心胸狭窄)

狗(鄙视)——dog(同情)

龙(高贵)——dragon(凶恶)

3.2.3 英汉文化差异导致语义错位

语义学中词语的上下义关系理论既涉及词汇的同义现象，也涉及词义的多义现象和蕴含性。语义错位是指两种语言的上义词和下义词之间不对称。语义错位有时是和文化密切相关的。如果某一社会对某类事物非常重视，或者某类事物对于该文化社会来说非常重要，在这种文化的语言中往往会产生许多下义词来描述该事物。例如，汉语中的“酒”包括葡萄酒、白酒、啤酒等，那么“酒”就是上义词，葡萄酒、啤酒、白酒就构成了“酒”的下义词。而在英语中存在葡萄酒(wine)、啤酒(beer)、威士忌(whisky)这样的下义词，却没有与“酒”对应的上义词。于是在翻译“酒文化”这样的词语时就会遇到麻烦。同样，英语中有许多与汉语中“杯子”对应的下义词，例如glass(玻璃杯)、cup(茶杯)、goblet(高脚杯)等，但却找不到与汉语中“杯子”对应的上义词。因此，要翻译“去买个杯子！”这样十分简单的句子，必须要首先弄清句子中的“杯子”到底指哪种杯子，是“glass”还是“cup”，抑或“goblet”。

3.2.4 英汉文化差异导致语用含义差异

在中国，对别人的健康状况表示关心是有教养、有礼貌的表现。但对西方人的健康表示关心，就不能按中国的传统方式了。一个中国学生得知其美籍教师生病后，会关切地说“you should go to see a doctor !(你应该到医院看看)”。不料，这句体贴的话反而使这位教师很不高兴。因为在这位教师看来，有病看医生这种简单的事情连小孩都知道，用不着任何人来指教。如果就某种小事给人以忠告，那显然是对其能力的怀疑，从而大大伤害其自尊心。

中国人在饭桌上的热情好客经常被西方人误解为不文明的行为。因西方人认为：客人吃多吃少完全由自己决定，用不着主人为他加菜添酒；而且饮食过量是极不体面的事情，因此客人吃饭后，主人不必劝他再吃。一位美国客人看到中国主人不断地给他夹菜很不安，事后他抱怨说"主人把我当猪一样看待"。

中国人路遇熟人时，往往会无所顾忌地说："啊呀，老兄，你近来又发福了！"或者以关切的口吻说："老兄，你又瘦了，要注意身体啊！"而西方人若听你说"you are fat"或"you are so thin"，即使比较熟悉，也会感到尴尬和难以回答。

西方人崇拜个人奋斗，尤其为个人取得的成就自豪，从来不掩饰自己的自信心、荣誉感以及在获得成就后的狂喜。相反，中国文化不主张炫耀个人荣誉，而是提倡谦虚。中国人反对王婆卖瓜式的自吹自擂，然而中国式的自我谦虚或自我否定却常常使西方人大为不满。"Your English is very good." "No，no，my English is very poor"；"you've done a very good job." "No，I don't think so. It's the result of joint efforts."这种谦虚，在西方人看来，不仅否定了自己，还否定了赞扬者的鉴赏力。这种中国式的谦虚在资本主义的竞争市场是行不通的。

我国早有"民以食为天"这一思想，因而吃饭问题也就成了人们经常挂在口头的话题。中国人路遇熟人总爱寒暄道："吃饭了吗？""吃过了吗？"河南农民在村头田边远远看见路过的陌生人爱说"吸烟吧？""喝茶吧？"之类的话。在多数情况下人们并不是十分关心别人是不是吃饭了或喝不喝茶，而只是一种招呼罢了。中国人听到这些问话也只是回答说"吃了"或"不啦，不啦"，实际上是个应酬，表示谢谢问话人的关心或热情。在我们看来这是一种有礼貌的打招呼用语，而若你跟西方人这样打招呼"Have you had your meal？"他们心理上首先的反应是"Yes，I have." "No，I haven't."或"Do you mean to invite me to dinner?"他们会认为你想请他吃饭或者干涉其私事，会引起误解。而汉语中习惯讲的这些打招呼用语亦不能翻译成英语的招呼用语。像汉语中这样的招呼语应视情况译成"Hello!" "How do you do!" "Nice day，isn't it?"等。

对于"饭桶""吃不开""吃不了兜着走""吃不消""吃不住""吃老本""吃软不吃硬""吃闲饭"和"吃香"等一系列汉语表达只好分别翻译成"good-for-nothing" "be unpopular" "land oneself in serious trouble" "more than one can stand，too much" "be unable to bear or support" "live off one's past gains" "be open to persuasion，but not to coercion" "lead an idle life" "be very popular"等才能基本如实传达原文的含义，尽管没有一条译文用"eat"一词。

对于别人的赞扬，中国人通常表示谦虚，并有一套谦虚之词，像"惭愧""哪里""寒舍""拙文"等。而西方人总是高兴地回答"Thank you"以表接受。或译成"Thanks for saying so. I'm flattered."。

中国人送客人时，主人与客人常说：“慢走！”“小心点！”“再见，走好啊！”“你们进去吧！”“请留步”等。而西方人只说：“Bye Bye!”“See you later!”“See you next time!”，所以我们翻译的时候一般用“Take care!”或“Mind your step!”。

3.2.5 英汉文化差异对商标翻译的影响

西方人习惯以姓氏给公司命名，像爱迪生公司、迪士尼公司、福特公司，威尔逊公司等。但是华人通常喜欢以喜庆、吉祥的词汇给公司命名，如“百盛”“嘉禾”“东来顺”“全聚德”“醉美”“九美斋”等。那么国外品牌进入中国市场就要仔细考虑这些因素，“家乐福(carrefour)”就是很成功的译例。中国人向往福、禄、喜、寿，追求家庭和睦，希望事业发达，长盛不衰。家乐福这样的名字很是符合中国人的口味。就连到美国的语言考试也取名为“托福”来博取国人的认同。

由于受东西方文化传统、宗教信仰、语言崇拜、地理环境等方面的影响，数字的神化存在着东西方的差异。如我国有“666”“999”“金六福”“三元”“十三香”等这些数字用作商标的商品，近年来生产的上海“三枪”名牌内衣，英文译名为“Three Guns”。这一产品若销往日本、哥伦比亚和北非地区，定会倍受欢迎，因为three 这个数字在这些地区代表“积极”意义。但若要销往乍得、贝宁、博茨瓦纳等地，则应更换译名。因为在乍得，奇数被视为具有“消极”意义；在贝宁，“3”则有“巫术”的含义。要把“666”“十三香”这样的商品出口到英美就会遇到麻烦，因为“six”象征魔鬼。thirteen是不吉利的数字，因为忌讳，西方人千方百计避免和“13”接触。在荷兰，人们很难找到13号楼和13号的门牌。他们用“12A”取代了13号。在英国的剧场，你找不到13排和13座。法国人聪明，剧场的12排和14排之间通常是人行通道。此外，人们还忌讳13日出游，更忌讳13人同席就餐，13道菜更是不能接受了。在日语中，“4”和“死”读音相同，“14”与“重死”同音，“24”与“二重死”也同音，因而成为禁忌数字。“7”在欧美国家有积极意义，所以 在欧美同样可以看到以“7-Up”“Mild Seven(柔和七星牌香烟)”“7-Eleven(早7点开晚11点关的商店)”等商标的商品。

我国出口一种口红，商标叫“芳芳”，在汉语中这个名字确实很好，我国人一看到“芳芳”二字就不禁在心中生起美的联想：不仅仿佛看到了一位花容月貌的少女，而且好像闻到了她周身传来的香气。可是这商标音译成汉语拼音“Fangfang”，英文读者一看心中不由得生起一种恐怖之感，因为fang恰好是一个英文单词，其意是①a long，sharp tooth of a dog；②a snake's poison tooth(狗的长牙或蛇的毒牙)。于是他们想象的不是一位涂了口红的少女，却是条张牙舞爪的恶狗、或毒汁四溅的毒蛇，像中国人看到了青面獠牙的“鬼怪”。由于翻译的这一败笔，口红的销路可想而知。

关于“轻身减肥片”的译名，为了迎合大众心理，也需要做出适当的变通。此药是著名的杭州中药二厂的拳头产品，原来的译名为Obesity-reducing Tablets，但美国人看了译名，以为是专给obese people(肥胖患症者)吃的，所以许多胖子(并非肥胖症患者)出于面子，不愿问津。其实此药除了能治单纯性肥胖症之外，还能减肥。为了投顾客所好，将原译名改为Slimming Pills，其销量情况大有改善。

综合练习

一、请指出以下汉语商标英文译本存在的问题，并试着给出合适的翻译

1. “白象”牌电池——“White Elephant” brand battery
2. “芳草”牌牙膏——“Fang Cao” brand toothpaste
3. “金鸡”牌鞋油——“Gold Cock” brand shoe blacking
4. “银耳”汤——“White Fungus” soup
5. “金三角”经济开发区——a special economic development zone: a “Golden Triangle”
6. “藕粉”——“Lotus Root Starch”

参考译文

1. Silver Elephant或Baixiang(“White Elephant”在英语中是固定表达，意思是“昂贵却无用的东西”)；
2. Fragrant Grass(fang恰好是一个英文单词，其意是①a long，sharp tooth of a dog；②a snake's poison tooth 狗的长牙或蛇的毒牙)；
3. Golden Rooster(“cock”一词在英美国家等除有“雄鸡”一意之外，还有“雄性器官之意”)；
4. Silver Mushroom Soup(fungus一词也指其他不可食用或不可口的物种)；
5. Golden Delta(Golden Triangle习惯上用于指东南亚的一个生产和走私毒品的地方)；
6. Lotus Root Pudding/Powder(杭州的西湖藕粉是自古出名的滋养品，历史上曾作为“供粉”每年进献给皇帝，许多中国人都知道这一点，但对英美人来说却鲜为人知。“starch”一词有“淀粉”的意思，因为多吃淀粉容易发胖，而许多西方人都怕发胖。)

二、试将下列句子译成英语，注意句子的语用含义

1. 惭愧！(不敢当；哪里)
2. 欢迎，欢迎(幸会；久仰)
3. 再会(保重；有空来玩)
4. 请笑纳(别嫌弃；一点小意思)

5. 您太客气(让你破费；不好意思)

6. 多谢(有劳您了；谢您了)

7. 别客气(别见外；没什么)

8. 劳驾(有劳您；请问……)

9. 不见不散啊！

10. 恭喜发财！

11. 一路顺风！

12. 该死！

13. 没错。

14. 没门儿！

15. 完全同意

参考译文

1. I'm pleased that you think so.(I'm pleased to hear that. You flatter me. Thank you for your compliment.)

2. Glad to meet you. (I'm pleased to see you. It's such a pleasure to see you.)

3. Goodbye. (Take care. See you. Do come again.)

4. I hope you will like it.(Please accept it.)

5. It's so lovely! (Thank you for the gift.)

6. Thanks. (Many thanks. I'm obliged.)

7. Don't mention it. (It's a pleasure. Not at all. You're welcome. Never mind.)

8. Excuse me... (Could you be so kind as to...Would you please...? May I trouble you...? Would you mind...?)

9. Be there or be square.(Till then；See you；I'll be waiting for you.)

10. Good luck.

11. Plain sailing. (Have a good journey.)

12. Damn it!

13. You bet.(No mistake. Certainly.)

14. No way.

15. I couldn't agree more.

第4章

词义的确定、引申和褒贬

词汇是人类语言和生活最紧密的衔接点。正是有了一个个词汇，人们才能将自己在生产活动、娱乐活动、文化活动及心理情感活动中的经验感受准确清楚地表达出来。这一方面说明词汇在人类语言和生活中的重要性，同时也说明词汇的意义和使用不可避免地要受到语言所产生的地理环境与人文环境的制约。不同地区的人在表达相同或相近的事情时，也许会选择不同的词汇，这样就造成了不同语言在词义上的差异。英国语言学家艾里克·帕特里奇(Eric Partridge) 说英语“词本无义，义随人生”(Words do not have meanings; People have meanings for words)。Dr Johnson也说：“The idea that for every word in anyone language there is another word accurately equivalent to it in every other language, is not in accordance with the facts. In his search for the equivalent of a word the translator meets many difficulties.”而汉语词义比较严谨，词的含义范围比较窄，比较精确固定，词义的伸缩性和对上下文的依赖性较小，独立性较大。

4.1 词义的确定

英国哲学家维特根斯坦(Ludwig Wittgenstein)说“The meaning of word is its use in the language.”(词义取决于它在语言中的使用)。

弗思(John Rupert Firth)则更进一步说“Each word when used in a new context is a new word.”(每个单词在一个新的上下文里就是一个新的单词)。

4.1.1 根据上下文及习惯搭配确定词义

英语同其他许多语言一样，一词多类、一词多义的现象很普遍，如果只记住某个单词的一两种意思，便不加区别地套译原文，往往会使译文生硬难懂，甚至歪曲原义词。判断一词多义的手段主要是看词的联立关系(the frame of words)，即从词的组合、搭配中判断词义。由于一个词语不是孤立的，而是置身于一篇文章中的，一篇文章是上下密切相关的有机体，因此要受到来自各方面因素的影响，譬如同样一个人，在父母面前是儿子，在子女面前是父母，在领导眼里是自己的职员，在下属面前又成为领导等等，他的称呼就会在不同的场合发生相应的变化。

看下面几例：

(1) He is the *last* man to come. 他是**最后**来的

(2) He is the *last* man to do it. 他**决不会**干那事

(3) He is the *last* person for such a job. 他**最不配**干这个工作

(4) He should be the *last* to blame. 怎么也**不该**怪他

(5) He is the *last* man to consult. 根本**不宜**找他商量

(6) This is the *last* place where I expected to meet you. 我怎么也**没想到**会在这个地方见到你

关于“last”的词义我们最熟悉的意思是“最后、末尾”，但由于上下文不同，翻译就完全不一样。

翻译要准确，并不是靠死记住单词的各种意义，而是围绕中心意义(central meaning)，通过上下文来调整它的次要意义(secondary meaning)。另外，要确定词义，准确翻译，掌握词项的习惯搭配也是很重要的。对于多义词，不同的词义常有不同的搭配限制。因此，这些词义可以通过它们的典型搭配显示出来。如“fat”一词：

fat pork **多脂肪**的猪肉

fat income **优厚的**收入

a *fat* pig **肥壮的**猪

fat kitchen **贮足食物的**厨房

再例如“soft”：

soft music **轻**音乐

soft drink **软**饮料

soft money **纸**币

soft fire **文**火

soft heart **软**心肠

soft head **无主见**者

soft water **软**水

soft goods **纺织**品

soft soaper **奉承**者

soft ware **软**件

“picture”一词原意为“图片”，学生往往反复诵读、记忆，不自觉在心中把这个词义与英文连为一体，而在翻译中形成“条件反射”，认为“picture”的意思就是“图片”。其实“picture”不作“图片”解的例子是不少的：

The park is a *picture* when the flowers are in bloom.

花开时公园里景色如**画**。

The book gives a good *picture* of everyday life there.

这本书生动地**描绘**了那里人们的。

The *picture* is much clearer with the new aerial.

装上新天线后**图像**清晰多了。

Have you seen her latest *picture*?

你看过她最新拍的**电影**了吗？

Are you in the *picture* now?

你现在知道是**怎么回事**了吗？(实情)

再如对“story”一词的翻译：

(1) This war is becoming the most important *story* of this generation.

这场战争行将成为这一代人最重大的**事件**。

(2) It is quite another *story* now.

现在的**情况**完全不同了。

(3) Some reporters who were not included in the session broke the *story*.
有些没让参加那次会议的记者把**内情**捅出去了。

(4) He'll be very happy if that *story* holds up.
如果这一**说法**当真，那他就太高兴了。

(5) The girl's *story* is one of the saddest.
那个姑娘的**遭遇**算是最惨的了。

(6) A young man came to Scotti's office with a *story*.
一个年轻人来到斯科特的办公室**报案**。

(7) ...，but officials refused to confirm the *story*.
但官员们拒绝证实这条**消息**。

(8) The *story* about him became smaller and by and by faded out from the American TV.
报道中对他的渲染减少了，不久就从美国电视上销声匿迹了。

即使是同一个意思也有不同的表现方法，在翻译的时候要考虑到上下文，选择确切的措辞，如"He spoke *slowly*."可译成"他**慢条斯理地**说"；"He is *slow* of speech."可译作"他口齿**不伶俐**"；"The police were *slow* in coming."可译为"警察**姗姗来迟**"；"We enjoyed a *slow* Sunday at home."可译成"我们在家里**悠闲地**度过了一个星期天"；"He waved his hand *slowly* in contempt."可译为"他**懒洋洋**地挥了挥手，一副不屑一顾的样子"。

其实slow在不同的上下文里还有其他引申的含意，如：

slow season **淡季**

slow time (与夏季时间相对的) **标准**时间

a tennis court with a *slow* surface **不利于跑动的**网球场

a *slow* starter (拳击中)**开始时采取守势而后猛攻**的选手

Business was rather *slow* last month. 上个月生意**不太景气**。

The book is rather *slow*. 这本书很**乏味**(不精彩)。

What a *slow* party it is! 一个多么**索然无味**的聚会呀!

He is *slow* at speech with women yet. 跟女人说话，他还有点**笨嘴拙舌**。

4.1.2 根据冠词的有无确定词义

中文里没有冠词，英文里有冠词。在英语表达中有冠词和无冠词，有时意思相差很大，这是我们做翻译时必须注意的。当前面几个选择词义的方法都用过后，如果还有矛盾或意思不通，可以考虑一下是否由于冠词的缘故。为什么根据冠词的有无可以选出合适的词意？

(1) 因为冠词原意有“那”“这”“该”的意思。没有冠词时，当然就无这种意思。我们把它的含义表达出来，就是它在该处的恰当词义了。如：

“They are *members of* the Department.” 可以译为“他们是该系的**部分成员**”。而“They are *the members of* the Department.” 则可译为：“他们是该系的**全体成员**”。

(2) 冠词有习惯用法。按照习惯，有些结构有冠词，构成一定的意思。有些结构无冠词，也有一定的意思。顺着这些习惯，就可以选出合适的意思。如：

Out of question 毫无疑问

out of the question 不可能的

Every one can be successful，which is not *out of the question*，but *out of question*.

每个人都能成功，这不是**不可能的**，而是**毫无疑问的**。

(3) 表示颜色的词前无冠词表示具体的颜色；有冠词表示抽象的颜色或颜色之形象化。例如：

She is dressed *in pink*.

她穿着粉**红色的**衣服。

She seems to be *in the pink*.

她看起来身体**非常健康**。

(4) 许多词，前面无冠词，是具体的意思；前面有冠词，词义则有点转意。例如：

My watch is *behind time*.

我的表**走慢**了。

My watch is *behind the time*.

我的表**过时**了。

That style of dress comes into *fashion*.

那种衣服的式样**流行**。

He can speak and write English *in a fashion*.

他多少会说点、写点英语，但**不太好**。

4.1.3　了解文化背景知识确定词义

翻译是将一种文化环境里产生的作品移植到另一种文化环境里，因此是一种跨文化活动。整个翻译过程中，原语文化和译入语文化都在以不同方式起制约作用。而中西文化在风俗习惯、思维方式、宗教信仰等方面有很大差异，只有了解这种文化差异，才能在翻译中确定词义进行正确表达，使译文既保持原文相关的文化色彩，又符合译入语习惯。

广州别名“五羊城”不宜译为“Five-goat city”，因为“goat”在西方人的观念里是一种淫荡的动物，具有好色、淫秽的联想意义。“You old goat”表示“你这个老色鬼”，而在中国人眼里“羊”则有一种温顺、服从的象征意义。陈小尉教授(福大外语系)认为“五羊城”宜译为“Five-Ram city”。

“龙”是中华民族的象征，代表一种气势磅礴的民族精神，成为历代帝王的象征。所以我们是“龙”的子孙“龙”的传人。而“dragon”一词在西方则是一条拖着长尾、满身长鳞、口中喷火、有双翼的巨大晰蝎(胡文仲1995)，是罪恶的象征。因此“望子成龙”应根据文化差异译为“to long to see one’s son succeed in life”(汉英词典)。

Politicians *shed crocodile tears* over the plight of the unemployed.

面对陷入困境的失业人群，政客们**虚情假意地**表示同情。

crocodile是一种凶残的爬行动物。在西方传说中，鳄鱼是一面吞食捕获的动物，一面流着眼泪，以诱使更多的动物上当受骗。crocodile tears 喻指“假仁假义、假慈悲”。

It was *Friday* and soon they’d go out and get drunk.

星期五发薪日到了，他们马上就会出去喝得酩酊大醉。

译文中的发薪日并非胡乱翻译。在英国Friday是发薪的日子。我们只有懂得英国文化，才能正确翻译。而在美国有“black Friday”之说，我们却要把它译为“黑色星期五”。因为在美国历史上，1869 年9月24日爆发了一轮经济危机，四年后的1873年9月19日又发生了另一轮危机，十分凑巧的是这两个日子均是星期五。

That guy’s got a *Midas touch*.

在翻译这句子时，首先要弄懂“Midas touch”是什么意思，这句话要表达的文化内涵是什么。“Midas touch”源于希腊故事，它指的是希腊国王Midas的点金术(the Golden Touch)。在明白了这一典故之后，我们还要结合社交语境(如商务活动)，最终能推断出它的意思是说那人很会做生意，他无须花太多气力，就会像点物成金那样轻松赚钱。所以可以把它译为：他**很会做生意，轻轻松松赚大钱**。

The United States has now set up a *loneliness industry*.

离开美国社会环境，这句话是很难翻译的。所谓loneliness industry 指的是美国社会福利的一部分。由于美国社会的大量孤寡老人乏人照顾，成了社会问题，于是，美国政府部门就建立一种名为loneliness industry 的社会服务项目。根据这一语境知识，我们可以把它译为：美国政府建立了一种**为孤寡老人服务的社会服务项目**。

语言本身不仅是文化的重要组成部分，也是文化的载体。每一种语言都是一个国家、民族文化发展的产物，都有其久远的历史背景和丰富的文化内涵。

翻译时，要处理好语言和文化的矛盾，要分析和比较两种语言的结构和表达方式的异同，在准确理解原文的基础上，根据原文提供的语境，理解和把握语言深层所蕴含的文化内涵，才能在译文中忠实、准确地表达原文的内容，体现原著的风格与文化背景，再现原文的语言特色和艺术形象，让读者领会异国的风土人情，增长见识。同样，由于中西生产生活方式不一样，存在不同的政治、历史背景，不同的风俗习惯，只有对此有所了解，才能在翻译中确定词义，选用合适的表达方式，使译文具有可读性。例如，英语中“bridal shower”是指在英美等国家新娘出嫁前家人为她举行的点心茶话会(high tea party)，一般只允许女子参加，新娘的女友常常给她赠送一些小礼品。如果将其直译为“新娘淋浴”就是误译，应根据这种风俗习惯，与中国民间风俗结合起来意译为“待嫁酒会”。与之相对应“bachelor's party”也不宜译为“单身汉聚会”，因为“bachelor's party”是指新郎在娶亲前一两天所举行的茶话会或酒会，一般只允许男子参加，可以译为“告别单身汉酒会”。

4.2　词义的引申和褒贬

有学者认为：翻译中学会抓住精神实质，摆脱原文表层结构的束缚，防止从“实”到“实”的转换，做到“licentious (破格、自由)”是至关重要的问题。英汉两种语言在表达方式上存在着许多差异。有时一个单词在词典上找不到合适的词义。如果死译、硬译，不仅会使译文生硬晦涩，词不达意，而且还有可能弄巧成拙，引起误解。在这种情况下，就必须采用灵活的手法，从一个词或词组的字面意思加以引申，然后再选出比较恰当的汉语来表达。此外，有些词还随着时代的发展而被赋予了新的含义，翻译时就必须采用词义引申的办法。

4.2.1　词义的引申

在文章或句子中词义的具体化与抽象化引申(即用一个表示具体形象的词来表示一种抽象的概念，或者用一个代表抽象概念或属性的词来表示一种具体的事物)，这是英语中经常使用的修辞手段，在很多情况下都不能“对号入座”直译成汉语。有时会遇到某些词在英语辞典上找不到适当的词义，如果任意硬套或逐词死译，就会使译文生硬晦涩，不能确切表达原意，甚至会造成误解。这时就应根据上下文和逻辑关系，从该词的根本含义出发，进一步加以引申。引申时，往往可以从以下几个方面来加以考虑。

1 抽象化引申

在文章或句子中词义的抽象化与具体化引申是英语中经常使用的修辞方法。词义抽象化是指把原文中某些意义比较具体和形象的词在译文中引申为意义比较抽象和一般的词。英语中，特别在现代英语中，常常用一个表示具体形象的词来表示一种属性、一个事物或一种概念。翻译这类词时，一般可将其词义作抽象化的引申，译文才能流畅、自然。

There is much *woman* about him.

他的**举止颇带女人气**。

He is a *rolling stone*.

他是个**见异思迁的人**。

Obviously there is much *room* for improvement in the design.

显然，设计还大有改进的**余地**。

He is prepared to *put his hand into her pocket*.

他准备**解囊捐钱**给她。

Today is the *link* between yesterday and tomorrow.

今天是昨天和明天之间的**桥梁**。

There is a mixture of *the tiger and ape* in the character of the imperialists.

帝国主义既有**残暴的**一面，也有**狡猾的**一面。

I have no *head* for mathematics.

我没有数学方面的**天赋**。

2 具体化引申

具体化是指在译文中，用所指意义较窄的词或词组替换原文中所指意义较广的词或词组。英语中有些词在特定的上下文中，其含义是清楚的，但译成汉语时还必须作具体化的引申，否则就不够清楚。

以虚代实的抽象名词能大大简化英语的表达，是一种常见的语言现象。就其特征而言，此类抽象名词可大致分成两大类。一类是指形形色色的"人"的抽象名词，如：

Is Jane a *possibility* as a wife for Richard?

简是做理查德妻子的**合适人选**吗？

His new car made him the *envy* of every boy in the neighborhood.

他拥有一辆新轿车，为此他成了邻里男孩们的**羡慕者**。

The car in front of me stalled and I missed *the green*.

我前头的那辆车停住了，我错过了**绿灯**。

The Great Wall is a *must* for most foreign visitors to Beijing.

长城是任何一个外国游客**必不可少的参观游览项目**。

Two years' working is *a must* to those who want to take the entrance examination for MBA. (Master of Business Administration)

对于参加MBA考试的人来说，两年的工龄是**必备条件**。

4.2.2　词义的褒贬

语言本身虽没有阶级性，但在具体使用时不可能不为一定的阶级服务。为了忠实于原文的思想内容，翻译时必须正确理解原作者的基本政治立场和观点，然后选用适当的语言来加以表达。

词汇按照感情色彩可以分为褒义词、贬义词和中性词。英语中有些词本身就带有褒义和贬义，译成汉语时应当把原有的褒贬义相应地译出来。例如：

He was a man of high *renown* (fame).

他是位**有名望的**人。(褒)

The tasks carried out by them are *praiseworthy*.

他们进行的事业是**值得赞扬的**。(褒)

Henry keeps *boasting* that he has talked to the President.

亨利总是**吹嘘说**他曾同总统谈过话。(贬)

"He was *polite* and always gave advice *willingly*," she recalled.

她回忆说，"他**彬彬有礼**，总是**诲人不倦**。"(褒)

We were shocked by his *coarse* manners.

我们对他的**粗暴**态度感到震惊。(贬)

英语中有些词义是中立的，本身不表示褒义或贬义，但在一定的上下文中可能有褒贬的意味，汉译时就应该用具有褒贬意味的相应的词来表达。例如：

The *aggressive* nature of imperialism will never change.

帝国主义**侵略的**本性是绝对不会改变的。(贬义)

He is an *aggressive* student who does his work quite well.

他是一个**有进取心的**学生，他的工作干得很出色。(褒义)

He is always *flattering* her by saying that she is the most beautiful woman he has ever seen.

他总是**奉承**她说她是他所见过的最漂亮的女人。(贬义)

She felt greatly *flattered* when she received the invitation to deliver a lecture.

当她接到去做演讲的邀请时，她感到非常**荣幸**。(褒义)

综合练习

一、试将以下词组译成汉语，注意"soft"及"delicate"在不同语境下的含义

1. soft pillow
2. soft music
3. soft cushion

4. soft wood
5. soft money
6. soft drink
7. soft breeze
8. soft light
9. soft voice
10. soft fire
11. soft hat
12. soft words
13. soft answer
14. soft goods
15. soft heart
16. soft water
17. a soft glance
18. delicate skin
19. delicate porcelain
20. delicate upbringing
21. delicate living
22. delicate health
23. delicate stomach
24. delicate vase
25. delicate diplomatic question
26. delicate difference
27. delicate surgical operation
28. delicate ear for music
29. delicate sense of smell
30. delicate touch
31. delicate food

参考译文

1. 软枕
2. 轻柔的音乐
3. 靠垫

4. 软木，软质木材

5. 纸币，支票

6. 不含酒精的饮料

7. 和风，柔和的微风

8. 柔光

9. 低声

10. 文火

11. 呢帽

12. 和蔼的话

13. 委婉的回答

14. 毛织品，纺织品

15. 软心肠

16. 软水

17. 充满深情的一瞥

18. 娇嫩的皮肤

19. 精致的瓷器

20. 娇生惯养

21. 奢侈的生活

22. 虚弱的身体

23. 容易吃坏的胃

24. 易碎的花瓶

25. 微妙的外交问题

26. 细微的差别

27. 难做的外科手术

28. 对音乐有鉴赏力

29. 灵敏的嗅觉

30. 生花妙笔

31. 美味的食物

二、试将以下句子译成汉语，注意词语在不同语境下的含义

1. He *saw* a man *sawing* trees with a *saw*.

2. Eat what you *can* and *can* what you *cannot*.

3. That woman *walks the streets*.

4. I'll *report* that official.

5. The boss *gave her the sack*.

6. That girl student is *in the green*.

7. The old lady has *gone to her rest*.

8. That young man has *lost his heart*.

9. That fellow did hard *labor* for 3 years.

10. The woman in *labor* is his wife.

11. I'm *not a little* afraid of snakes.

12. I have *seen* him *through*.

13. Where is the *Book*?

14. Don't *call him names*!

15. The little boy is a *love child*.

16. He is *disinterested* in the affairs.

17. Every life has its *roses* and *thorns*.

18. We have the situation well in *hand*.

19. It is not *right* for children to sit up late.

20. She tried her best to *right* her husband from the charge of robbery.

21. I want you to *account for* every cent you spent.

22. If the stove isn't *made up*, it will go out.

23. Society is *made up* of people with widely differing abilities.

24. They *made up* a bed on the sofa for the unexpected visitor.

25. He saw dim *figures* moving towards him.

26. The invention of machinery had brought into the world a new era—the Industrial Age. Money had become *King*.

27. John was an *aggressive* salesman who did his job quite well.

28. Hans was too obviously *flattering* the gentleman by saying he was the most courageous man he had ever seen.

29. The boxer was *knocked out* in the second round.

30. The Department of Justice was reluctant to bring *poor cases* into court.

31. Other media closer to the scene dismissed Carter as a *poor loser*.

32. He *bombarded* her with questions.

33. The director's *eyes and ears* are run to everything the actor does.

34. We see that surface is covered with tiny "*hills* and *valleys*."

35. He writes in a *round hand*.

36. His *hand* is out.

37. Give me a *hand*，please.

38. The office is short of *hands*.

参考译文

1. 他看见一个人正用锯子锯树。
2. 能吃的吃掉，吃不掉的就做成罐头。
3. 那个女人是妓女。
4. 我要检举那位官员。
5. 老板解雇了她。
6. 那女学生正值豆蔻年华。
7. 那个老太太安息了。
8. 那个青年人处于热恋之中。
9. 那个家伙服过三年劳役。
10. 分娩的妇女是他的妻子。
11. 我很怕蛇。
12. 我帮助他过难关。
13. 圣经在哪?
14. 别骂他!
15. 那个小男孩是个私生子。
16. 他在此事上公正无私。
17. 每个人的生活都有甜有苦。
18. 我们能很好地把握局面。
19. 孩子们睡得晚不好。
20. 她尽力为她丈夫被控抢劫申冤。
21. 我要你把花费的每分钱都交代清楚。
22. 如不添柴，炉子就会熄灭。
23. 社会是由具有迥然不同能力的人组成的。
24. 他们把沙发收拾一下让这位不速之客睡。
25. 他隐约看见一个人影正在向他眼前移动。
26. 机器的发明使世界进入了一个新纪元即工业时代，金钱成了主宰一切的权威。
27. 约翰是个积极肯干的推销员，他工作干得很出色。
28. 汉斯说，这位先生是他所见到过的最有胆识的人。这种阿谀奉承未免过于露骨。

29. 该拳击手在第二个回合中被淘汰了。

30. 司法部不愿意将没有把握打赢官司的案子拿到法庭上。

31. 对此事比较了解的其他媒体鄙夷地认为，卡特是一个输不起的人(输了会发脾气的人)。

32. 他连珠炮似的向她提出了许多问题。

33. 导演的注意力完全放在了演员的一举一动上。

34. 我们看到，该表面凹凸不平。

35. 他的字写得很圆润。

36. 他的技能荒废了。

37. 请帮我一下。

38. 这个办公室缺人手。

第5章

翻译技巧(一)词类转换

英译汉时的词类转换能使译文流畅，表意确切。为了使译文既忠实于原文又符合汉语习惯，翻译时不能一味拘泥于某些词汇在原文的词性，必要时应该采取词类转换的方法，对原词类进行适当的转换。

5.1 翻译中进行词类转换的原因

按照绝大多数语法书的分类，汉英词类的数量大致相等，类别基本上对应。汉语的词类大致有十类左右，实词类有：动词、名词、形容词、代词、副词、数词和量词，虚词有连词、介词、助词、叹词等。英语也有十大类词：其中实词类包括名词(Noun)、动词(Verb)、形容词(Adjective)、副词(Adverb)、数词(Numeral)、代词(Pronoun)，虚词类有：介词(Preposition)、连词(Conjunction)、冠词(Article)和感叹词(Interjection)。

英汉两种语言属于不同的语系，英语属于印欧语系(Indo-European Family)，汉语则属于汉藏语系(Sino-Tibetan Family)。这两种语言的词汇构成和使用习惯均存在着一定的差异。汉语是分析型(analytic) 语言，其典型特征是没有屈折变化(inflection)，即汉语的名词不会改变自身的形式(form) 变为复数，动词也不用改变自身的形式表示过去时、现在时或将来时，汉语的词也没有表示阳性和阴性的词缀。汉语词语组合成句子依靠词序(word order) 和虚词(empty word)。而英语是分析型和综合型(synthetic) 语言，其分析型特征体现在词序和助词(auxiliary)的组句功能上，其综合型特征体现在它有丰富的屈折变化形式。英、汉两种语言在词的分类、词的兼类、词类的句法功能以及使用频率等方面都有所不同。英语的词类依据是语法，而汉语的词类是根据词的意义来划分的。有些词类英语中有而汉语中没有，如冠词、引导词、关系代词、名词性物主代词、关系副词分词、动词不定式、动名词等；同样，有些词类汉语中有而在英语词汇中却难觅其踪，如量词、助词。汉语词大部分是一词一类，仅有少量兼类词，而一词多类却是英语中的普遍现象。

词类划分的差异必然导致词类转换法的广泛应用。例如，冠词虽然数量微少，却是英语中用法繁多，使用频率很高的功能词之一。因为汉语里没有冠词，也没有与之绝对等同的词语，当冠词在句中只起语法作用时往往将其省略不译。然而，对于在句中具有不同程度的词汇意义的冠词，则不能简单地将其忽略不译。为了恰如其分地表达冠词的意义，只有采取词类转译的方法，如将具有明显数字意味的冠词转译成汉语数词，将具有明显指代意味的冠词转译成汉语代词。

英、汉两种语言在词类的句法功能上亦有很大的差异。汉语一个词类能充当的句子成分比较多，一般无须转换词类。英语一个词类能充当的句子成分少，充当不同的句子成分，需要转换词类。例如，英语中只有动词才能作谓语，而汉语中，除动词外，许多其他词类也能作谓语，如副词、形容词、名词、数量词等。英、汉两种语言中各类词的使用频率不同，习惯用法不同亦会促成翻译中的词类转换。因此在大多数情况下，英译汉时很难将两种语言的词汇一一对应，所以要“打破语言的外壳，保持实质内容”，有时需要词性变化，否则句子结构欧化，不符合汉语习惯。为了使译文符合汉语习惯，翻译时不必拘泥于原文的表层结构，在忠实原意的前提下，可将原文中某些词的词类转换为汉语的其他词类，从而使译文更加通顺、自然。

5.2　词类转换技巧应用

首先，让我们看看什么是词类转换。在翻译时，由于两种语言在语法和习惯表达上的差异，在保证原文意思不变的情况下，译文必须改变词类，这就叫词类转换(或词类转移)。词类转换分为以下6种。

5.2.1　转译成动词

英语和汉语比较起来，汉语的动词用得较多，这是一个特点。一个英语句子中，往往只有一个动词，而在一个汉语句子中却可以有几个动词。因此，英语中有不少词类，尤其是名词、介词、形容词和副词，在译成汉语时都可翻译成动词。

1 英语名词转译成汉语动词

英语中名词占优，尤其在科技英语中，名词倾向化是突出之势。名词转换为动词的现象很普遍，常见的有如下几种。

(1) 英语中动词派生的名词，如liberation、abolition、exploration、application、connection、conclusion、treatment和detection等以及具有动作意义的名词如sight、thought、glance、glimpse等在英译汉中要转译成汉语的动词。这类名词后面常常跟有一个介词短语作定语，转换的结果是名词与短语中的名词成了动宾结构。

Even those parents who seemed hard and demanding would just melt at the *thought* of their child in tears over a failed test or a broken fingernail.

即使看上去强硬而又苛求的家长，**一想到**他们的子女因考试不及格或弄破了手指而掉眼泪的时候，也会立即心软。

Not all mergers，however，are the result of global economic trends，political change or technological innovation. BMW’s *takeover* of the Rover Group injected much needed investment into the struggling UK car manufacturer whilst extending BMW's product range.

然而，并非所有的合并都是经济全球化趋势、政治变化或者技术革新所带来的结果。德国宝马汽车公司**接管了**罗福汽车集团(The Rover Group)，给这个在挣扎中求生存的英国汽车制造公司注入了急需的资金，同时有拓展了宝马汽车公司本身的产品范围。

All peaceloving people demand the unconditional *prohibition* of atomic weapons.

一切爱好和平的人民都要求无条件地**禁止**原子武器。

One after another，speakers called for the *down fall* of imperialism，*abolition* of exploitation of man by man，*liberation* of the oppressed of the world.

发言人一个接一个表示要**打倒**帝国主义，要**消灭**人剥削人的制度，要**解放**世界上的被压迫人民。

(2) 作为固定词组主体的名词往往可以转译成动词。如：make use of，have a look at，have a rest，make no mention of，pay attention to等。例如：

One way an organization can find staff for job vacancies is to recruit outside the company. It may opt to put an advertisement in a newspaper or magazine which *gives a short description of* the job and invites introductory letters from applicants.

企业机构找人补充职位空缺的办法之一是公司实行对外招聘。它可以选择在报纸或杂志上登广告，**简要介绍**工作职务的情况并征集应聘者的自荐信。

He *has a perfect command of* English.

他**精通**英语。

School leaders *showed great concern for* the students' health.

校领导**很关心**学生的健康。

It's an honor to *make acquaintance with* Your Excellency.

得识阁下，不胜荣幸。

(3) 某些由动词+ er 或or 构成的名词，有时在句子中并不指其身份和职业，而含有较强的动作意味，往往可转译成汉语动词。

A *lover* of mankind，he never had a wife or family to love him.

他**热爱**人类，却又从未有过妻儿家庭的爱抚。

He is a good *eater* and *sleeper*.

他**能吃能睡**。

I am no *drinker*，nor *smoker*.

我既不**喝酒**，也不**抽烟**。

2 英语介词转译成汉语动词

英语中含有动作意味的介词，如in、across、through、for、against等，以及作表语用的介词短语，作原因、目的的介词短语，作方式、陪衬状语用的短语，都可转译为动词。例如：

They seem to do everything in a rush，with an eye *on* the clock，as if they had only a short time to live.

他们办事似乎都很匆忙，眼睛老是**盯着**钟表，好像剩下的日子不多了。

I teach because I enjoy finding ways of getting myself and my students *out of* the ivory tower and *into* the real world.

我教书，是因为我喜欢想方设法使自己和我的学生从象牙塔里**走出来**，**步入**现实世界。

He was out in the field *on* this case for three days.

他在野外待了三天，**处理**这一案件。

3 英语形容词转译成汉语动词

英语中表示知觉、情感、愿望等心理状态的形容词，在联系动词后作表语时往往转译成汉语动词。如able、afraid、angry、ashamed、aware、anxious、careful、cautious、certain、concerned、confident、content、doubtful、glad、grateful、ignorant (不知道)，sorry、thankful等，这些都是常用作补语的表示心理状态的形容词，可译为动词。有些由动词派生出来的英语形容词也可以译成汉语动词。例如：

We were all *convinced* that the plan would work.

我们都**深信**这计划可行。

The manager is *grateful* to the customers for their valuable suggestions.

经理**感谢**顾客们提出的宝贵意见。

He is not *skilled* at dealing with complaints.

他不**擅长**处理投诉案件。

You are *ignorant* of the hazards of smog.

你**没有意识到**烟雾的危害性。

4 英语副词转译成汉语动词

当具有动作意义的副词做表语或宾补时，可译成汉语动词。

As he ran out，he forgot to have his shoes *on*.

他跑出去时，忘记**穿**鞋了。

No difficulty can hold us *back*.

没有任何困难能**阻止**我们前进。

I must be *off* now. I have other fish to fry.

我得**告辞**了，我还有别的要紧事要做。

She opened the window to let fresh air *in*.

她把窗子打开，让新鲜空气**进来**。

5.2.2 转译成名词

1 英语动词转译为汉语名词

英语中有很多由名词派生或转用的动词，其概念很难用汉语动词来表达，如果找不到相应的动词，可以将其译成名词。

He was deeply *impressed* by what they did in the critical moment.

他们在关键时刻的行为给他留下了深刻的**印象**。

The design *aims* at automatic operation，easy regulation，simple maintenance and high productivity.

设计的**目的**在于自动操作，调节方便，维护简易，生产率高。

The products of this factory are chiefly *characterized* by their fine workmanship and durability.

该厂产品的主要**特点**是工艺精湛，经久耐用。

Such materials are *characterized* by good insulation and high resistance to wear.

这些材料的**特点**是：绝缘性好，耐磨性强。

We are wrongly *informed*.

我们得到的**消息**不对头。

2 英语形容词、副词转译成汉语名词

英语中有些表示事物特征的形容词用作表语时，往往转译成汉语名词。有时往往可以在其后加“性”“度”“体”等词。例如：

In the fission processes the fission fragments are very *radioactive*.

在裂变过程中，裂变碎片具有强烈的**放射性**。

Computers are more *flexible*，and can do a greater variety of jobs.

计算机具有更大的**灵活性**，因此能做许多种不同的工作。

Stevenson was *eloquent and elegant* but soft.

史蒂文森**有口才**、**有风度**，但很软弱。

Glass is more *transparent* than plastic cloth.

玻璃的**透明度**比塑料布要好。

另一种为前加定冠词表示与其有关的一类人，这样的词有sick、wounded、poor、rich、young、old、blind等。

Therefore *the rich* were buried with precious stones and *the poor* with their tools.

因而**有钱人**用宝石陪葬，而**穷人**用工具陪葬。

A trained dog can be a guide to *the blind*.

一条经过训练的狗可以给**盲人**当向导。

英语中有些副词，尤其是以“- ly”结尾的副词，虽然在句子中作次要成分，但其表达的意义和概念却在句子中占有重要地位。这类副词可转译为汉语名词。如：

He is *physically* weak but *mentally* sound.

他**身体**虽弱，但**思想**建康。

5.2.3　转译成形容词

(1) 英语中一些表示特殊身份或性格特征的名词，如fool、gentleman、master、friend、traitor、knave(恶棍，骗徒，纸牌的杰克)、blunderer以及由形容词派生出来的名词如necessity、stupidity、importance等在英译汉时可翻译为形容词。例如：

They wanted a generation of Americans conditioned to *loyalty* and *duty*.

他们都希望把下一代美国人训练得**忠于**祖国，**尽职尽责**。

I am sure you will be *gentleman* enough to make an apology for the language you have just said.

我相信你会**彬彬有礼**地对你刚才所说的话表示歉意。

He was *blunderer* enough to repeat his mistake.

同样的错误他犯两回可是够**傻**的。

Even in these days，when divorce is so easy and family ties are supposed to be weak，it would probably be a *mistake* to underestimate the influence of families on presidential politics.

即使在家庭纽带十分脆弱、离婚成了常事的今天，低估了家庭在总统政治中的影响力，也是**错误的**。

(2) 表示时间、地点的副词，常可作名词的后置定语，可将其译为汉语定语形容词。

The pressure *inside* equals the pressure *outside*.

内部压力等于**外部**压力。

The equations *below* are derived from those *above*.

下面的方程式是由**上面的**那些方程式推导出来的。

(3) 当英语中动词或形容词译成汉语中的名词时，引起原来修饰动词或形容词的副词转换成修饰名词的形容词。

The President had *prepared meticulously* for his journey.

总统为这次出访做了十分**周密的准备**。

The film "Carve Her Name with Pride" *impressed* him *deeply*.

《女英烈传》这部电影给了他**深刻的印象**。

(4) 有些表数量的名词，以"(a+形容词) +名词+of"形式出现时，可译成形容词。

A good many of the houses were destroyed by the fire.

许多房子被大火烧毁。

A number of clever criminals are finding ways to break computer codes.

不少聪明的罪犯正在想方设法来破译计算机密码。

5.2.4 转译成副词

(1) 当英语名词翻译为汉语动词时，通常修饰该名词的形容词转译成汉语的副词。

Warm discussions arose on every corner as to his achievements.

到处都在**热烈地**讨论他的成就。

He had a *careful* study of the map before he started off.

出发前他**仔细地**研究了地图。

We place the *highest* value on our friendly relations with developing countries.

我们**高度地**珍视同发展中国家的友好关系。

(2) 英语名词转译成汉语副词。英语中有些意义抽象的名词或名词短语与句子其他成分之间存在一定的逻辑关系时，可以根据其意义转译成汉语副词或相应的状语成分。例如：

I have the *honor* to inform you that your request is granted.

我**荣幸地**通知您，您的请求已得到批准。

The new Mayor earned some appreciation by the *courtesy* of coming to visit the city poor.

新市长**有礼貌地**前来访问城市贫民，获得了他们的一些好感。

It would be wise to handle this delicate problem *with calmness and patience*.

冷静耐心地处理这个微妙的问题是明智的。

Day and night the nurses took care of the sick.

护士**夜以继日地**照顾着病人。

He is so *heart and soul* with us.

他是如此**真心实意地**和我们站在一起。

(3) 英语中有些动词具有汉语副词的含义，翻译时可转换成汉语副词。

I *succeeded* in persuading him.

我**成功地**劝说了他。

We've had an ongoing stream of founders from outside the US, and they *tend to* do particularly well, because they're all people who were so determined to succeed that they were willing to move to another country to do it.

我们一直不断地有来自美国之外的创业者，他们**往往**表现得非常好，因为他们全部都是那种下定决心，一定要成功的人，所以他们愿意到另外一个国家来创业。

综合练习

一、运用词类转换技巧试将下列句子译成汉语

1.Too much *exposure* to TV programs will do great harm to the eyesight of children.

2. Rockets have found *application* for the exploration of the universe.

3. The *adoption* of this new device greatly cut down the percentage of defective products.

4. When he *catches a glimpse* of a potential antagonist, his instinct is to win him over with charm and humor.

5. Until such time as mankind *has the sense* to lower its population to the points where the planet can provide a comfortable support for all, people will have to accept more "unnatural food".

6. He is no smoker, but his father is a *chain-smoker*.

7. Unfortunately, I was a bit bossy and I was not a good *listener*.

8. My young brother is a better *teacher* than I.

9. They are *after* fame and position.

10. *Through* the corridor, you will see his garden.

11. This is not John's fault. He was *against the* plan from the very beginning.

12. We marched on *against* the piercing wind.

13. When the switch is *off*, the electricity circuit is *open*.

14. The cultivation of a hobby and new forms of interest is therefore a policy of first *importance* to a public man.

15. The medicine is used in the *treatment* of cancer.

16. The thief made a trembling *confession* of his wrongdoing.

17. An *acquaintance* of world history is helpful to the study of current affairs.

18. A *visit* to his grave is scheduled after *conversation*.

19. There is a big *increase* in demand for all kinds of consumer goods in every part or our country.

20. Several of the ladies wept *at the sight of* so much suffering.

21. They are very much *concerned about* the future of their country.

22. My experience ought to be a warning to those who are too *confident* in their own opinions.

23. Are you *sure* that she is innocent?

24. As he was a perfect *stranger* in the city，I hope you will give him the necessary help.

25. I'm a *stranger* to the operation of computer.

26. We found *difficulty* in controlling the air pollution.

27. He acknowledged the *truth* of his statement.

28. Independent thinking is an absolute *necessity* in study.

29. Your financial support is of *great value* to us.

30. Keeping your head is of *great importance*.

31. My *conviction* remains that if you want to make poverty history，you have to make corruption and bad leadership history.

32. The products of this factory are chiefly *characterized* by their fine workmanship and durability.

33. As a result，*the rich* became all the richer.

34. Volvo，the Swedish automotive，energy and food group，increased its profits by ten point nine percent in the first quarter of this year despite a *fall* of five percent in group turnover.

35. He declared that for himself he was still *for* the Charter，details，name，and all.

36. The dominant factor in the growth of the company throughout the years has been its success in maintaining technical superiority in product design and manufacturing techniques.

参考译文

1. 孩子们看电视过多会大大地损坏视力。

2. 火箭已经用来探索宇宙。

3. 采用这种新装置极大地降低了废品率。

4. 发现有可能反对他的人，他就本能地要以他的魅力和风趣把这个人争取过来。

5. 除非人类终于意识到要把人口减少到这样的程度，使地球能为所有的人提供足够的饮食，否则将不得不接受更多的“人造食品”。

6. 他倒不抽烟，但他爸爸却一支又一支不停地抽。

7. 遗憾的是，我这人有点儿专横，不大善于听取别人的意见。

8. 我弟弟比我教得好。

9. 他们在追求荣誉和地位。

10. 穿过走廊，你就可以看到他的花园了。

11. 这不是约翰的过错，他从一开始就反对这项计划。

12. 我们冒着刺骨的寒风前进。

13. 闭上开关，电路断开。

14. 因此，对于一个从事社会活动的人来讲，培养一种爱好和新的情趣方式，乃是至关重要的对策。

15. 这种药用于治疗癌症。

16. 小偷战战兢兢地坦白了所干的坏事。

17. 读一点世界史，对学习时事是有帮助的。

18. 讨论后，我们将祭扫他的陵墓。

19. 我国各地对各种消费品的需要量已大大增加。

20. 几位女士看到如此的惨状而哭泣。

21. 他们非常关心国家的前途。

22. 我的经历，对于那些太坚信自己意见的人来说，应该是一个警钟。

23. 你敢肯定她是无辜的吗?

24. 他对这座城市完全陌生，所以我希望你能给他必要的帮助。

25. 我对计算机操作比较陌生。

26. 我们感到控制空气污染是困难的。

27. 他承认他讲的是真的。

28. 在学习中独立思考是必需的。

29. 你对我们的经济援助是很有价值的。

30. 保持头脑冷静是至关重要的。

31. 我依然坚信想让贫困成为历史，就必须让腐败和不良领导成为历史。

32. 该厂产品的主要特点是工艺精湛，经久耐用。

33. 结果，富者更富。

34. 沃尔沃是瑞典的汽车、能源和食品集团公司。本年度第一季度，尽管它的总营业额下降了5%，但利润增加了10.9%。

35. 他声称他本人仍然拥护宪章，拥护它的细则，拥护它的名称，拥护它的一切。

36. 该公司多年来发展壮大的主要因素是一贯成功地保持了产品设计和制造工艺上的技术优势。

二、将下列段落译成汉语

Enchantment of the South Sea Islands

The mighty Pacific washes the shores of five continents – North America, South

America, Asia, Australia, and Antarctica. Its waters mingle in the southeast with the Atlantic Ocean and in the southwest with the Indian Ocean. It is not on the shores of continents, nor in the coastal islands, however, that the soul of the great Pacific is found. It lies far out where the fabled South Sea Islands are scattered over the huge ocean like stars in the sky.

Here great disturbances at the heart of the earth caused mountains and volcanoes to rise above the water. For hundreds of years tiny coral creatures have worked and died to make thousands of ring-shaped islands called atolls.

The air that sweeps the South Sea Islands is fragrant with flowers and spice. Bright warm days follow clear cool nights, and the rolling swells break in a never-ending roar on the shores. Overhead the slender coconut palms whisper their drowsy song.

When white men first came to the Pacific Islands, they found that the people living there were like happy children. They were tall men and beautiful women who seemed not to have a care in the world. Coconut palms and breadfruit trees grew at the doors of their huts. The ocean was filled with turtles and fish, ready for the net. The islanders had little need for clothing. There was almost no disease.

Cruel and bloody wars sometimes broke out between neighboring tribes, and canoe raids were sometimes made on nearby islands. The strong warriors enjoyed fighting. Many of the islanders were cannibals, who cooked and ate the enemies they killed. This was part of their law and religion. These savages, however, were usually friendly, courteous, and hospitable. Some of the early explorers were so fascinated with the Pacific Islands that they never returned to their own countries. They preferred to stay.

Notes and Explanations:

1. the South Sea Islands南太平洋诸岛，South Sea南半球诸海洋的，南太平洋的
2. wash *v.* 波涛冲洗、拍打
3. mingle with混合，汇合(注意此句中方位的表达顺序)
4. fabled *a.*虚构的，富有神奇色彩的
5. atoll *n.* 环状珊瑚岛，环礁
6. worked and died 繁衍、死亡
7. rolling swells 滚滚巨浪；注意此句翻译中所采用的词类转换的技巧
8. drowsy song催眠曲
9. filled with turtles and fish, ready for the net 鱼鳖成群，张网可得
10. canoe raid 乘独木舟进行攻击；注意此句中将被动语态转为主动的翻译方法
11. cannibal *n.*吃人的人

参考译文

迷人的南太平洋诸岛

太平洋气势磅礴，滚滚波涛拍打着五洲海岸——北美洲、南美洲、亚洲、大洋洲和南极洲。太平洋在东南方与大西洋汇合，在西南方与印度洋相接。然而，浩瀚的太平洋最精美之处不在其大陆海岸，也不在沿海诸岛，而是在远离陆地的海域。在那里，富有神奇色彩的南太平洋诸岛像天上的繁星一样散布在广阔的海面上。

那里，由于地心引力的剧烈运动，一道道山脉、一座座火山升出水面。千百年来，微小的珊瑚虫在这里繁衍、死亡，形成了数不胜数的叫作环礁的环状岛屿。

散发着鲜花和香料芬芳的微风轻轻地吹拂着南太平洋诸岛。在那里，白日明媚温暖，夜晚清激凉爽。滚滚浪花拍打着海岸，发出永不休止的轰鸣。头顶上空，纤纤椰树沙沙作响，低声吟唱着令人昏昏欲睡的催眠曲。

白人首次登上这些太平洋海岛时，发现生活在那里的人们都像孩子一样欢快。男子身材高大，妇女婀娜多姿，似乎对世上的一切都不用操心。他们茅舍门前长着一丛丛椰子树、面包树；海洋里鱼鳖成群，张网可得。岛上的人几乎不需要穿什么衣服，也几乎见不到任何疾病。

邻近部落之间有时会爆发残酷的血战。他们有时乘独木舟去攻击附近的岛屿。这些强悍的勇士乐于战斗。岛民中的许多居民都有吃人的习俗。他们把杀死的敌人煮熟吃掉。这种习俗是他们的法律和宗教的一部分。然而，这些野蛮人通常是友善、谦恭和好客的。一些早期的探险家因为太迷恋这些太平洋岛屿而不再返回自己的国家。

第6章

翻译技巧(二)增词法

英汉两种语言由于词法结构、语法结构和修辞方法的差异，在翻译过程中，往往出现词的增加和减少的现象。所谓增词(amplification)，就是在译文中增加一些原文字面上没有的词、词组，甚至句子，这是由于英汉两种语言在用词、造句以及思维方式上各有特点所造成的。增词的目的，或是为了补足语气，或是为了连接上下文，有的则是为了避免译文意义含混。增词是有一定规律可循的，主要体现在词汇、语法、逻辑、修辞和谚语等方面。

一般而言，增词法在大的方面有两种情况：一是把原文句子里“隐含”(implication)或上下文意思清楚而没有写出来的词在译文里补进去，以便汉语能清楚地(explicitly)表达原文的意思，也就是说这样的增词是出于语义上的需要；另一种增词则是出于句法上的考虑，把原文中省略的句子成分补充进去，使译文的句子有完整的意思。

6.1 根据意义上或修辞上的需要增词

由于意义上的需要及英汉语言上的差异，英语中重复用词的情况较少，而汉语有时为了达到一定的修辞效果，经常使用重叠或排比句，翻译成汉语时需要在名词前增加动词。

6.1.1 增加动词

增词就是增加原文中虽然无其词而有其意的一些词。当原句为避免用词重复时，可能省去再次出现的相同动词，汉译时要表达出来；当原句的主语或宾语直译成汉语时，译文可能不通顺，或不符合汉语习惯，这种情况下可增译动词。例如：

In every Chinese city，we *got into* the streets，shops，parks，theatres and restaurants.

在中国，我们每到一个城市就**逛**大街、**购**物、**游**公园、**看**演出、**品**名菜。

My part-time job，*my English* and *my old classmates* were more than enough to fill my summer vacation.

我要**做**兼职，**学**英语，还要与老同学**聚聚**，这些占去了我暑假的全部时间。

They *build* roads，houses，bridges，ships，pipelines，and canals.

他们**修**路、**盖**房、**架**桥、**造**船、**铺**管道、**挖**运河。

6.1.2 增加形容词、副词

根据上下文，有些名词、动词或形容词前要增加恰当的形容词或副词，才能使意思明确。例如：

Army will make a *man* of him.

军队会把他锻炼成一个**堂堂正正的男子汉**。

This is grasping at *straws*.

抓住**救命稻草**。

The crowds *melted away*.

人群**渐渐散开了**。

Inflation has now reached *unprecedented* level.

通货膨胀现在已经发展到**空前严重**的地步。

6.1.3 增加名词

1 在不及物动词后增加名词

英语中有些动词有时用作及物动词，有时用作不及物动词；当它作不及物动词时，宾语实际上隐含在动词后面，译成汉语时候应该把它译出来，例如：

Mary *washes* before meals.

玛丽饭前**洗手**。

Mary *washes* before going to bed.

玛丽睡前**洗脚**。

Mary *washes* for a living.

玛丽靠**洗衣**度日。

Mary *washes* in a restaurant.

玛丽在饭店**洗碗**。

Their host *carved*，*poured*，*served*，cut bread，talked，laughed，proposed healths.

热情的主人又是**切肉**，又是**倒茶**，又是**上菜**，又是切面包，有说有笑，还不断敬酒，忙个不停。

Since her earliest walking period she had been as the right hand of her mother. *Scrubbing*，*baking*，errand-running，and *nursing*—what there had been to do she did.

她很小的时候她就是母亲的好帮手：擦地板，烤面包，跑差事，照顾弟弟妹妹，样样都是她做的事儿。

2 在形容词前加名词

英语中的形容词表现力很强，携带的信息也很丰富。某些形容词本身就暗含了名词的意义，在英译汉时常常需要将隐含的名词补译出来。例如：

This camera is easy to operate，*versatile*，*compact* and has a pleasing modern design.

这种照相机操作简便，**功能**齐全，**结构**紧凑，造型美观。

Compared with those ones，these cameras are *small*，*light* and *cheap*.

与那些照相机相比，这些照相机的**体积小**、**重量轻**而且**价格便宜**。

Keith：A *little*，*yellow*，*ragged*，beggar.

凯斯是个要饭的，**身材矮小**，**面黄肌瘦**，**衣衫褴褛**。

3 在抽象名词后增加名词

某些由动词或形容词派生来的抽象名词，翻译时可根据上下文在其后面增添适当的名词，使译文更合乎规范。例如：

to persuade 说服　persuasion 说服工作

to prepare 准备　preparation 准备工作

backward 落后　backwardness 落后状态

tense紧张　tension 紧张局势

arrogant 自满　arrogance 自满情绪

mad 疯狂　madness 疯狂行为

antagonistic 敌对　antagonism 敌对态度

We were all greatly moved by his *loftiness*.

我们都被他那种**崇高品质**所深深打动。

They wanted to ease the *tension* in the Middle East.

他们试图缓解中东的**紧张局势**。

I was deeply *impressed* by the backwardness of the mountain area.

这一山区的**落后状况**给我留下了深刻印象。

6.1.4　增加表示名词复数的词

汉语名词的复数没有词性变化，很多情况下不必表达出来。但是要表达多数人的名词时，可在其后加"们"，如the teachers(教师们)，或者在前面加"诸位"或"各位"，如ladies and gentlemen(诸位女士和先生)。此外，英语名词复数汉译时还可以增加重叠词、数词或其他词表示复数。如：

He stretched his legs which were scattered with *scars*.

他伸出双腿，露出腿上的**道道伤痕**。

Every summer，*tourists* go to the coastal cities.

每到夏季，旅游者**纷纷**涌到海滨城市。

The ASIAN countries have designated 1992 as "Asian Tourism Year"，and are cooperating in a drive to convince the world's pleasure-and-culture-seekers of their *attractions*.

亚洲几个国家将1992年指定为"亚洲旅游年"，携手合作发起一场宣传攻势，旨在让世界各地的那些猎奇探胜的游客确信，他们这些国家也有**许多引人入胜的旅游景观**。

Cargo insurance is to protect the trader from *losses* that many dangers may cause.

货物保险会使贸易商免受许多风险所可能造成的**种种损失**。

New buildings，massive in span and artful in design，have sprung up everywhere. A plethora of *stores and shops* have sprouted everywhere.

一幢幢新建的高楼大厦在各处拔地而起，规模宏伟，设计精美。到处冒出了大大小小的数不胜数的商店。

6.1.5　增加表达时态的词

英语动词的时态靠动词词形变化(如write，wrote)或加助动词(如will write，have written)来表达的。汉语动词没有词形变化，表达时态要靠增加汉语特有的时态助词或一些表示时间的词。如：翻译完成时往往用“曾”“已经”“过”“了”；翻译进行时往往用“在”“正在”“着”；翻译将来时往往用“将”“就”“会”“便”“就要”等等。除此之外，为了强调时间概念或强调时间上的对比，往往需要加一些其他的词。

The English language *is* in very good shape. It *is changing* in its own undiscoverable way，but it *is* not *going* rotten like a plum dropping off a tree.

英语**目前**的情况很好，它**正**按照它那不易为人发现的方式在起着变化，而不是像一只树上掉下来的李子那样**在逐渐**腐烂。

I *had imagined* it to be merely a gesture of affection，but *it seems* it is to smell the lamb and make sure that it is her own.

原来我以为这不过是一种亲热的表示，但是**现在看来**，这是为了闻一闻羊羔的味道，来断定是不是自己生的。

I *knew* it quite well as I *know* it now.

我**当时**和**现在**了解得一样清楚。

The old man *said*，“They *say* his father *was* a fisherman. Maybe he *was* as poor as we *are*.”

老头儿说：“听人说，**从前**他爸爸是个打鱼的。他**过去**也许跟我们**现在**一样穷。”

6.1.6　增加量词

英语中的数词(包括不定冠词a)与可数名词往往直接连用，他们之间没有量词，而汉语往往借助量词。因此翻译时应根据汉语表达习惯恰当地增加表示其形状、特征或材料等的量词。如：

first thing第一件事　the first oil well第一口油井　a pack of cigarette一包香烟

a carton of cigarette一条香烟　a bike一辆自行车　a typewriter一架打字机

a tractor一台拖拉机　a mouth一张嘴　a full moon一轮满月　a bad dream一场噩梦

He was so absorbed in the work that he hasn't had *a bite* since this morning.

他工作得这么专心致志，从早晨到现在连饭都没来得及吃上**一口**。

A red sun rose slowly from the calm lake.

一轮红日从风平浪静的湖面冉冉升起。

Into the dim clouds was swimming *a* crescent moon.

一钩新月渐渐隐没在朦胧的云彩里去了。

A stream was winding its way through the valley into the river.

一弯溪水蜿蜒流过山谷，汇合到江里去了。

英语中有些动词或动作名词，译成汉语动词时常需增加一些表示行为、动作量的动量词。例如：have a rest(休息一下)；make a stop(停一下)，等等。

Once，they *have a quarrel*.

有一次，他们争**吵了一番**。

He squeezed his sister too and *gave her a gentle push*.

他也捏了一下他的妹妹并且把她轻轻**推了一下**。

Herb *gave her a sly look*.

赫伯**狡猾地看了她一眼**。

I was extremely worried about her，but this was neither place nor the time for *a lecture* or *an argument*.

我真替她万分担忧，但此时此地，既不宜**教训她一番**，也不宜与她**争论一通**。

6.1.7 增加反映背景情况的词

The *New York Times*，the *Guardian*，*Le Monde*，the *People's Daily* and the *United Morning Post* all reported the nuclear crises in Korean Peninsula.

美国的《纽约时报》、**英国的**《卫报》、**法国的**《世界报》、**中国的**《人民日报》以及**新加坡的**《联合早报》都对朝鲜半岛的核危机进行了报道。

Duma corresponds to the Senate in America.

俄国杜马相当于美国国会。

The *Pentagon* made no responds to this incident.

五角大楼**(指美国国防部)**对这一事件没有做出任何反应。

6.1.8 增加概括词

英语和汉语都有概括词。英语中的in short、and so on、etc.等等，翻译时可以分别译为“总之”“等等”“……”。有时候英语句子中没有概括词，而翻译时可增加“两人”“双方”“等等”“凡此种种”等概括词，同时省略掉英语中的连接词。例如：

We must enable everyone who receives education to develop *morally*, *intellectually and physically*.

我们应该使受教育者在德育、智育、体育**三个方面**都得到发展。

They talked about *inflation*, *unemployment*, *financial investment and environmental protection*.

他们谈到了通货膨胀、失业、金融投资以及环保**等问题**。

The *Americans and the Japanese* conducted a completely secret exchange of messages.

美日**双方**在完全保密的情况下互相交换了信件。

The thesis summed up the new achievements made in *electronic computers*, *artificial satellites and rockets*.

论文总结了电子计算机、人造卫星和火箭**三方面**的新成就。

6.2　根据句法上的需要增词

在了解英语和汉语句法结构差别的基础上，在准确理解原文的基础上，判断原文在什么地方有省略或需要增加词句，才能用另一种语言准确表达出来。在翻译时，增加适当的词，准确、通顺地表达原文的思想内容。

6.2.1　增补原文回答句中的省略部分

Few children can eat when excited with the thoughts of a journey; *nor* could I.

孩子们一想到要去旅行，心情激动，很少能吃下东西，我也同样吃不下去。

Is this your book? Yes, *it is*.这是你的书吗？**是我的**。(Yes, it is = Yes, it is mine.)

Rebecca: "What! Don't you love him (Amelia's brother)?" Amelia: "Yes, of course, *I do*."

里贝卡：“怎么？你不爱他(爱米丽的哥哥)？”爱米丽：“**我当然爱他**。”

(Yes, of course, I do = Yes, of course I love him.)

6.2.2　增补原文句子中所省略的动词

Reading *makes* a full man; conference (...) a ready man; writing (...) an exact man.

读书使人充实，讨论使人机智，写作使人准确。

An eagle and a fox had long *lived* together as good neighbors； the eagle (...) at the summit of a high tree， the fox (...) in a hole at the foot of it.

一只鹰和一只狐狸长期友好地**住**在一起，鹰**住**在一棵高高的树顶上，狐狸**住**在树下一个洞里。

We don't *retreat*， we never have (...) and never will (...).

我们不**后退**，我们从没有**后退**过，将来也决不**后退**。

6.2.3 增补原文比较句中的省略部分

Better be wise by the defeat of others than *by your own*.

从别人的**失败中**吸取教训比从**自己的失败中**吸取教训更好。

He is more *concerned* about others than about himself.

他**关心**别人胜于**关心**自己。

The footmen were as ready to *serve* her as they were their own mistress.

仆人们愿意**服侍**她，就像他们愿意**服侍**他们的女主人一样。

综合练习

一、将下列句子译成汉语

1. Not to educate him (the child) is to condemn him to repetitious *ignorance*.
2. *Oxidation* will make iron and steel rusty.
3. This *lack of resistance* in very cold metals may become useful in electronic computers.
4. You have to overcome your *complacency*.
5. What a *leader* he is!
6. What a *sight*!
7. He was always looking for a shortcut to *fame and fortune*.
8. Miss Havisham sent her out to *attract* and *torment* and do mischief， with the malicious assurance that she was beyond the reach of all admirers.
9. Aunt Harriet used to *entertain* lavishly.
10. *Long-stemmed* models walked through the lobby.
11. This typewriter is indeed *cheap and fine*.
12. He is a *complicated* man—*moody*， *mercurial*， with a *melancholy streak*.
13. He felt the *patriot* rise within his breast.

14. He allowed the *father* to be overruled by the *judge*, and declared his own son guilty.

15. In general, the metals are good conductors, with silver *the best* and copper *the second*.

16. Courage in excess becomes foolhardiness(愚勇), affection *weakness*, thrift *avarice*(贪婪).

17. The molecules of hydrogen get closer and closer with the *pressure*.

18. Mary *washes* after getting up.

19. Sept. 11 delivered both a shock and a surprise—*the attack*, and *our response to it*—and we can argue forever over which mattered more.

20. He was *wrinkled* and *black*, with scant gray hair.

21. Man, *was*, *is* and always *will be* trying to improve his living conditions.

22. When I turned around, John was grinning, *expectant*, studying my face intently to see if he had pleased me. He *had*.

23. Fortune knocks at every man's door once in a life, but in a good many cases, the man is in a neighboring saloon and does not hear *her*.

24. They *had always been* able to control things. *Now* control *was getting away* from all of them.

25. We *don't regret*, we *never have had*, we *never will*.

26. I *was*, and *remain*, grateful for the part he played in my release.

27. The high-altitude plane *was* and still *is* a remarkable bird.

28. I *had* never thought I'd be happy to find myself considered unimportant. But this time I *was*.

29. Can you manage *without* help?

30. *Past retirement age*, Dr. Masefield is as vigorous as ever.

31. Hydrogen burns in air or oxygen, *forming* water.

参考译文

1. 如果我们不对儿童进行教育的话，那就要使儿童沦入世世代代的愚昧状态。

2. 氧化作用会使钢铁生锈。

3. 这种在甚低温金属中没有电阻的现象可能对电子计算机很有用处。

4. 你必须克服自满情绪。

5. 他真是一个出类拔萃的领袖！

6. 多么美的景色啊！

7. 他一直在寻觅成名成家、发财致富的捷径。

8. 郝薇香小姐把她放出去招蜂引蝶，去折磨男人，去害男人，其恶毒用心就是让追求她的男人对她永远望尘莫及。

9. 哈丽特阿姨时常慷慨地款待客人。

10. 身材修长的模特儿们走过大厅。

11. 这部打字机真是物美价廉。

12. 他是一个性格复杂的人——喜怒无常，反复多变，有些忧郁寡欢。

13. 他感到一种爱国热情在胸中激荡。

14. 他让法官的职责战胜父子的私情，而判决他儿子有罪。

15. 一般来说，金属都是良好的导体，其中以银为最好，铜次之。

16. 勇敢过度，即成蛮勇；感情过度，即成溺爱，俭约过度，即成贪婪。

17. 随着压力增加，氢分子越来越近。

18. 玛丽起床后洗脸。

19. 9•11事件带给我们的是震惊和意外——令人震惊的是这场袭击，令人意外的是我们对这一事件的反应——至于哪一个更要紧我们可能会永远争论不休。

20. 他满脸皱纹，皮肤黝黑，头发灰白稀疏。

21. 人类过去、现在而且将来总是在尽力改善生活条件。

22. 我转过身，只见约翰正咧着嘴笑，满脸期待的神情；他热切的目光想从我的脸上探明他是否博得了我的欢心。他确实博得了我的欢心。

23. 每个人的一生中，幸运之神都只来敲一次门，可是许多情况下，那个受到眷顾的人竟在隔壁的酒馆里，听不见她敲门。

24. 他们从前一向是能够控制局面的，现在局势失控了。

25. 我们不后悔，我们从来就没后悔过，我们将来也不会后悔。

26. 我的获释是他成全的，对此我过去很感激，现在仍然很感激。

27. 该高空飞机过去是，现在仍然是一种了不起的飞机。

28. 以往我从未想过，当我发觉人们认为我无足轻重时，我会感到高兴。但这次情况确实如此。

29. 如果没有人帮忙，你能应付得了吗？

30. 虽然已经过了退休年龄，可梅斯费乐德博士仍然和以前一样精力充沛。

31. 氢气在空气或氧气中燃烧，就会形成水。

二、将下列段落翻译成汉语

September 11 Attacks

Sept.11 delivered both a shock and a surprise—the attack, and our response to it – and we can argue forever over which mattered more. There has been so much talk of the goodness that erupted that day that we forget how unprepared we were for it. We did not expect much from a generation that had spent its middle age examining all the ways it failed to measure up to the one that had come before all fat，no muscle，less a beacon to the world than a bully，drunk on blessings taken for granted.

It was tempting to say that Sept. 11 changed all that，just as it is tempting to say that every hero needs a villain，and goodness needs evil as its grinding stone. But try looking a widow in the eye and talking about all the good that has come of this. It may not be a coincidence，but neither is it a partnership：good does not need evil，we owe no debt to demons，and the attack did not make us better.

It was an occasion to discover what we already were. "Maybe the purpose of all this，" New York City Mayor Rudy Giuliani said at a funeral for a friend， "is to find out if America today is as strong as when we fought for our independence or when we fought for ourselves as a Union to end slavery or as strong as our fathers and grandfathers who fought to rid the world of Nazism." The terrorists，he argues，were counting on our cowardice. They've learned a lot about us since then. And so have we. For leading that lesson，for having more faith in us than we had in ourselves，for being brave when required and rude where appropriate and tender without being trite，for not sleeping and not quitting and not shrinking from the pain all around him，Rudy Giuliani，Mayor of the World，is TIME's 2001 Person of the Year. (From *Time*，December 31，2001)

参考译文1

9·11事件带给我们的是震惊和意外——令人震惊的是这场袭击，令人意外的是我们对这一事件的反应——至于哪一个更要紧我们可能会永远争论不休。对于当天涌现出的可歌可泣事迹，我们已经谈得太多了，但却忘记了我们当时对袭击毫无防备。我们对这一代人本没有太多期许，因为他们把自己的中年时代全都花费在检讨自己为何不如上一代人的原因上，最终却只落得脑满肠肥，毫无力量和生气。与其说他们是世界的引路人，不如说是欺凌弱小、陶醉于上帝恩赐的一代。

我们也许很容易就说9·11事件改变了这一切，就像我们会说每个英雄都需要一个坏人来反衬，善良需要邪恶来砥砺一样。但让我们反观9·11罹难者遗孀的眼神，再来谈谈人们在这一事件中所彰显出的美德，我们可能会看到这也许并非是一个巧合。善良并不需要邪恶相伴，我们也并不亏欠这些魔鬼一丝一毫，而这次袭击也没有使我们变得更好。

这次袭击给了我们一个重新认识自己的机会。在参加一个朋友的葬礼时，纽约市市长鲁迪·朱利亚尼这样说道："也许这一切的目的就是要考验我们，看看今天的美国是否仍像我们当年为独立而战时那样强大；今天的美国是否仍像我们当年团结一致，为废止奴隶制而战时那样强大；今天的美国是否仍像我们的父辈当年为摧毁纳粹而战时那样强大。”他有力地说道：恐怖分子们希望我们胆小怯懦。但从此以后他们会对我们更加了解，当然我们也更深刻地认识了我们自己。他领导有方，比我们自己更信任我们，必须时临危不惧，必要时态度强硬、温文尔雅，却又绝不迂腐；他废寝忘食，虽身处危局却决不退缩放弃。他，就是鲁迪·朱利亚尼，当今世界最出色的市长，2001《时代》周刊年度人物。(摘自2001年12月31日《时代》周刊)

参考译文2

“9·11”事件既令人感到震惊，也令人感到意外。震惊的是攻击事件本身，意外的是我们对事件的反应。至于说这两者哪个更为重要，人们也许永远会争论下去。对于当天一下子涌现出来的可歌可泣的事迹，我们已经谈得不少了。在一片谈论声中，我们居然忘了，面对这些令人敬佩的行为我们当时是多么感到意外。因为我们本来就没有对这代美国人抱有多大期望。他们的中年是在自叹不如的心境中度过的，他们和上一代美国人比来比去，总感到自己望尘莫及。他们虚浮有余，坚实不足，根本谈不上是世界的灯塔，倒却是横行的恶霸，沉醉于福荫之中，总觉得受之无愧。

我们也许会脱口而出地说，是“9·11”事件改变了这一切，正如我们会脱口而出地说，英雄需要有恶棍来陪衬，善良需要有邪恶来砥砺。但当你望着“9·11”死难者遗孀的双眼时，你难道还能侃侃而谈“9·11”事件所引发的好处吗？不错，善恶并存也许确非巧合，但它们也绝非相互依存的伙伴：善用不着恶陪伴左右，我们并不亏欠魔鬼，“9·11”事件也没有把我们变成更好的人。

它只是一次机会，我们不过借此发现了自己的本色。纽约市市长朱利安尼在朋友的葬礼中说得好：“也许这一切的目的就是要考验一下，看看今日的美国是否仍像当年为争取独立而战时那样坚强，是否仍像当年为结束奴隶制而团结奋战时那样坚强，是否仍像当年我们的父辈为消灭纳粹而战时那样坚强。”他认为，恐怖主义者就指望我们会胆怯。但自“9·11”事件以来，他们想必对我们已有所了解。当然我们对自己也有了不少认识。由于朱利安尼在这次考验中堪称表率，由于他对我们的信心远胜于我们对自己的信心，由于他该勇敢时就勇敢，该鲁莽时就鲁莽，他温情流露，但那绝非应景之俗套，由于他不分昼夜，不停工作，虽被痛苦包围，却能勇敢面对，因此这位天下第一市长当选为2001年《时代周刊》的年度风云人物。

——叶子南译

第7章

翻译技巧(三)重复法

翻译作为语际交流，不仅仅是语言的转换过程，而且是文化移植的过程。王佐良先生曾经说过：“翻译的最大困难是两种文化的不同。”因此，解决好翻译中文化差异的问题是保证译作成功的关键。

英语中的Repetition(反复)也是一种极常用的修辞格，用以强调某种事物的意义，形成优美的节奏。但从总体上说，英语是一种忌重复(redundancy)的语言，主张“言贵简洁(Brevity is the soul of the wit)”；为了强调有时也使用重复手段，但一般不重复原词，多用代词复指以使行文简练。

英语回避重复的主要方法：指代法——代词；换词法——范畴词、同义词，或准同义词；替代法——替代词语和替代句型；省略法——省略相同的词语；保留介词法；紧缩法。

7.1 重复的意义

“汉语的重复作为一种修辞手段有两种作用。一是为了强调，重复表达一个意思，或增添修饰语，加强语义。二是为了便于词语搭配，或平衡节奏，增加可读性。”前者称为语义性重复，后者称为修辞性重复。这些具有重复语义的词语或句子，可有效地增强语势、强化语义、增强表达效果。

汉语喜欢重复，英语崇尚简洁，这是汉英民族审美心理差异所形成的不同的审美标准，翻译时对于汉语的重复词语或重复结构必须有所删削省略，以使译文适应读者的审美心理，符合英语的表达习惯。

汉语中的某些成语为了音韵整齐、语义对称而使用两组同义词，英译时往往只需译出其中一组词义，以避免重复。如：

花言巧语——fine words

油嘴滑舌——glib-tongued/a smooth tongue

捕风捉影——to catch at shadows

铜墙铁壁——bastion of iron/ Guards and Wards

精疲力竭——exhausted/ be worn out/be run down/be tired out

随波逐流——to swim with the stream

水深火热——in deep waters

咬牙切齿——to gnash one's teeth

土崩瓦解——to fall apart

自吹自擂——to blow one's own trumpet

汉语中为了讲究句子的平衡、气势或音韵节奏，还常连续使用两组结构相似、语义相同的平行结构，英译时也往往只需译出其中一组词义。如：

此时鲁小姐卸了浓妆，换几件雅淡衣服，公子举目细看，**真有沉鱼落雁之容，闭月羞花之貌**。(吴敬梓：《儒林外史》)

By this time Miss Lu had changed out of her ceremonial dress into an ordinary gown, and then Zhu looked at her closely, *he saw that her beauty would put the flowers to shame.*

句中“沉鱼落雁之容”和“闭月羞花之貌”都是形容女性之娇美，这种对仗的修辞形式有结构对称、增强语势之效，读起来还具有音韵之美，英译时却只需译出主要语义即可。

英语中代词的使用频率大大高于汉语，对于汉语中重复出现的名词，英译时可用相应的代词指称汉语名词，这是避免重复、简化译文语句的有效方法。

此外，汉语和英语中的排比句是一种常见的、富有表现力的修辞手法，通常采用三个或三个以上结构相同、语义相关、语气连贯的词组或句子排列成串，以达到“壮文势，广文义”的目的；但“英语的排比强调结构上的整齐匀称，汉语的排比不仅强调齐整美，而且还强调反复美。共同词语反复出现是构成汉语排比辞式齐整的重要标志。”对于排比句的翻译，有时可照原文结构直译，但有时为适应英美读者“言贵简洁”的审美心理，对其中反复出现的共同词语或结构必须予以简化，以符合英语的表达习惯。如：

We must *adhere* to the socialist road，the people’s democratic dictatorship(i.e. the dictatorship of the proletariat)，the Communist Party’s leadership and Marxism-Leninism and Mao Zedong Thought.

我们必须**坚持**社会主义道路，**坚持**人民民主专政即无产阶级专政，**坚持**共产党的领导，**坚持**马列主义、毛泽东思想。

Let us stretch out our arms to embrace *spring*，which is *one* of the revolutions，of the people，and of science.

这是革命的**春天**，这是人民的**春天**，这是科学的**春天**！让我们张开双臂，热烈拥抱这个**春天**吧！

汉民族历来有求偶对称的审美心理，崇尚对称工整所造就的形式美。中国古代四方形的城郭，北京的四合院民居，故宫、庙宇中的四方形大殿等，无不流露着“对称工整”的审美构思。《周易·系辞上》记述：“易有太极，是生两仪，两仪生四象，四象生八卦。”这也许是汉民族求偶对称的心理渊源。

汉语成语大多采用四字结构，在古诗赋和骈文中也采用四字句的行文格式，此外还有大量的按固定格式形成的“四字格”，由于它们读起来铿锵悦耳，连用排比起来，颇有行云流水或势如破竹之感，对人们的日常表达和文学语言有着广泛而深远的影响，故四字结构在汉语中是非常常见的语言现象。现举数例：

秦孝公据**崤函之固**，拥**雍州之地**，**君臣固守**，**以窥周室**，有**席卷天下**、**包举宇内**、**囊括四海**之意、**并吞八荒**之心……(贾谊：《过秦论》)

The garden was a paradise on earth，with more food and clothes than could be consumed and more money than could be spent.

花园里面是人间的乐园，有的是吃不完的**大米白面**，穿不完的**绫罗绸缎**，花不完的**金银珠宝**。(周而复：《上海的早晨》)

原文中的“大米白面”“绫罗绸缎”“金银财宝”分别指“吃的”“穿的”“用的”，可直截了当地译为food、clothes和money，这样词义凝练通俗，行文简洁流畅；

如将“大米”“白面”“绫”“罗”“绸”“缎”“金”“银”等物质名词逐字译出，译文势必显得累赘、臃肿、拖沓，不符合英语的表达习惯。

江岸上**彩楼林立**，**彩灯高悬**，**旌旗飘扬**，呈现出一派**喜气洋洋**的节日场面。**千姿百态**的各式彩龙在江面上游弋，舒展着优美的身姿，有的**摇头摆尾**，**风采奕奕**，有的**喷火吐水**，**威风八面**。

(何志范：《乐山龙舟会多姿多彩》)

High-rise buildings ornamented with colored lanterns and bright banners stand out along the river banks. On the river itself，gaily decorated dragon-shaped boats await their challenge，displaying their individual charms to their hearts' content. One boat wags its head and tail；another spits fire and sprays water.

原文辞藻华丽，文采斐然，描述生动，场面壮观；但若照原文直译，则原文的结构和过多的修饰语会使译文累赘冗余，令人厌读，很可能产生适得其反的效果。译者充分考虑了西方读者的审美情趣，灵活处理了中英文在行文习惯上的差异，调整句子长度并删去了“呈现出一派喜气洋洋的节日场面”“风采奕奕”“威风八面”等词句，通过“gaily decorated”和“displaying their individual charms to their hearts' content”，以简洁明快的语句，表达原文中龙舟赛场壮观热烈的气氛和千姿百态的龙舟风采。

7.2 重复法应用

重复法是指在译文中适当地重复原文中出现过的词语，以使意思表达得更加清楚；或者进一步加强语气，突出强调某些内容，收到更好的修辞效果。一般而言，英语往往为了行文简洁而尽量避免重复。所以，英语经常借助替代、省略或变换等其他表达方法。相反，重复却是汉语表达的一个显著特点。在许多场合某些词语不仅需要重复，而且也只有重复这些词语，语义才能明确，表达才能生动。为了达到汉语译文准确、通顺和完整的翻译标准，在翻译中，常常需要对一些关键性的词加以重复。

7.2.1 重复名词

重复英语中作宾语或表语的名词。例如：

Big powers have *their* strategies while *small countries* also have *their own* lines.

强国有强国的策略，小国有小国的路线。

Marketing economy is itself the *product* of long course of development，of a series of revolutions in the modes of production and of exchange.

市场经济本身是一个长期发展过程的**产物**，是生产方式和交换方式一系列变革的**产物**。

The three most important *effects* of electric current are heating，magnetic and chemical effects.

电流最重要的三种**效应**就是热**效应**、磁**效应**和化学**效应**。

7.2.2 重复动词

英语句子中动词后有介词时，在第二次或者第三次出现时往往只用介词而省略动词，在汉语译文中则要重复动词。

He encouraged this bumptious young man to *write* of his own region—of its bleak poverty and of its women old before their time.

他鼓励这个狂妄的年轻人**写**自己的故乡——**写**故乡的荒凉和贫困，**写**故乡未老先衰的女人。

Then he *spoke of* the rise of charity and popular education，and in particular of the spread of wealth and work.

接着他**谈到**了慈善事业的兴起和教育的普及，特别**谈到**了财富和工作面的扩大。

But his wife kept *dinning* in his ears *about* his idleness，his carelessness，and the ruin he was bringing on his family.

可他老婆总是在他耳边唠叨个没完。**说**他懒惰，**说**他粗心，还**说**他一家人都要毁在他的身上。

7.2.3 重复代词

(1) 英语代词的使用非常频繁，汉语中除非必要，一般不宜多用代词。因此，在翻译中，除了适当地将原文中的一些代词直译外，还经常将某些代词所替代的名词重复译出，以使译文意思清楚明了。例如：

Even as the doctor was recommending *rest*，he knew that *this* in itself was not enough，that one could never get real rest without a peaceful mind.

尽管医生建议**休息**，他也知道**休息**本身是不够的，如果心情不平静，是休息不好的。

Jesse opened his *eyes*. *They* were filled with tears.

杰西睁开**眼睛**，**眼**里充满了泪水。

He hated *failure*；he had conquered *it* all his life，risen above *it*，despised *it* in others.

他讨厌**失败**，他一生中曾战胜**失败**，超越**失败**，并且藐视别人的**失败**。

(2) 当英语用物主代词its、his、their等代替句中作主语的名词(有时附有修饰语)时，翻译时往往可以不用代词而重复其作主语的名词(有时附有修饰语)，以达到明确具体的目的。

Happy families also had *their own* troubles.

幸福的家庭也有**幸福家庭**的苦恼。

Each country has *its own* customs.

各国有**各国**的风俗。

(3) 在翻译英语中的关系代词which、that或关系副词whoever、whenever、wherever等时，往往使用重复法处理。

As each currency's *value* is stated in terms of other currencies, French francs, then, have a value in US dollars, *which* have a value in British pounds, which have a value in Japanese yen.

由于每一种货币的**价值**是用另外的货币表现出来的，那么法国法郎的**价值**可以用美元来体现，美元可以用英镑来体现，英镑可以用日元来体现。

Needs are the basic, often instinctive, human *forces* that motivate a person to do something.

各种需要是人类基本的、通常又是出于本能的**驱动力**，**各种驱动力**促使一个人去从事某件事情。

Wherever there is oppression, there is resistance.

哪里有压迫**哪里**就有反抗。

7.2.4 其他情况下的重复

(1) 在重复法中，有时采用两字重叠、四字重叠或四字对偶等修辞手段，使译文更生动。

There has been too much *publicity* about that case.

这件事已经闹得**满城风雨**，**沸沸扬扬**。

Easy *come*, easy *go*.

来得容易**去得**快。

No pains, *no* gains.

一分耕耘，**一分**收获。

Nothing venture, *nothing* gain.

不入虎穴**焉得**虎子。

(2) 为了强调，英语中往往重复关键词，以使读者加深印象。汉译时可以采用同样手段。英文中有重复的词，译文也重复同样的词。

And that government of *the people*，by *the people*，for *the people*，shall not perish from the earth.

并且使这个**民**有、**民**治、**民**享的政府永世长存。

Gentlemen may cry *peace*，but there is no *peace*.

先生们尽管高喊**和平**，**和平**，但是依然没有**和平**。

Kids are *kids*.

孩子终究是**孩子**。

综合练习

一、将下列句子译成汉语

1. You can *do* that work very well if you care to.

2. Light *travels* more quickly than sound does.

3. People use natural science to understand and change *nature*.

4. A good play serves to educate and inspire *the people*.

5. Students must be cultivated to have the ability to analyze and solve *problems*.

6. For the purpose of attaining freedom in the world of nature，man must use natural science to understand，conquer and change *nature* and thus attain freedom from nature.

7. We *talked* of ourselves，of our prospects，of the journey，of the weather，of each other—of everything.

8. Ignorance is *the mother* of fear as well as of admiration.

9. *Whoever* violates the disciplines should be criticized.

10. *Wherever* there is matter，there is motion.

11. The use of poison gas is a clear *violation* of international law—in particular of the Geneva Convention.

12. For China，the first thing is to *throw off* poverty. To do that we have to find a way to develop fairly rapidly.

13. "Stop thief! Stop thief！" There is a magic in the sound. The tradesman *leaves* his counter，and the carman his wagon；the butcher *throws down* his tray，the baker his basket，the milkman his pail，the errand-boy his parcels，the schoolboy his marbles，the pavior his pickaxe，the child his battledore.

14. Oh，thought she，I have been very wicked and *selfish*—selfish in forgetting their

sorrows—selfish in forcing George to marry me. I *know* I am not worthy of his—I know he would have been happy without me—and yet—I *tried*, I tried to give him up.

参考译文

1. 如果你肯做那项工作，你就能做得很好。

2. 光传播的速度要比声音传播速度快得多。

3. 人们利用自然科学来理解自然改变自然。

4. 一部好的电视剧可以教育人，启发人。

5. 必须培养学生分析问题和解决问题的能力。

6. 人们为了要在自然界里得到自由，就要用自然科学来了解自然、征服自然和改造自然。

7. 我们谈到自己，谈到前途，谈到旅程，谈到天气，谈到彼此的情况——谈到所有的一切事情。

8. 无知是羡慕的根源，也是恐惧的根源。

9. 谁违反了纪律，谁就应该受到批评。

10. 哪里有物质，哪里就有运动。

11. 使用毒气很明显违背国际法，尤其违背日内瓦公约。

12. 对于中国首要的事情就是摆脱贫穷，而为了摆脱贫穷我们必须找到一条快速发展的道路。

13. “捉贼！捉贼！”这个声音里有一种魔力。商人离开了柜台，赶车的离开了车子，屠夫放下了盆子，面包师放下了篮子，挤牛奶的放下了提桶，杂役放下了包裹，小学生丢下弹子，铺路工人丢下尖锄，小孩子丢下球拍。

14. 她暗暗想到：“唉，我真混账，真自私。爸爸妈妈那么可怜，我不把他们放在心上，又硬要嫁给乔治，可见我只顾自己。我明知自己配不上他，明知他不娶我也很快乐，可是——我努力想叫自己松了手让他去吧，可是总狠不下心。”

二、将下列段落译成汉语

Think it over...

Today we have higher buildings and wider highways, but shorter temperaments and narrower points of view;

We spend more, but enjoy less;

We have bigger houses, but smaller families;

We have more compromises, but less time;

We have more knowledge, but less judgment;

We have more medicines, but less health;

We have multiplied out possessions, but reduced out values;

We talk much, we love only a little, and we hate too much;

We reached the Moon and came back, but we find it troublesome to cross our own street and meet our neighbors;

We have conquered the outer space, but not our inner space;

We have higher income, but less morals;

These are times with more liberty, but less joy;

We have much more food, but less nutrition;

These are the days in which it takes two salaries for each home, but divorces increase;

These are times of finer houses, but more broken homes;

That's why I propose, that as of today;

You do not keep anything for a special occasion, because every day that you live is a SPECIAL OCCASION.

Search for knowledge, read more, sit on your porch and admire the view without paying attention to your needs;

Spend more time with your family and friends, eat your favorite foods, visit the places you love;

Life is a chain of moments of enjoyment; not only about survival;

Use your crystal goblets.

Do not save your best perfume, and use it every time you feel you want it.

Remove from your vocabulary phrases like "one of these days" or "someday";

Let's write that letter we thought of writing "one of these days"!

Let's tell our families and friends how much we love them;

Do not delay anything that adds laughter and joy to your life;

Every day, every hour, and every minute is special;

And you don't know if it will be your last.

参考译文

今天我们拥有了更高层的楼宇以及更宽阔的公路，但是我们的性情却更为急躁，眼光也更加狭隘；

我们消耗的更多，享受到的却更少；

我们的住房更大了，但我们的家庭却更小了；

我们妥协更多，时间更少；

我们拥有了更多的知识，可判断力却更差了；

我们有了更多的药品，但健康状况却更不如意了；

我们拥有的财富倍增，但其价值却减少了；

我们说的多了，爱的却少了，我们的仇恨也更多了；

我们可以往返月球，但却难以迈出一步去亲近我们的左邻右舍；

我们可以征服外太空，却征服不了我们的内心；

我们的收入增加了，但我们的道德却少了；

我们的时代更加自由了，但我们拥有的快乐时光却越来越少；

我们有了更多的食物，但所能得到的营养却越来越少了；

现在每个家庭都可以有双份收入，但离婚的现象越来越多了；

现在的住房越来越精致，但我们也有了更多破碎的家庭；

这就是我为什么要说，让我们从今天开始；

不要将你的东西为了某一个特别的时刻而预留着，因为你生活的每一天都是那么特别。

寻找更多的知识，多读一些书，坐在你家的门廊里，以赞美的眼光去享受眼前的风景，不要带上任何功利的想法；

花多点时间和朋友与家人在一起，吃你爱吃的食物，去你想去的地方；

生活是一串串的快乐时光；我们不仅仅是为了生存而生存；

举起你的水晶酒杯吧。

不要吝啬洒上你最好的香水，你想用的时候就享用吧。

从你的词汇库中移去所谓的“有那么一天”或者“某一天”；

曾打算“有那么一天”去写的信，就在今天吧！

告诉家人和朋友，我们是多么爱他们；

不要延迟任何可以给你的生活带来欢笑与快乐的事情；

每一天、每一小时、每一分钟都是那么特别；

你无从知道这是否是最后一刻。

第8章

翻译技巧(四)省略法

英汉两种语言在语法上差异较大，例如：英语有冠词，而汉语却没有；英语重形合、连接词较多，汉语重意合、连接词较少；英语中介词丰富，多达280多个，汉语中介词则较少，只有30几个；英语中经常使用代词，尤其是经常使用人称代词、关系代词等，而汉语中代词则用得较少。因此，英译汉时可根据具体情况将冠词、连接词、介词、代词略去，使译文简练通畅。

省略法(omission)，也叫减省译法，是指在翻译中，原文中有些词在译文中可以省略，不必翻译出来。因为译文中虽然没有这个词，但是已经具有了原文这个词所表达的意思，或者这个词在译文中的意义是不言而喻的。

一般来说，汉语较英语简练。英译汉时，许多在原文中必不可少的词语要是原原本本地译成汉语，就会成为不必要的冗词，译文会显得十分累赘。因此省略法在英译汉中使用得非常广泛，其主要目的是删去一些可有可无、不符合译文习惯表达法的词语，如实词中的代词、动词的省略；虚词中的冠词、介词和连词的省略等，使译文更加通顺流畅，更符合译入语表达习惯。省略要遵循如下原则：不能把原文的某些思想内容删去，不能改变原文的意思。

由于汉语意合句多，不强调形式上的完整，只要不妨碍意义的表达，即可省去形式上的东西；英语形合句多，注重把各种关系用语言形式表达出来。所以在汉译英时往往需要增补必要的关联词(连词、介词等)；在英译汉时则往往可以省去这些关联词。

8.1 按句法需要省略

有些词语在英语中使用比较广泛(如关联词、代词)或者不能随便省略(如冠词、虚词it、联系动词等)，而在汉语却使用较少或可以省略；有些词语在汉语中使用比较广泛(如范畴词、量词、语气助词等)而在英语中却可以省略或较少使用。

8.1.1 省略代词

滥译代词，与滥译冠词一样，是造成生硬牵强的“翻译腔”的重要原因。相对于英语，汉语最常见的省略是主语的省略，出现的频率相当高。这种人称代词的省略实际上是采用零前指(zero anaphora)的照应形式进行语篇的衔接。请看下面的例子：

贾母一面说，一面来看宝玉，只见今日这顿打，不比往日，又是心疼，又是生气，也抱着哭个不了。(曹雪芹，《红楼梦》，Chap. 33)

From the sight that met *her* eyes *she* could tell that this has been no ordinary beating. *It* filled *her* with anguish for *the* sufferer and fresh anger for *the* man *who* had inflicted it，and for a long time *she* clung to the inert form and wept... (D. Hawkes，Trans. *The Story of the Stone*)

上文中，主语“贾母”只在文首出现一次，之后就全部省略了。

李讷和汤普森(转见胡壮麟1994：65- 66) 指出，汉语使用零式指称远多于英语，并且由于汉语是意合语言，零式指称不受句法限制。他们通过实验，得出“零式指称才是汉语的常规”这一结论。鉴于李讷和汤普森的语料取自中国古典白话小说，胡壮麟(1994：66) 又从现代汉语的角度加以说明。许余龙(1992：249) 对三部现代汉语小说中的零前指照应和人称照应进行了分析，零前指的运用受以下因素的影响。

(1) 篇章的信息结构和结构特征。如当段落中相连句子的话题涉及同一个人或事物，构成一个话题链时；或段落中相连的句子都比较短且结构简单，就有利于采用零前指。

(2) 篇章的整体语义因素和局部语义因素。如某一人或事物是整个篇章语义结构的组织核心；再如各句中动词、名词等成分表达的施事、动作、受事等关系能表达哪类人干哪类事，且前后句子联系明显，就容易出现零前指。

(3) 语用因素。如作者一般都遵守合作原则，如果他认为读者能确定零前指的照应项，则会倾向于使用零前指。

(4) 语体风格因素。如在法律文件、科技文体等正规严谨的文体中，零前指的使用频率会大大降低。

(5) 主题显著。只有在主题显著的语言里才有可能采用零前指的形式。汉语是主题显著的语言，零前指的使用符合汉语重意合、具有开放性、竹节式结构的特点。

在语篇行文与表达习惯上，英汉的重要差异之一就是代词的使用频率。英语中每个句子(包括从句)都有主语，但汉语却习惯于：前一部分已有主语，后一部分如果与前一部分的主语相同，则要求省去，以免重复。中国古典文学之精华的唐诗宋词元曲，代词使用频率极低。一部《宋词三百首》很难找出50个代词来。例如：

昨夜西风凋碧树，
( )独上高楼，
( )望尽天涯路。
( ) 欲寄[ ]彩笺兼尺素，
山长水阔( )知[ ]何处。

——晏殊《蝶恋花》

原文实际上一个代词都没有，用形式化句法分析，可以认为省略了括号中的六个代词，即四个(我) 两个[你]。

而对于英语，代词使用极为频繁，原因多样。语法上讲，英语作为印欧形态语言的一支，句子主谓二分，主语不可省略；及物动词必有宾语，介词必有宾语。而为了避免不断地重复名词词组，这些主语、宾语之类就常常使用代词。另外，物主代词之使用也常为英语的语法要求。如“He put a book on his head”中“his”就是语法上必须有的。

英汉在代词频率上的差异，有诗为证：

松下问童子，
言师采药去。
只在此山中，
云深不知处。

——贾岛《寻隐者不遇》

其英语译文为：

A Note Left For an Absent Recluse
I ask your lad neath a pine-tree.
“My master’s gone for herbs，” says he.
“Amid the hills I know not where，
For clouds have veiled them here and there”

——许渊中译，2000

原诗中任何形式的代词都没有，而许渊冲译文使用了6个人称代词。

中国语言学家申小龙研究汉语特点，打破了“主谓二分”的印欧语言句子观对汉语的束缚，提出全新的汉语句型系统，即主题句、施事句、关系句三分天下。其中，施事句成分有时空坐标、施事者、事件，只有事件是必不可少的核心，而这个核心是动词组的铺排，而不是带主语的小句。

《人民日报》上一例语篇，是一位14 岁英国男孩写的汉语短文，对英语翻译很有启示意义。短文内容如下：

今年我在英国上学，**我的**学校是一个寄宿学校。第一个月时，我人生地不熟，但**我的**朋友很友好，所以那学期过得很快。**我的**学校里有很多同学，**他们**分别来自日本、英国、中国、法国和德国。在**我们的**学校里**你**能做不少的事情。

——安(英国)《人民日报》2005 年5 月18 日

英国男孩写此短文时，学汉语已有五年。他的汉语水平从短文看还是很不错的，然而很明显，他受到母语代词高频现象的影响，用了过多的代词。实际上六个黑体代词统统可以省略，而且六个代词的省略，不仅不会导致意义含混，反而会使短文更地道，更接近中国人的自然表达。

从这篇英国男孩的短文可以猜测，很可能是先用英语思考，后用汉语翻译的产物，像最后一句话有可能译自“In our school you can do a lot of things. ”。六个代词若回译过去，正好全都是英文必需使用代词之处。这篇短文的外国味主要就反映在代词的过多使用上，若省略六个代词，短文就立刻更有中国味了。这个活生生的例子，对英汉翻译不乏启示作用。

在英语中，完整的句子(祈使句除外)都有主语。当谓语动词是及物动词时，宾语往往必不可少，因此代词会反复出现；而汉语句子中，前后若指的是同一人或事物，后面的主语就不再重复，宾语也经常会因为前面已提到过而省略。所以在汉语的译文中，重复出现的代词大多可以省略。因此，在进行英汉翻译时要省略多次出现的主语人称代词、泛指人称代词、部分宾语代词和物主代词。请看下面的例子。

1 省略作主语的人称代词

根据汉语习惯，前句出现一个主语，后句如仍为同一主语，就不必重复出现。英语中通常每句都有主语，因此人称代词作主语往往多次出现，这种人称代词汉译时常常可以省略。英语中，泛指人称代词作主语时，即使是作第一个主语，在汉语译文中往往也可以省略。

The products should be sampled to check *their* quality before *they* leave the factory.

产品出厂前应该进行抽样检查。

I had many wonderful ideas，but *I* only put a few into practice.

我有很多美妙的想法，但是只有少数付诸实践了。

The significance of a man is not in what he attained but rather in what *he* longs to attain.

人生的意义不在于所得，而在于追求。

We live and learn.

活到老，学到老。

Your face used to be red and now *it's* pale. You were thin and now *you're* fat. I can't believe that it's you，Mr. White.

你的脸过去是红红的，现在变苍白了。你过去瘦瘦的，现在胖乎乎的。我简直不敢相信，这就是你呀，怀特先生。

2 省略作宾语的代词

英语中有些作宾语的代词，不管前面是否提到过，翻译时往往可以省略。

The more he tried to hide his mistakes，the more he revealed *them*.

他越是想要掩盖他的错误，就越是容易暴露。

Please take off the old picture and throw *it* away.

请把那张旧画取下来扔掉。

3 省略物主代词

英语句子中的物主代词出现的频率相当高。一个句子往往会出现好几个物主代词，如果将每个物主代词都翻译出来，那么汉语译文就显得非常啰嗦。所以在没有其他人称的物主代词出现的情况下，在翻译时物主代词大多被省略。试比较：

Jeff was about to head into the freezing air when *his* mother stopped *him* and，*she* carefully put *his* gloves on *his* hands.

译文(1)：天气极为寒冷，Jeff正要出门，被母亲叫住了，细心地给他戴上手套。

译文(2)：天气极为寒冷，Jeff正要出门，他的母亲叫住了他，她细心地把他的手套戴在他的手上。

英文原文五个代词，译文(1)省略了四个，译得比较自然，而译文(2)不注意代词的适当省略，比较生硬。再看下面的例子：

The mother and the eldest daughter weeded the ridges，passing before the others...A younger son，of twelve years，brought sea sand in a donkey's creels from a far corner of the field. They mixed the sand with the black clay. The fourth child，still almost an infant，staggered about near *his* mother，plucking weeds slowly and offering them to *his* mother as gifts.

母亲和大女儿在除垄上的草，把旁人甩在后面……二儿子十二岁，从老远的地头把海滩上的沙子装进鱼篮，赶着毛驴驮了回来。他们把黑土掺上了沙子。老四还是个小不点儿，在母亲身边摇摇晃晃转悠着，慢吞吞地拔起杂草，当礼物送给母亲。

He shrugged *his* shoulders，shook *his* head，cast up *his* eyes，but said nothing.

他耸了耸肩，摇了摇头，两眼看着天，一句话也没说。

4 非人称代词“it”的省略

“it”起着代词的作用，在译文中，当它被用作非人称或没有意义的时候，往往可以省略。

(1) 非人称代词“it”常用来表示天气、季节、时间、距离等概念，多在句中作主语。根据汉语表达习惯，常不译出。例如：

It is six miles to the nearest hospital from here.

离这儿最近的医院也有6英里。

It was about nine o'clock in the evening. Outside the window *it* was completely dark and *it* was raining cats and dogs.

晚上9 点钟左右，窗外一团黑漆，大雨倾盆。

(2) 强调句中“it”的省略。在强调句型“it is (was) ...that...”中，汉译时“it”必须省略，否则会不知所云。例如：

It is the joint venture that he has wanted to visit.

他一直想参观的正是那家合资公司。

It was after he heard Prof Li's report on environmental pollution that he further realized the importance of protecting our environment.

听了李教授的有关环境污染的报告后，他才进一步意识到保护环境的重要性。

(3) 先行词“it”的省略。英语中常用先行词“it”作形式主语或形式宾语，将真实主语(或真实宾语) 放置在其后。汉译时“it”不必译出。

It hasn't been clear when the new flyover is open to traffic.

新立交桥何时通车尚不清楚。

It is only shallow people who judge by appearances.

只有浅薄的人才会以貌取人。

It is commonly believed in the United States that school is where people go to get an education.

在美国，人们通常认为上学是为了受教育。

8.1.2 省略冠词

英语有冠词，汉语没有冠词；因此，英语中用来表示一类或独一无二的事物的冠词在英译汉时应该省略。

Any substance is made up of atoms whether it is *a solid*, *a liquid*, or *a gas*.

任何物质，不论是**固体**、**液体**或**气体**，都由原子组成。

A teacher should have patience in his work.

当**老师**的应该有耐心。(省略表示类别的冠词)

The moon was slowly rising above *the sea*.

月亮慢慢从**海上**升起。(省略表示独一无二的定冠词)

但是，当不定冠词用来表示数量时不可省略。例如：

He left without saying *a word*.

他**一句话**都没说就离开了。

8.1.3　省略介词

一般说来表示时间或地点的英语介词译成汉语时若放在句首常可省去，例如：

Rumors had already spread *along the streets and lanes*.

大街小巷流言四起。

Now complains are heard *in all parts* of that country.

该国**各地**怨声载道。

On Oct. 12, *1492*, Columbus discovered a new world.

1492年10月12日，哥伦布发现了新大陆。

值得注意的是：紧接在动词后面的介词汉译时一般不能省略，例如：

His uncle passed away *on* September 15, 2004.

他的叔父**于**2004年9月15日去世。

He stood *by* the desk.

他站在桌子**旁边**。

She hid *behind* the door.

她藏在门**后**。

8.1.4　省略连词

汉语词语之间连接词用得不多，其上下逻辑关系常常是暗含的，由词语的次序来表示。汉语可通过语序的排列把各句子成分和句与句之间的关系理顺，也可通过上下句的搭配，把原因、结果、条件、时间等逻辑关系隐含地表达出来。英语则不然，连接词用得比较多。因此，英译汉时，可以省略某些连词。例如：

Take the whole into consideration, *but* do the job bit by bit.

大处着眼，小处着手。

One's mind works fast *when* it is in great danger.

急中生智。(省译了引出时间状语从句的连词when)

While the prospects are bright，the road has twists and turns.

(形合)前途是光明的，道路是曲折的(意合)。

If you confer a benefit，never remember it. If you receive on，remember it always.

施恩勿记；受恩勿忘。

8.1.5 省略动词

英语中一般要有谓语动词，但是汉语中谓语不一定要用动词充当，形容词或名词都可以，因此在英语翻译成汉语的时候，有时我们会省略英语的谓语。主要有两种情况：

(1) 省略一些联系动词。

They *are* to be had very cheap and good.

它们物美价廉，随处可得。

When the pressure *gets* low，the boiling point *becomes* low.

气压低，沸点就低。

(2) 省略一些与有动作含义的名词搭配用的动词。

Solids expand and contract as liquids and gases *do*.

如同液体和气体一样，固体也能膨胀和收缩。

For this reason television signals *have* a short range.

因此，电视信号的传播距离很短。

8.2 因修辞需要省略

在翻译过程中，从汉语的修辞需要和汉语的表达习惯出发，在不影响原句的完整性和不违背原文意思的前提下，为了修辞的需要，我们常将某些词语、句子成分甚至是从句省略不译或从简译出，以求得译文干净利落，流畅精炼。例如：

Part-time work applicants who had worked at a job would receive preference *over those who had not*.

应聘业余工作的人士，有工作经验者优先录取。

A small island has played a *disproportionately* large role in the thinking of evolutionary biologists.

岛屿虽小，但在影响进化论生物学家思维的过程中起到的作用却非常大。

本句中的disproportionately一词主要是说small与large之间比例失调，说得直接些，一个这么小，而另一个居然那么大。所以中文表达时可以将disproportionately省掉，而用其他表达法将该词的意思结合到整句之中，如“却非常大”。

I felt a trifle shy at the thought of presenting myself to a total stranger with the announcement that I was going to *sleep under his roof*，eat *his food* and drink *his whisky*，till another boat came in to take me to the port for which I was bound.

我要去见一个素不相识的陌生人，向他宣布我得住在他家、吃他的、喝他的，一直等到下一班船到来，把我带到我要去的港口为止——想到这儿，我真有点不好意思了。

这里，如把“sleep under his roof，eat his food and drink his whisky”直译为“睡在他的屋顶下、吃他的食物、喝他的威士忌”，会使语言极为繁冗，不够精练。译文采用减省译法处理原文，既准确地传达了原意，又使行文简洁，气韵十足，一气呵成。

Her dark eyes made little reflected stars. She was looking at him as *she was always looking at him* when he awakened.

她那双乌黑的眼睛就像亮晶晶的星星在闪烁，他平素醒来的时候，她也是这样望着他。

此句中有两个“she was looking at him”，如不作省略而译为“她像平常那样望着她一样望着他”，汉语就显得啰嗦繁复，佶屈聱牙。

综合练习

一、将下列句子译成汉语

1. If *I* had known *it*，I would not have joined in *it*.
2. When will he arrive? —*You* can never tell.
3. But *it's* the way I am，try as I might，I haven't been able to change *it*.
4. *If* you give him an inch，he will take a yard.
5. After getting up，I wash *my* face，brush *my* teeth，and comb *my* hair.
6. He put his hands into *his* pockets and then shrugged *his* shoulders.
7. They held *their* position.
8. I put on *my* zip suit and went out.
9. *He* who idles away the time is nothing but a living death.
10. Any excuse will serve，if *one* has not a mind to do it.
11. *A* wise man will not marry *a* woman who has attainments but no virtue.

12. Her dark hair waved untidy across her broad forehead, *her* face was short, *her* upper lip short, showing a glint of teeth, *her* brows were straight and dark, *her* lashes long and dark, *her* nose straight.

13. As I know more of mankind *I* expect less of *them*, and I'm now ready to call a man a good man more easily than formerly.

14. *It* will be a waste of time going to the railway station too early.

15. Smoking is prohibited *in* public places.

16. *In* 1405, the great Chinese navigator Zheng He sailed from China to Sumatra, that is, 90 years before Columbus.

17. The soft can overcome the hard, *and* the weak can defeat the strong.

18. He looked gloomy *and* troubled.

19. Like charges repel each other *while* opposite charges attract.

20. Early to rise *and* early to bed makes a man healthy.

21. *As* it is late, you had better go home.

22. *If* winter comes, can spring be far behind?

23. He was so tired *that* he could hardly keep his eyes open.

24. *Before* the night was far advanced, the soldiers began to move against the enemy.

25. *In the course of* the same year, war broke out in that area.

26. In *actual* fact, the United States is pursuing a policy of encouraging the aggressor...

参考译文

1.早知如此，我就不参加了。

2. 他什么时候到？——说不准。

3. 我就是这个脾气，虽几经努力，却未能改变。

4. 他这个人得寸进尺。

5. 起床后，我洗脸，刷牙，然后梳头。

6. 他将双手放进衣袋，然后耸了耸肩。

7. 他们守住了阵地。

8. 我穿上拉链服，走了出去。

9. 虚度年华者，虽生犹死。

10. 如果不想做，总会找到借口。

11. 聪明的人是不会娶有才无德的女子为妻的。

12. 她的黑发蓬蓬松松地飘拂在宽阔的前额上，脸是短短的，上唇也是短短的，露出一排闪亮的牙齿，眉毛又直又黑，睫毛又长又黑，鼻子笔直。

13. 随着我对人类了解越多，我的期望就越低，我现在说人家是好人比过去容易得多了。

14. 过早去火车站是浪费时间。

15. 公共场所不准吸烟。

16. 1405年中国伟大的航海家郑和从中国航行到了苏门答腊岛，这比哥伦布早了90年。

17. 柔能克刚，弱能制强。

18. 他看上去有些忧愁不安。

19. 同性电荷相斥，异性电荷相吸。

20. 早睡早起身体好。

21. 不早了，你得回家了。

22. 冬天来了，春天还会远吗?

23. 他很疲倦，连眼睛都睁不开了。

24. 入夜不久，士兵们开始向敌人进攻。

25. 同年，该地区爆发了战争。

26. 实际上，美国在推行一种鼓励侵略者的政策……

二、将下列段落译成汉语

Thoughts for a New Year

Most of us look away when we pass strangers. It is the exceptional person who stops to help the woman maneuvering her kids and groceries up the staircase. We rarely give up in line or on the subway or bus. Locked into our automobiles，we prefer gridlock to giving way.

These daily encounters，when they are angry or alien，diminish our lives. When they are pleasant，we feel buoyed. Yet when we sit at home and make resolutions，we think about what we can accomplish in private spaces：home，work. Too many have given up the belief that they control the shared，the public world.

As individuals we can change the contour of a day，the mood of a moment，the way people feel. The demolition and reconstruction of public life is the result of personal decisions made every day：the decision to give up a seat on the bus；the decision to be patient or pleasant against all odds；the decision to let that jerk take a left—hand turn from a right—hand lane without rolling down the window and calling him a jerk.

It's the resolution to be a civil，social creature. This may be a peak period for the battle against the spread of a waistline and creeping cholesterol. But it is also within our will power to fight the spread of urban rudeness and creeping hostility. Civility doesn't stop nuclear holocaust and doesn't put a roof over the head of the homeless. But it makes a difference in the shape of a community，as surely as lifting weights can make a difference in the shape of a human torso.

参考译文

新年随想

当我们与陌生人擦肩而过时，多数人往往把目光移开。要是有人停下来帮妇女哄她的小孩和帮她把食品搬上楼梯，反而会被人看成另类。无论是排队还是乘地铁或公共汽车，我们很少让位于他人。坐在自己的汽车里，我们宁愿堵塞交通也不愿给人让路。

这些日常接触，要是气冲冲的或是使人反感的，那便会减少我们生活的乐趣，要是它们令人愉快，那便会使我们精神振奋。然而，当我们坐在家里做出各种决定的时候，我们考虑的仅是在个人天地——家庭和工作里可以实现的目标。太多的人已经放弃了他们也管理着共享的、公共的世界这一信念。

作为众人的一员，我们可以改变一天的面貌，一时的情绪，以及人们对某件事的感觉。公共生活的毁坏和重建是人们每日所做的种种个人决定的综合结果。这些决定包括：公共汽车上让座；面对逆境而能容忍或具有乐观精神；让那个笨蛋从右车道往左拐而不摇下车窗骂他蠢货。

这是做一个文明的、社会的人的决定。今天也许是人们为减少腰围和降低胆固醇而斗争的高峰期。然而，反对城市野蛮行为和人际敌对态度的蔓延，也是我们只要愿做就能做到的事。有礼貌不能制止核战争，也不能为无家可归者提供栖身之所，但它的确能改变一个社会群体的面貌，犹如举重能改变一个人的体形一样。(摘自*The World of English*)

第9章

翻译技巧(五)正说反译与反说正译

众所周知，语言是文化的载体，英汉文化都经历了长时间的积淀，有着各自的语言表达习惯，有时相同的自然陈述客体，人们却从不同的角度加以考察思考，因而出现了截然相反的表达。例如，放在公共场所刚刚刷过油漆的座椅边，可以看见“油漆未干”这样的警示语，汉语通过“未”这个否定词来直接提醒人们不可以坐那个椅子。而英语不用“The paint is not dry.”，而用“Wet paint.”，含蓄地把客观事实告诉人们。又如在中国许多地方都会遇到“游客止步”“闲人莫入”的告示，正确的英语表达是“Crew only”或“Private”，并不含有否定的形式。其否定意思(员工之外的人不许进入)是隐含的，是一种汉语少有而英语大量存在的“暗否定”。接电话时对方说“hold the line, please?”译成汉语却是“请别挂断电话”。英文中说“Be generous with your praise!”，汉语却是“不要吝惜对他人的赞扬!”这样的例子不在少数。

9.1 正反转换法的文化基础

英语和汉语有相同之处，那就是在表达同一事物或同一概念时，往往可以从正面叙述，也可以从反面叙述。比如我们可以说“很困难”(quite difficult)，也可以改成“很不容易”(far from easy)；说做某事“竭尽全力”(do one's best)，也可以说“不遗余力”(spare no effort)；可以说某个学生成绩“还好”(good)，也可以说“不错”(not bad)。但由于思维方式的不同，英语中有些从正面表达的东西在汉语中习惯从反面表达；而有些英语从反面来表达的东西在汉语中则习惯从正面来表达。因此，英译汉时常常有必要进行转换。这就是通常所说的“正说反译与反说正译”法。如英语中的“Wet Paint!”，汉语中常说成“油漆未干”，英语中说“I won't keep you waiting long ”汉语中却说“我一会儿就回来”。不论是正说反译还是反说正译，归纳起来主要要求有三种：保证语义明确、加强修饰效果、尊重汉语习惯，保证译文通畅易懂。

9.2 正说反译、反说正译的应用

所谓反面表达，是指英语中含有“not”“never”“no”“un-”“im-”“ir-”“in-”“dis-”“less-”等否定成分，汉语中含有“不”“没”“无”“未”“甭”“别”“休”“莫”“毋”“勿”“非”等否定成分的表达，不含这些成分的视为正面表达。

翻译方法很多，要根据具体语境来选择最佳的翻译方法。以下情况常常采用反译法。具体说来，用“反面表达”翻译英语“正面表达”的句子的情况有以下5种。

9.2.1 正说反译的应用

1 本身表示否定意义的谓语动词或动词词组

常见的谓语动词或动词词组本身表示否定意义的有：fail，fall short，be frustrated，fizzle out，escape，slip away，elude，stop，cease，overlook，ignore，neglect，refuse， grudge，disdain，reject，turn down，forbid，prohibit，exclude from，bar，ban，expire，be blind to，deny，avoid，omit，forget，prevent from，live up to，resist，miss，lack等，翻译成汉语时为了使译文通顺却要从反面表达。例如：

As a result，many people *avoided* the very attempts that are the source of true happiness.

结果，很多人**没有**尝试，而这些尝试正是幸福的源泉。

I *missed* what you have said because of the noise outside.

由于外面的噪音，我**没听清楚**你说的话。

The crops *failed* because of drought.

由于旱灾，农作物**没有收成**。

2 含否定之意的介词或介词短语

有些介词或介词短语是正面表达，翻译成汉语时为了使译文通顺要从反面表达，如：above，against，below，beneath，beyond，instead of，out of，without，but for。请看以下例子：

All international disputes must be settled through negotiations *instead of* any armed conflicts.

一切国际争端应通过谈判**而不是**武装冲突来解决。

The question is *above* the five-yea-old boy.

那个五岁的小孩**不懂**这个问题。

Out of sight，*out of* mind.

眼**不**见，心**不**烦。

But for the storm，we should have arrived earlier.

要是没有遇上暴风雨，我们早到了。

3 形式肯定意思否定的固定搭配

某些固定结构也是形式肯定，意思否定，例如：absent (from)，free from，safe from，different(from)，far from，few，little，alien to，anything but，know better than，too...to...，rather than，awkward(不熟练，不灵活，使用起来不方便)，bad(令人不愉快的，不受欢迎的，不舒服的)，blind to (看不到、不注意)，dead(无生命的、无感觉的、不毛的)，difficult(不容易的)，foreign to(不适于，与……无关)，short of(不足，不够)，poor(不好的，不幸的)，ignorant of(不知道)等。所以，翻译成汉语时为了使译文通顺要从反面表达，例如：

His work is *far from* satisfactory.

他的工作**远远不能**令人满意。

The problem is *anything but* easy.

这个问题**绝不**容易。

Some of the excuses were *more than* could be believed.

有些解释实在**不能**令人相信。

He is *more* brave *than* wise.

他**有**勇**无**谋。

4 含有if、before、unless、until、would rather的从句或虚拟语气的句子

有些含有if、before、unless、until、would rather 的从句或虚拟语气的句子，形式上是正面表达却要从反面翻译。例如：

She will die of hunger *before* she steals.

她**宁愿**饿死**也不**愿去偷。

5 某些正面表达的英语习语

有些英语习语从正面表达，汉语却习惯上从反面加以翻译，例如：

As the saying goes, "Men only weep when deeply hurt."

俗话说，"男儿有泪不轻弹，皆因未到伤心处"嘛。

Bite off more than one can chew.

贪多嚼不烂。

Let sleeping dogs lie.

莫惹是生非。

A bird in the hand is worth two in the bush.

双鸟在林不如一鸟在手。

9.2.2 反说正译的应用

相反地，有些从反面表达的英语句子，在直译的情况下要么词不达意，要么汉语读者无法接受，就要从正面加以表达，以恰当地再现原文的意思，我们不妨从以下4个方面加以分析。

1 双重否定

这容易理解，因为双重否定相当于肯定。这里所说的还有一种是否定词与含有否定意义的词连用，例如：

There is *no* rule that has *no* exception.

任何规则都有例外。

Nothing is *impossible* to a willing mind.

有志者事竟成。

There is *no* evil *without* compensation.

恶有恶报。

He can *hardly* open his mouth *without* talking shop.

他一开口总是三句话不离本行。

2 形式否定，意思肯定

有些否定的形式表示肯定的意思，例如：

She *couldn't* have come *at a better time.*

她来得**正是时候**。

Your article will be published *in no time.*

你的文章**很快**就会刊发的。

I *couldn't agree* with you *more.*

我**太赞成**你的看法了。/完全同意。

Don't lose time in posting this letter. (反面表达)

赶快把这封信寄出去。(正面表达)

综合练习

一、将下列短语译成汉语

1. ice-free harbour
2. nuclear-weapon-free zone
3. free from anxiety
4. take French leave
5. beyond dispute
6. free-frost refrigerator
7. crew only
8. free from arrogance and rashness
9. keep upright
10. keep Top Side Up
11. keep off the Grass
12. agreeable sweetness

参考译文

1. 不冻港
2. 无核武器区
3. 无忧无虑
4. 不辞而别
5. 无可争论
6. 无霜冰箱
7. 闲人莫入
8. 不骄不躁
9. 保持直立/竖放
10. 请勿倒置
11. 请勿践踏草坪
12. 甜而不腻

二、将下列句子译成汉语

A. 运用正说反译翻译技巧将下列句子译成汉语

1. Children were *excluded* from getting in the building.
2. To our disappointment，he *failed* to take the overall situation into account.
3. Such a chance was *denied* to me.
4. His parents *forbade* him to marry Mary.
5. Her child was in a terrible state of *neglect*.
6. The window *refuses* to open.
7. Learn how to be *instead of* do.
8. I gave him advice *instead of* money.
9. I have read your article. I *expected* to meet an older man.
10. There is *not* any advantage *without* disadvantage.
11. The beaten enemy had *no other* choice *than* to surrender.
12. He spent *not a little* on books.
13. He *sits out* the other guests.
14. He is *the last* man to accept a bribe.
15. He has a *short memory*.
16. I would rather die *before* I would betray my country.
17. The troops *would rather* take a roundabout way than tread on the crops.
18. He was utterly *in the dark* about what had happened in the department yesterday.

19. *Leave me alone*!

20. *Call a spade a spade*.

21. He *knows better than* to do such a thing.

22. It's *too* dark here for us *to* read the words on this slip of paper.

23. He yelled "*freeze*!"

24. The sea food *goes against* my stomach.

25. That's *all Greek* to me.

26. When you called on me this morning, I was still *in bed*.

27. His *lack of* consideration for the feelings of others angered everyone present.

28. Travelling alone, she was sitting *still* in the corner of the carriage.

29. It is gravity that *keeps* us *from* falling off the earth.

30. He raised his hand to scratch his head with *embarrassment*.

31. This book contained *too much* gossip, *too many* distortions and falsehoods *to* warrant comment.

32. A person who does a *regrettable* action is often regretful afterwards.

33. You are quite a *stranger* here.

34. The guerrillas would rather fight to death *before* they surrendered.

35. *Before* he could stop me, I had rushed out of the classroom.

36. *Opportunity knocks but once*.

37. *Fully clothed*, he fell across his bunk and was instantly sleep.

38. As a human being, we should demonstrate our intellectual and moral superiority by respecting others for who they are—*instead of* rejecting them for who/what they are not.

39. Work does *much more than* most of us realize to provide happiness and contentment.

40. She was *deaf to* all advice.

41. I *stayed awake* almost the whole night.

42. *Seats shall be reserved for warm body only*.

43. The explanation is pretty *thin*.

参考译文

1. 儿童不许进入这栋楼。

2. 我们失望的是他不顾大局。

3. 我没有得到这样一个机会。

4. 他的父母不许他与玛丽结婚。

5. 她的孩子简直没人管。

6. 窗户打不开。
7. 要学习如何做人，而不是做事。
8. 我给了他忠告，而不是钱。
9. 拜读了你的大作，没想到你这样年轻。
10. 有一利必有一弊。
11. 败军只有投降一条路。
12. 他买书花了许多钱。
13. 别的客人都走光了，他还不走。(反面表达)
14. 他决不会接受贿赂。(反面表达)
15. 他的记性不好。
16. 我宁可死，也不背叛我的祖国。
17. 部队宁可绕道走，也不踩庄稼。
18. 他对昨天系里发生的事全然不知。
19. 别管我！
20. 直言不讳。
21. 他不至于干这样的事。
22. 这里光线太暗了，看不出这个便条上写的字。
23. 他喊到“别动！”
24. 海鲜不合我口味。
25. 这我一窍不通。
26. 你早晨来看我的时候，我还没有起床。
27. 他只顾自己，不顾别人，使得大家都很生气。
28. 她没有同伴，只一个人坐在车厢一角动也不动。
29. 是重力使我们不至于从地球上抛出去。
30. 他不好意思地举起手来搔他的头顶。
31. 这本书里无聊的话太多，歪曲和弄虚作假之处太多，不值一评。
32. 一个人做了不该做的事，日后往往会懊悔。
33. 这儿的人都不认识你。
34. 队员们宁愿战斗到死也决不投降。
35. 在他还没来得及阻拦我之前，我已经跑出教室。
36. 机不可失。
37. 他衣服也没脱往床上横着一躺，很快就睡着了。
38. 作为人，我们应该不管他人的身份如何都尊重他们，从而显示出自己高超的智慧和道德，而不要因为他们没有某种身份或地位而去鄙视他们。

39. 工作对于获得幸福和满足起了很大的作用，我们大多数人对此却认识不足。

40. 她什么劝告都不听。

41. 我昨晚几乎一夜没睡。

42. 请勿用物品占位。

43. 这个解释站不住脚。

B. 运用反说正译翻译技巧将下列句子译成汉语

1. We must *never stop* taking an optimistic view of life.

2. You *cannot* make omelets *without* breaking eggs.

3. If that *isn't* what I want!

4. He *can't* see you quickly enough.

5. He is *no more than* a puppet.

6. A poor man is *no less* a citizen *than* a rich man.

7. *Nothing* is *more* precious than life.

8. He *can't* be more careless.

9. It *never* rains but it pours.

10. His speech leaves *no room* to improvement.

11. The music is like *nothing* on the earth.

12. The vast discrepancies in wealth and standard of living show clearly that such a country can make *no* claim to be building a state free from the exploitation of the laboring masses.

13. I *couldn't* feel *better*.

14. I *can't* agree with you *more*.

15. All the articles are *untouchable* in the museum.

16. Some people can eat what they like and get *no fatter*.

17. It is *no less than* blackmail to ask such a high price.

18. Not being grateful for what we have *until* we lose it，of not being conscious of health until we are ill.

19. No deposit will be refunded *unless* ticket produced.

参考译文

1. 我们对生活要永远抱乐观态度。

2. 有失才有得(正面表达)/不破不立(反面表达)

3. 我所要的就是这个呀!

4. 他很想尽快和你见面。

5. 他只是一个傀儡。

6. 穷人、富人都是人。

7. 生命最可贵。

8. 他太粗心了。

9. 不下则已，一下倾盆。/不鸣则已，一鸣惊人。

10. 他的演讲完美之至。

11. 此曲只应天上有。

12. 财富与生活水平悬殊的差别清楚地表明，这样的国家不能自称为是在建设一个劳工大众不受剥削的国家。

13. 我觉得身体好极了。

14. 我太赞成你的看法了。

15. 博物馆内一切展品禁止触摸。

16. 有些人爱吃什么就吃什么，照样瘦。

17. 只有勒索信才能要这么高的价格。

18. 物失方知可贵，病时倍思健康。

19. 凭票退回押金。

三、将下列语篇译成汉语

Thinness and Vainglory

No woman can be too rich or too thin.This saying often attributed to the late Duchess of Windsor embodies much of the odd spirit of our times. Being thin is deemed as such a virtue.

The problem with such a view is that some people actually attempt to live by it. I myself have fantasies of slipping into narrow designer clothes. Consequently I have been on a diet for the better—or worse—part of my life. Being rich wouldn't be bad either but that won't happen unless an unknown relative dies suddenly in some distant land leaving me millions of dollars.

Where did we go off the track? When did eating butter become a sin and a little bit of extra flesh unappealing if not repellent? All religions have certain days when people refrain from eating and excessive eating is one of Christianity's seven deadly sins. However until quite recently most people had a problem getting enough to eat. In some religious groups， wealth was symbol of probable salvation and high morals and fatness a sign of wealth and well-being.

Today the opposite is true. We have shifted to thinness as our new mark of virtue. The result is that being fat—or even only somewhat overweight—is bad because it implies a lack of moral strength.

Our obsession (迷恋) with thinness is also fuelled by health concerns. It is true that in this country we have more overweight people than ever before and that in many cases being overweight correlates with an increased risk of heart and blood vessel disease. These diseases however may have as much to do with our way of life and our high-fat diets as with excess weight. And the associated risk of cancer in the digestive system may be more of a dietary problem—too much fat and a lack of fiber than a weight problem.

The real concern then is not that we weight too much but that we neither exercise enough nor eat well. Exercise is necessary for strong bones and both heart and lung health. A balance diet without a lot of fat can also help the body avoid many diseases. We should surely stop paying so much attention to weight. Simply being thin is not enough? It is actually hazardous if those who get or already are thin think they are automatically healthy and thus free from paying attention to their overall life-style. Thinness can be pure vainglory (虚荣).

翻译要点注解：

1. No woman can be too rich or too thin.本句注意cannot...too...的译法，不可照字面直译，注意双重否定的翻译。

2. attribute...to... 认为……属于……。

3. Duchess of Windsor 温莎公爵夫人(1896-1986)，英王爱德华八世之妻。

4. live by 以……为生；designer clothes 时髦的服装；slip into 匆忙穿上；for betteror worse 不管是福是祸，不管是好是歹，不管结果怎样。

5. go off the track 出轨，背离常规；a little bit of extra flesh 稍稍多一点赘肉。

6. unappealing无感染力的。

7. repellent 讨人嫌的，令人反感的。

8. Christianity's seven deadly sins 基督教不可饶恕的七宗罪，分别是傲慢、妒忌、暴怒、懒惰、贪婪、贪食及色欲。

9. obsession 着迷；have as much to do with... as with...既与……，也与……有很大关系。

10. those who get (or already are) thin 那些瘦了身或本身就瘦的人。

11. free from paying attention 正说反译：不注意。

12. extra flesh赘肉。

13. unappealing *adj*. 无吸引力的，相貌平庸的。

14. repellent *adj*. 排斥的，令人厌恶的。

15. refrain *v*. 抑制；自制；避免；如：to refrain from smoking戒烟。

16. salvation(基督教)赎罪，得救(从罪恶的力量或惩罚中解救出来)。

17. Our obsession with thinness is also fueled by health concerns. 因对健康关心，我们对瘦身也越发痴迷。

18. obsession *n.* 迷住，困扰。

19. fuel *v.* 激起。

20. have as much to do with...as with...与……两者都很有关。

21. be more ofa dietary problem than...更多的是饮食问题而不是……。

22. but that we neither exercise enough nor eat well. 而是我们锻炼不够，吃得也不科学。(注意well不宜译作“好”)

23. balanced diet均衡的饮食。

24. those who get(or already are)thin那些瘦了或本来就瘦的人。

25. be free from没有……的，摆脱了……的。

参考译文

瘦身与虚荣

“女人的钱再多也不多，女人再瘦也不瘦。”这句常被认为是已故温莎公爵夫人说的话，很大程度上体现了时代的奇怪精神——瘦被视为难得的优点。

此观点的问题在于有些人实际上想以此为生活准则。我自己就幻想能轻松套上瘦小的时装。因此，我一生中的大部分时间都在节食——这真是糟糕极了。再说，有钱也不是什么坏事，但这种情况不会发生在我身上——除非一个不知名的亲戚突然死在某个遥远的国度，给我留下了千百万美元的遗产。

我们在何处背离了生活常规？什么时候吃黄油成了一种罪过？稍稍多一点赘肉不是令人厌恶，就是毫无魅力？所有宗教都有特定的禁食日，暴食是基督教不可饶恕的七宗罪之一。然而，直至前不久大多数人都还有吃不饱的问题。过去，在有些宗教团体中，财富是可能得到救赎和道德高尚的象征，而肥胖则是财富和康乐的象征。

今天恰恰相反。瘦已转变为美德的新标志，其结果便是肥胖成了坏事——哪怕稍稍偏重也不行——因为这意味着缺乏道德意志。

对健康的关心助长了人们对瘦身的痴狂。的确，目前美国体重超标的人比以往任何时候都多，而且在许多情况下，肥胖与增加心血管疾病的风险息息相关。不过除了超重，这些疾病也同样与我们的生活方式及高脂肪饮食习惯有很大关系。患消化系统癌症的相关风险可能更主要是饮食而非体重问题——食物高脂肪低纤维。

这么看来，问题的关键不是体重过重，而是我们既锻炼不充分，又吃得不科学。锻炼对强健骨骼、心肺健康都很必要。低脂肪均衡饮食也有助于身体远离多种疾病。我们绝对不应再过分注重体重了。仅仅瘦是不够的。如果那些瘦人认为他们自然而然就可保持健康，从而不注意总体生活方式，实际上会很危险。瘦可谓纯属虚荣。

——许建平.译

第10章

翻译技巧(六)定语从句译法

傅雷先生曾经说过：“东方人与西方人的思维方式有基本分歧，我人重综合，重归纳，重暗示，重含蓄；西方人则重分析，细微曲折，挖掘唯恐不尽，描写唯恐不周。”汉语学家王力先生指出：“西洋语法是硬的，没有弹性；中国语法是软的，富有弹性。……所以中国语法以达意为主。英国人写文章往往化零为整，而中国人写文章却往往化整为零。”

定语从句(attributive clause) 也叫形容词从句(adjective clause)，是由关系词(relative)引导的，在主从复合句(complex sentence) 中起形容词作用，修饰主句中名词或代词，或当名词用的其他类词的从句，被其修饰的词称为先行词(antecedent)。一般情况下，定语从句总是跟在它所修饰的先行词的后面。引导定语从句的有关系代词(relative pronoun：who，whose，that，which，as，but，than)和关系副词(relative adverbial：when，where，why)。关系代词和关系副词通常位于从句之首，它们除了连接主、从句的作用外，还是从句中的一个句子成分，在从句中，关系代词用作主语、表语、宾语，关系副词用作状语。

一般来说，英语句子常用各种形式手段，如连接词语、分句或从句，注重显性衔接(overt cohesion)，句子形式完整，结构紧凑严谨，注重以形显义。汉语造句少用或不用形式连接手段，注重逻辑事理顺序和句子的功能、意义，通过隐性连贯(covert cohesion)以神通形，结构简练明快。谈到这种句子结构差异时，庄绎传教授曾形象地说道："我感觉汉语句子结构好比一根竹子，一节一节地连下去；而英语的句子结构好比一串葡萄，主干可能很短，累累果实附着在上面。"虽然英汉两种语言在句子结构上存在本质上的差别，但按照杨莉藜的观点，可以粗线条地划分为主谓结构、支配结构、限定结构和并列结构。在翻译的过程中，这4种结构在语内和语际可以相互转换。英语中的定语从句属于限定结构，下面我们通过具体实例来看在翻译过程中这种结构是如何转换成汉语的不同结构的。

定语从句的修饰对象一直是翻译中经常遇到而难以把握的问题。要做出正确的判断必须具备多方面的知识。定语从句可以按照它与先行词在逻辑含义上的紧密程度分为限制性定语从句和非限制性定语从句两大类，而具体翻译方法也因其紧密程度的差别有所不同。值得注意的是有些定语从句和主句之间还存在着状语关系，这就要求译者根据具体的上下文加以辨别。在翻译定语从句时我们可以采用前置法、后置法、结构转换法、融合法、断句拆译法等把定语从句译成汉语中的偏正结构、介词结构、独立分句或融合成主句的一部分。

语言学家指出，英语的定语从句可以向右无限扩展；而汉语没有定语从句之说，作为修饰成分的定语习惯上放在被修饰词之前，呈封闭状。英汉定语结构的差异展示如下。

This is the cat.

这就是那只猫。

This is the cat that killed the rat.

这就是那只捕杀了老鼠的猫。

This is the cat that killed the rat that ate the cake.

这就是那只捕杀了偷吃了蛋糕的老鼠的猫。

This is the cat that killed the rat that ate the cake that lay in the room.

这就是那只捕杀了偷吃了放在房间里的蛋糕的老鼠的猫。

This is the cat that killed the rat that ate the cake that lay in the room that Jack lived in.

这就是那只捕杀了偷吃了放在杰克居住的房间里的蛋糕的老鼠的猫。

不难发现，汉语译文从第三句起便读不通了。要使译文通顺，就得将其切分开来处理：这就是那只捕杀了老鼠的猫。那只老鼠偷吃了放在房间里的蛋糕。而杰克就住在这间房里。

再请看下面的例子。

Nearly everyone knows the story of "the dog that worried the cat that caught the rat that a te the grain that lay in the house that Mr. Bubble built."

几乎人人都知道这个故事："冒泡先生盖了房，房里堆了粮，耗子把粮食吃光，猫把耗子抓伤，狗又把猫逼上房。"

因此，定语从句不一定都翻译成所修饰先行词的定语。根据具体的语境，翻译定语从句经常采用的方法与技巧一般有以下几种。

10.1 前置法

前置法顾名思义就是在翻译时将定语从句提到它所修饰的先行词之前。定语从句可以大体上分成限定性定语从句(restrictive attributive clause)和非限定性定语从句(non-restrictive attributive clause)。限定性定语从句和先行词(antecedent)的关系很密切，是对先行词的修饰限定，如果去掉，整个句子就显得不完整了。采用前置法翻译的定语从句一般来说是限定性定语从句，而且句子不太长，否则容易出现中间过于臃肿的现象。这时候，只要将其译成带"的"的定语词组放在被修饰词前即可将英语复合句译成汉语的简单句。例如：

There are probably no questions we can think up that can't be answered，sooner or later，inc luding even the matter of consciousness.

大概没有我们能想到却不能回答的问题，甚至包括意识的问题，这是迟早的事。

解析：that从句修饰questions；we can think up也是定语从句修饰questions，但省略了that。原译文：迟早可能不存在我们能想到但解答不了的问题，甚至包括我们意识到的问题。

He who has never tasted what is bitter does not know what is sweet.

没有吃过苦的人不知道什么是甜。

Chances favor the minds that are prepared.

唯有时刻准备的人才能抓住机遇。

Morality is not really the doctrine of how to make ourselves happy but of how we are to be worthy of happiness. —I. Kant

道德确实不是指导我们如何获得幸福的教义，而是指导我们如何才配得到幸福的学说。

——康德

10.2 后置法

所谓后置法就是保持原句的顺序，将原句的定语从句尤其是定语较长、较复杂的限制性定语从句和起补充说明的非限制性定语从句译成和主句并列的一个分句，放在主句之后。采用此种译法可以使用句号分开主句和从句，重复先行词，例如：

Tom，the book’s protagonist，took issue with a man who doted on his household pet yet，as a slave merchant，thought “nothing of separating the husband from the wife，the parents from the children”.

书中的主人公汤姆与一个男人发生了争执，这个男人虽然爱家中的宠物但作为一个奴隶贩子却认为：“夫妻离散骨肉分离没什么大不了。”

此句中who引导的定语从句为限制性定语从句，定语中有两个并列谓语dote和thought，用句号开分，重复使用先行词“这个男人”。若用前置法翻译这个定语从句会显得定语太长而不符合汉语习惯，因此采用后置法。

Our aim is to establish in Ghana a strong and progressive society... where poverty and illiteracy no longer exist and disease is brought under control；and where our educational facilities provide all the children of Ghana with the best possible opportunities for the development of their potentialities.

我们的目的是在加纳建立一个强大、进步的社会……在这里，贫困和文盲不再存在，疾病得到控制；在这里，我们的教育机构为加纳所有的孩子提供发展他们潜力的最好机会。(两个并列句，表示并列关系)

What should doctors say, for example, to a 50-year-old man coming in for a routine physical check up just before going on vacation with his family who, though he feels in perfect health, is found to have a form of cancer that will cause him to die within 5 months?

比如说，有位50岁的男士在与家人外出度假之前进行常规身体检查。虽然他自己感觉身体很好，却查出患有某种癌症，5个月之内就会死亡。这时候医生该说什么呢？

10.3 融合法（定语从句谓语化）

用从句的关系代词与主句某成分的代替关系，根据意思重新组织成汉语单句。此种译法主要适用于限制性定语从句，是把原句中先行词译成主语，定语从句译成谓语结构。英语中的There be结构就可以采用这种译法来处理译文。例如：

There is a man downstairs who wants to see you.

楼下有人要见你。

There are some metals that are lighter than water.

有些金属比水轻。

There have been many great men who have emerged from slums.

有很多伟人出身于贫民窟。

There were men in that crowd who had stood there every day for a month.

在那群人中，有些人每天站在那里，站了一个月。

The American middle-class family that once could count on hard work and fair play to keep itself financially secure has been transformed by economic risk and new realities.

美国中产阶级家庭曾经指望通过刻苦的工作和公平竞争来确保他们的经济稳定，但是这一点已经被经济风险和新的现实给改变了。

本句仍然是两个层次，主句为“The American middle-class family has been transformed by economic risk and new realities”，译为“美国中产阶级家庭已经被经济风险和新的现实给改变了”，从句是“that once could count on hard work and fair play to keep itself financially secure”，译为“曾经指望通过刻苦的工作和公平竞争来确保他们的经济稳定”。分别翻译后确定这两句是转折关系，说的是从前和现在。这个定语从句是一个转折状语从句。

10.4 译成状语性从句

定语从句和主句之间还存在着状语关系。从语义的角度看，这类定语从句一般相当于状语的作用，表达原因、结果、条件、时间、目的、让步等含义，其功能与状语从句大致相同。在翻译时我们一般都将状语性定语从句译为状语从句，使译文简练明了。此种译法在限制性定语从句和非限制性定语从句中均适用。下面我们从功能作用上来分析英语的状语性定语从句译法。

10.4.1 表示原因

这类定语从句从上下文语言环境来分析，其意义与原因状语从句大致相当。从句在主从句中所表示的原因逻辑关系，均可用表示原因的从属连词because、since、as 等来改写。限定性定语从句和非限定性定语从句均可表示原因，而以非限制性定语从句为主。例如：

The Carter Administration has tentatively decided against the sale to Taiwan of long-range F-4 Phantom fighters that could be used to attack China，Administration officials said today.

一些政府官员今天说，卡特政府已初步决定不向台湾出售F-4幻影远程战斗机，因为台湾当局极可能使用这种战斗机来攻打中国大陆。

Rushing throngs，who was blinded by the darkness and the smoke，rushed up on a street and down the next，trampling the fallen in a crazy fruitless dash toward safety.

由于黑暗和浓烟蒙蔽了视线，狂奔的人群沿着大街小巷奔跑，践踏着倒下的躯体，慌乱而徒劳地向着安全地方冲闯。

Vegetarianism is definitely unsatisfactory for growing children，who need more protein than they can get from vegetable sources.

对生长发育中的儿童来说，素食肯定是不可取的。因为他们需要的蛋白质不可能全部从植物类食品中获得。

We know that a cat，whose eyes can take in many more rays of light than our eyes，can see clearly in the night。

我们知道由于猫的眼睛比我们人的眼睛能吸收更多的光线，所以猫在夜里也能看得很清楚。

10.4.2 表示结果

当从句所表示的是主句中某一动作或状态所产生的结果时，其意义相当于so that引导的结果状语从句，修饰主句的谓语动词。在翻译时，根据其意义及汉语的表达习惯，可加上适当的连词。例如：

Copper，which is used so widely for carrying electricity，offers very little resistance.

铜的电阻很小，所以广泛用于传输电力。

The sun warms the earth，which makes it possible for plants to grow.

太阳温暖了大地，这才使植物有可能生长。

He changed his mind，which made me very angry.

他改变了主意，这使我很生气。

10.4.3 表示条件

表示条件的状语性定语从句既可表示真实条件又可表示非真实条件。表示真实条件含义时，这类从句通常表达一种先决条件，可以翻译成“如果……”“只要……”等。表示非真实条件含义的时候，定语从句往往用虚拟语气来表达一种假设的情况，汉语可译为“假如……”“要是……”等。

Men become desperate for work，any work，which will help them to support their families. (=...as long as it will help them to support their families.)

人们极其迫切地要求工作，不管什么工作，只要它能够维持家人的生活就行。

It may seem somewhat odd to get water from fire，but we shall find that water is a common by-product of any fire in which hydrogen takes part.

火中取水，似乎有点离奇？但我们不难发现：水乃是火燃烧后所产生的一种常见的副产品；只要燃烧过程中有氢气的存在，便会产生水。

Nowadays it is understood that a diet which contains nothing harmful may result in serious disease if certain important elements are missing.

现在人们已经懂得，如果饮食中缺少某些重要成分，即使其中不含任何有害物质，也会导致严重疾病。

10.4.4 表示时间

当从句所表示的动作与主句所表示的动作几乎同时发生时，其含义相当于由连词when、while或as等引导的时间状语从句，修饰主句中的谓语动词。这类定语从句可以处理成时间状语从句，在翻译时，往往需要加上相应的连词“当……的时候”。这类从句表示时间时，其语义功能与when、while 引导的时间状语从句不尽相同。如：

It was a keen disappointment when I had to postpone the visit which I had intended to pay to China in May.

原计划五月来华，后不得不推迟，深表遗憾。

An electrical current begins to flow through coil，which is connected across a charged condenser.

当线圈同充电的电容器相连接时，电流就开始流经线圈。

I came across our English teacher，Miss Howe，who was taking a walk in the park yesterday afternoon.

昨天下午，我们英语老师豪小姐在公园里散步时，我碰巧遇见了她。

10.4.5 表示目的

当从句所表示的是主句中某一动作或状态发生的目的或动机时，其含义相当于由连词so that、in order that等引导的目的状语从句，用来修饰主句的谓语动词。这类定语从句可以转换成目的状语从句。例如：

Private schools in the United States have a wide range of programs that(=so that they) are offered to meet the needs of certain students.

美国私立学校设课繁多以期满足某些学生的不同的要求。

In the late 1960s，a type of filter was introduced in Britain and elsewhere that would have made cigarettes safer.

60年代后期，英国和其他一些国家曾采用一种过滤嘴来减少香烟的危害。

I'll try to get an illustrated dictionary dealing with technical glossary，which will enable me to translate scientific literature more exactly.

我要设法弄一本有插图的科技词典，以便把科学文献译得更准确。

10.4.6 表示让步

当从句所表示的是主句中某一动作或状态与从句中的某一动作或状态在逻辑上有一定矛盾，但并不影响主句的事实或语气的突然转折时，其含义相当于由连词though、although引导的让步状语从句。在翻译时，需要加上“但是”“然而”“却”等连词使行文流畅，语气连贯。如：

Although we have suffered heavy losses by assisting the French and during the Dunkirk evacuation，we have managed to husband our air fighter strength in spite of poignant appeals from France to throw it improvidently into the great land battle，which it could not have turned decisively.

在援助法国和敦刻尔克大撤退中，我们损失惨重，但还是设法保存空战实力，我们没有因为法国的强烈呼吁而草率投入地面战斗。即使当时我们这样做，也是回天乏术，败局已定。

Glass，which breaks at a blow，is capable of withstanding great pressure.

尽管玻璃一打就碎，仍然能承受很大压力。

A gas occupies all of any container in which it is placed。

气体不论装在什么容器里，都会把容器装满。(译成条件状语从句)

Electronic computers，which have many advantages，cannot carry out creative work and replace man.

尽管电子计算机有许多优点，但是它们不能进行创造性的工作，也不能代替人。

综上所述，不难看出，理解和翻译定语从句的时候不仅要重视语句形式的研究，还要从实际意义着手进一步探讨其语义功能。只有这样，才能正确地理解和翻译状语性定语从句，忠实传达原文所表达的含义。无论是翻译普通意义的定语从句还是状语性定语从句，都应体现英语里一个貌似形合、实则意合的现象，翻译时译者需要仔细领会原句所蕴含的深层逻辑意义，然后准确无误地译出其内涵意义。

综合练习

一、将下列句子译成汉语

A. 用前置法翻译下列定语从句

1. If marriage exists only as an intimate relationship that can be terminated at will，and family exists only by virtue of bonds of affection，both marriage and family are relegated to the marketplace of trading places，with individuals maximizing their psychological capital by moving through a series of more or less satisfying intimate relationships.

2. We are not conscious of the extent to which work provide the psychological satisfaction that can make the difference between a full and an empty life.

3. And someone with a history of doing more rather than less will go into old age more cognitively sound than someone who has not have an active mind.

4. The root is that part of the vegetable which least impresses the eyes.

5. People tend to be more impressed by evidence that seems to confirm some relationship.

6. A person who is a sack of all trades has many skills.

7. The time of day when you feel more energetic is when your cycle of body temperature is at its peak.

8. An electric field is a space where an electric force exists.

9. Pollution is a pressing problem which we must deal with.

10. A man, who bites others, gets bitten himself.

11. Even a skilled writer probably could not describe all the features that make one face different from another.

12. Have you set the day when you will move?

13. Creating a "European identity" that respects the different cultures and traditions which go to make up the connecting fabric of the Old Continent is no easy task and demands a strategic choice.

14. Furthermore, humans have the ability to modify the environment in which they live, thus subjecting all other life forms to their own peculiar ideas and fancies.

15. My brother- in- law's laugh, which was very infectious, broke the silence.

16. A youngster, who has no playmates of his age living nearby, may benefit greatly from attending nursery school.

参考译文

1. 如果婚姻只是一种可以任意终结的亲密关系，而家庭只是靠爱情的纽带来维持，那么婚姻和家庭则沦为可以自由买卖的市场，每个人都可以穿梭于一系列或多或少会让自己心满意足的亲密关系，从而使自己的心理资本得到最大的增值。

2. 我们不了解工作给人们带来的能把充实的生活与空虚的生活区分开来的心理满足的程度有多大。

3. 习惯于多动脑的人，在进入老年后，要比一个从来不积极动脑的人认知能力健全。

4. 根是植物中最不引人注目的部分。

5. 人们往往对看上去能证实某种关系的迹象有更深刻的印象。

6. 一个全才的人是一个掌握许多技能的人。

7. 一天中人们精力最充沛的时刻是体温循环处于巅峰的时刻。

8. 电场就是电力存在的空间。

9. 污染是我们必须解决的一个迫切问题。

10. 害人者，反害己。

11. 即使是高明的作家，也可能无法描写出将一个面孔与另一个面孔区别开来的全部特征。

12. 你搬迁的日子定了吗？

13. 不同的文化和传统把欧洲大陆编织成一体，要创造出一种尊重这些不同文化和传统的"欧洲特征"绝非易事，需要做出战略选择。

14. 而且，人类还有能力改变自己的生存环境，从而让所有其他形态的生命服从人类的独特想法和想象。

15. 我姐夫那富有感染力的笑声打破了沉默。

16. 周围没有同龄伙伴和自己玩的儿童，上托儿所可以得到很多的益处。

B. 用后置法翻译下列定语从句

1. In Europe，as elsewhere，multi-media groups have been increasingly successful; groups which bring together television，radio，newspapers，magazines and publishing houses that work in relation to one another.

2. When that happens，it is not a mistake：it is mankind's instinct for moral reasoning in action，an instinct that should be encouraged rather than laughed at.

3. Although there are some men who like children and may have considerable experience with them，others do not particularly care for children and spend little time with them.

4. Behaviorists suggest that the child who is raised in an environment where there are many stimuli which develop his or her capacity for appropriate responses will experience greater intellectual development.

5. They are striving for the ideal which is close to the heart of every Chinese and for which，in the past，many Chinese have laid down their lives.

6. In conclusion，I wish to acknowledge my deep obligation to Dr. X，and to Prof. Y，both of whom have read the manuscript and offered the most helpful criticism.

参考译文

1. 在欧洲，像在其他地方一样，多媒体集团越来越成功；这些集团将相关的电视、广播、报纸、杂志和出版社组合在一起。

2. 产生这种反应并没有错，这是人类用道德观念进行推理的本能在起作用。这种本能应得到鼓励，而不应遭到嘲笑。

3. 尽管有些男人喜欢孩子而且对抚养孩子有相当多的经验，其他男人却不是特别关心孩子，几乎不和孩子待在一起。

4. 行为主义者认为，如果孩子在一个有许多刺激物的环境中长大，而这些刺激物又能培养他做出适当反应的能力，这个孩子就会有更大的智力发展。

5. 他们正在为实现理想而努力，这个理想是每个中国人所珍爱的，在过去，许多中国人为了这个理想而牺牲了生命。

6. 最后，我要对X博士和Y教授表示深切的谢意。他们两位都曾审阅了原稿并提出了极为有益的批评。

C. 用融合法翻译下列定语从句

1. There are some countries in the world where there is little rain at any time.

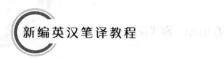

2. I don't know any parent who would choose the word fun to describe raising children.

3. There are some Americans some years ago who said that the United States should play the so-called China card. That is absurd. China is not a card that the United States can play.

4. I saw a cow that was grazing under a tree.

5. We are a nation that must beg to stay alive.

6. In recent years an interesting fact has been brought to public attention: As educational levels, salaries, and the cost of living have increased, more and more people are now having fewer and fewer children to the point where schools in many cities have to close down.

7. There was a promotional campaign that emphasized cheer as an effective "all temperature" detergent was lost on the Japanese who usually wash clothes in cold water.

参考译文

1. 世界上有些国家终年少雨。

2. 我认识的为人父母的人中，没有谁认为抚养小孩好玩。

3. 几年前曾有一些美国人说美国应打所谓中国牌，这是荒谬可笑的。中国不是一张可以任美国打的牌。

4. 我看见一头牛在树下吃草。

5. 我们这个国家不讨饭就活不下去。

6. 最近几年一个有趣的情况引起人们的注意：随着教育水平、工资和生活消费的提高，越来越多的人不想多生孩子，已经到了许多城市的学校不得不关门的地步。

7. 有个促销活动重点强调该洗涤剂适用于任何温度，在日本却反应平平那是因为日本人习惯于用冷水洗衣服。

D. 将下列定语从句译为相应的状语从句

1. In learning a foreign language, say English, one should first pay attention to speaking, which is the groundwork of reading and writing.

2. Again he adjusted his tie after loosening the knot which seemed to make his breathing hard and heavy.

3. You must grasp the concept of "work" which is very important in physics.

4. The computer, which(because it) seems to play the role of a human brain, is often called an electric brain.

5. The coffee, which had been boiling for a long time, tasted rancid.

6. He turned a deaf ear to our demands, which enraged all of us.

7. The ambassador was giving a dinner for a few people whom he wished especially to

talk to or hear from.

8. Scientists say this could lead to design changes in airplanes that would save hundreds of millions of dollars in fuel costs.

9. The first computers used the same types of component which made equipment very large and bulky.

10. She is clever and quick at work，for which(=so that)she is honored with the title of model worker.

11. For any machine whose input and output forces are known，its mechanical advantage can be calculated.

12. Anyone who should do such a thing would be a great fool.

13. He who laughs last laughs best.

14. How can anyone hope to be a qualified teacher，who doesn't know what the students are thinking and demanding?

15. Nothing is difficult in the world for anyone，who dares to scale the height.

16. Anybody who commits the land power of the United States on the continent of Asia ought to have his head examined.

17. They amounted to near twenty thousand pounds，which to pay would have ruined me.

18. "No man is fit to be a naturalist，" said he， "who does not know how to take care of specimens".

19. The thief，who was about to escape，was caught by the policemen.

20. A driver mustn't talk with others or absent-minded who is driving the bus.

21. Samuel O. Bruh was just an ordinary-looking citizen like you and me，except for a curious，shoe-shaped scar on his left cheek，which he got when he fell against a wagon-tongue in his youth.

22. Chinese trade delegations have been sent to African countries，who will negotiate trade agreements with the respective governments.

23. They are trying to provide better controls，which may eliminate these troubles.

24. They have built up a new college here，where students will be trained to be engineers and scientists.

25. He insisted on building another house，which he had no use for.

26. His wife insisted on buying another handbag，which she had no use for.

27. Tom，who had been prevented by illness from studying，passed the examination.

28. The books，some of which had already been damaged，were sold out.

参考译文

1. 学习一门外语，比如说英语，首先要注意说，因为说是读和写的基础。

2. 他松了一下领结，又整了整领带，好像是领带使他感到呼吸困难和急促。

3. 你必须掌握“功”这个概念，因为它在物理学中很重要。

4. 由于计算机起着类似人脑的作用，所以常常被称作电脑。

5. 这咖啡因为煮的时间长了，所以尝起来味道不新鲜。

6. 他对我们的要求充耳不闻，以致使得我们大家都很生气。

7. 大使打算设宴招待一些人，因为他希望专门与他们交谈或听取他们的意见。

8. 科学家们说，这项成就将引起飞机设计上的变化，从而可以在飞机燃料费用方面节约数亿美元。

9. 首批计算机采用同类元件，致使设备既庞大又笨重。

10. 她工作出色，效率高，因此荣获模范工作者的称号。

11. 对任何机器，如果知其输入力和输出力，就能求出其机械效益。

12. 无论是谁，只要是做这样的事，都是个大傻瓜。

13. 谁笑到最后，谁笑得最好。

14. 一个人如果不知道他的学生在想什么，需要什么，怎么指望自己成为一个合格的教师呢?

15. 世上无难事，只要肯登攀。

16. 如果谁要把美国的地面部队派遣到亚洲大陆，那他就应该检查一下他的脑子是否正常。

17. 金钱总额将近两万英镑，如果要我个人赔，非要了我的命不可。

18. “假如一个人不知道如何保管好标本，”他说，“那他绝不适合做博物学家。”

19. 小偷正要逃跑时，被警察抓住了。

20. 司机开车时，不能说话，也不能走神。

21. 萨缪尔·布鲁这位老兄相貌平平，犹如你我，只不过年少时有一回摔倒，撞在大车辕杆上，从此，左颊留下了一道疤痕；那疤痕倒也别致，形状像只小小的鞋印，令人感到好奇。

22. 中国贸易代表团前往非洲各国，届时将与非洲各国政府进行贸易协定谈判。

23. 他们正在设法提供较好的控制方法，去消除这些故障。

24. 他们已在这里建了一所新的学院，以培养工程师和科学家。

25. 他坚持要再建一幢房子，尽管他并无此需要。

26. 他的妻子执意要再买一个包，尽管她用不上。

27. 尽管汤姆生病耽误了学习，可是他考试也及格了。

28. 那些书虽然有些已损坏，但都卖光了。

二、翻译下列段落，注意定语从句的处理

One way an organization can find staff for job vacancies is to recruit outside the company. It may opt to put an advertisement in a newspaper or magazine which gives a short description of the job and invites introductory letters from applicants.Since the company would not desire applicants who do not have a good profile，it is important that an application form sent to a prospective applicant should request clear information about such things as the applicant's age，qualifications and work experience as well as references from other individuals who know the applicant well.This information assists the company's management in making a final decision on those applicants they can short-list for an interview.The staff conducting an interview together are called an "interview panel"，who，prior to the interview，carefully review the job descriptions，personnel specifications，and applications. To help the panel in their selection，an interview assessment form is often used during the interview when each applicant is checked according to a number of criteria indicated on the form.

参考译文

企业机构找人补充职位空缺的办法之一是公司实行对外招聘。它可以选择在报纸或杂志上登广告，简要介绍工作职务的情况并征集应聘者的自荐信。由于公司不会录用个人材料不佳的申请者，因此向有希望的应聘者寄发包括诸如年龄、资历、工作经验等简明信息的申请表，并向了解应聘者情况的有关人士征求参考意见是很重要的。这些信息有助于公司管理部门缩小范围并最终确定面试人员名单。主持面试的工作人员组成"面试小组"。他们在面试之前要仔细审阅工作职位情况介绍、人事要求和求职信。为了有助于面试小组做出选择，在面试中经常使用面试评定表以根据表上的若干标准对应聘者进行考评。

第11章

翻译技巧(七)名词性从句译法

名词性从句包括主语从句、表语从句、宾语从句、同位语从句。在翻译时，大多数语序可以不变，即可按原文的顺序译成相应的汉语。但有时也需要一些其他处理方法。

11.1 主语从句的译法

构成主语从句的方式有下列两种。

11.1.1 关联词或从属连词位于句首的主语从句

关联词引导的主语从句是指连接副词或连接代词引导的主语从句。它们一般是放在句首，作为主从复合句的主语。这样的词有关联词how、why、when、where、whenever、wherever、what、which、who、whatever、whoever及从属连词that、whether、if。例如：

Whether the Government should increase the financing of pure science at the expense of technology or vice versa often depends on the issue of which is seen as the driving force.

结构分析：句子的框架是Whether...or...often depends on...。Whether...or引导了主语从句作句子的主语，financing这里根据上下文要译成经费投入；介词结构of which is seen as the driving force是宾语the issue的后置定语，of介词结构中又包含了which引导的介词宾语从句。

参考译文：政府究竟是以减少对技术的经费投入来增加对纯理论科学的经费投入还是相反，这往往取决于把哪一方看作驱动的力量。

How well the predictions will be validated by later performance depends upon the amount，reliability，and appropriateness of the information used and on the skill and wisdom with which it is interpreted.

结构分析：句子的框架是How...depends on...and on...。句子的主语由how引导的主语从句担任；谓语动词词组depends on后面跟了两个由and连接的并列宾语，在第二个宾语中，介词with+which引导的定语从句修饰先行词the skill and wisdom。

参考译文：这些预测在多大程度上为后来的表现所证实，这取决于所采用信息的数量、可靠性和适宜性，以及解释这些信息的技能和才智。

What could be a key to jetlag(时差综合征) and winter blues is the hormone melatonin(褪黑激素)，which is known to regulate body rhythms.

结构分析：句子的框架是What...is the hormone melatonin which is...。what引导了一

个主语从句，而谓语部分中由which引导了非限制性定语从句修饰hormone melatonin。句中jetlag是时差综合征，blues不能译成蓝色，而是忧郁之意。

参考译文：能解除时差综合征和冬季忧郁症的关键是荷尔蒙褪黑激素，众所周知，这种激素能够调节人体节奏。

11.1.2 it+谓语+that(whether)引导的主语从句

如果先译主句，可以顺译为无人称句。有时也可先译从句，再译主句。如果先译从句，便可以在主句前加译“这”。例如：

And it is imagined by many that the operations of the common mind can by no means be compared with these processes of scientists，and that they have to be acquired by a sort of special training.

结构分析：句子的框架是And it is imagined...that...，and that...。这是典型的句型It+is+p.p.(过去分词)+that clause。It是形式主语，句子真正的主语是两个并列的that引导的主语从句，由连词and连接。operations此处不能译成操作，根据上下文应译成“活动”，这里的processes要译成“思维过程”，而不能简单地理解成过程。

参考译文：许多人以为，普通人的思维活动根本无法与科学家的思维过程相比，认为这些思维过程必须经过某种专门训练才能掌握。

Furthermore，it is obvious that the strength of a country’s economy is directly bound up with the efficiency of its agriculture and industry，and that this in turn rests upon the efforts of scientists and technologists of all kinds.

结构分析：句子的框架是Furthermore，it is obvious that...，and that...。这是典型的句型It + is + objective + that clause。It是形式主语，真正的主语是由连词and连接的两个并列的主语从句：A. that the strength of...bound up with...，B. and that this...rests upon the efforts...。第一个主语从句中的词组be bound up with是与……有关联之意；在第二个主语从句中，代词this指代前文的the efficiency of its agriculture and industry，译为效率的提高。

参考译文：再者，显而易见的是一个国家的经济实力与其工农业生产效率密切相关，而效率的提高则又有赖于各种科技人员的努力。

It is a matter of common experience that bodies are lighter in water than they are in air.

分析：有时为了使译文成分完整，可以补充上泛指的主语(如人们、大家……)。

参考译文：物体在水中比在空气中轻，这是一种大家共有的经验。

类似的结构还有：

it is(universally)known that...大家都知道……

it is believed that...人们都相信……

It is strange that she should have failed to see her own shortcomings.

真奇怪，她竟然没有看出自己的缺点。

11.2 表语从句的译法

表语从句是位于主句的联系动词后面、充当主句表语的从句，它也是由that、what、why、how、when、where、whether等连词和关联词引导的。一般来讲，可以先译主句，后译从句。例如：

Nutritional experiments have made it evident that vitamins are indispensable for one's growth and health.

营养实验证明：维生素对人们的健康和生长是不可缺少的。

Galieo's greatest glory was that in 1609 he was the first person to turn the newly invented telescope on the heavens to prove that the planets revolve around the sun rather than around the Earth.

伽利略的最光辉的业绩在于他在1609年第一个把新发明的望远镜对准天空，以证实行星是围绕太阳旋转，而不是围绕地球。

Things are not always as they seem to be.

事物并不总是如其表象。

在that(this)is why...句型中，如果选择先译主句，后译从句，可以译成这就是为什么……，这就是为什么……的原因，这就是……的缘故等。如果选择先译从句，再译主句，一般可以译为……原因就在这里，……理由就在这里等。如：

That is why heat can melt ice，vaporize water and cause bodies to expand.

这就是为什么热能使冰融化，使水蒸发，使物体膨胀的原因。

在this(it)is because...句型中，一般先译主句，再译从句，译成是因为……，这是因为……的缘故，这是由于……的缘故。如：

This is because the direct current flows in a wire always in one direction.

这是由于直流电在导线中总沿着一个方向流动的缘故。

在this is what...句型中，如果先译主句，后译从句，通常译为这就是……的内容，这就是……的含意等。如果先译从句，后译主句，通常译为……就是这个道理，……就是这个意思等。如：

This is what we have discussed in this article.

这就是我们在本文中所讨论的内容。

If I have seen farther than other men, it is because I have stood on the shoulders of giants. —Newton

假如我比别人望得远，这是因为我站在了巨人的肩上。

11.3 宾语从句的译法

宾语从句可以分为两种：一种是动词引导的宾语从句；另一种是介词引导的宾语从句。

翻译宾语从句时，句子顺序一般不变。例如：

There are now 31million kids in the12-to-19 age group, and demographers(人口学家) predict that there will be 35 million teens by 2010, a population bigger than even the baby boom at its peak.

结构分析：句子的框架是There are...kids..., and demographers predict that...。这是一个并列复合句，在第二个并列分句中，谓语动词predict后面跟了一个that引导的宾语从句；在that宾语从句中，a population bigger than even the baby boom at its peak是35million teens的同位语。

参考译文：12岁至19岁年龄组的孩子目前有3100万，人口学家预测，到2010年他们将达到3500万，比二战后生育高峰期出生的孩子还多。

If parents were prepared for this adolescent reaction, and realized that it was a sign (that the child was growing up and developing valuable powers of observation and independent judgment), they would not be so hurt, and therefore would not drive the child into opposition by resenting and resisting it.

结构分析：句子的框架是If parents were..., and realized that..., they would not...and...。句子的主句是they would not be so hurt, and therefore would not..., 里面有两个并列的谓语would not be和would not drive，在第二个谓语词组中，有介词词组by resenting and resisting it，it指代前文中的this adolescent reaction；在if引导的状语从句中，仍然有两个并列的谓语部分were prepared for... and realized that...，在第二个谓语部分中，that引导的宾语从句作realized的宾语，that宾语从句中又包含了that引导的同位语从句that the child was growing up... and independent judgment作a sign的同位语。

参考译文：如果做父母的对这种青少年的反应有所准备，而且认为这是一个显示出孩子正在成长、正在发展珍贵的观察力和独立的判断力的标志，他们就不会感到如此伤心，所以也就不会因对此有愤恨和反对的情绪而把孩子推到对立面去。

Taking his cue from Ibsen's *A Doll's House*，in which the heroine，Nora，leaves home because she resents her husband's treating her like a child，the writer Luxun warned that Nora would need money to support herself；she must have economic rights to survive.

结构分析：句子的框架是Taking...，the writer Luxun warned that...。句子开头现在分词短语taking his cue from...like a child作状语，在此短语中，in which引导的非限制性定语从句修饰先行词Ibsen's *A Doll's House*，而非限制性定语从句中又包含了because引导的原因状语从句；主语部分中，that引导的宾语从句作动词warned的宾语，宾语从句中有两个并列分句由分号隔开。

参考译文：易卜生的剧作《玩偶之家》中的女主人公娜拉离家出走，因为她憎恶她的丈夫像对待孩子一样来对待她。作家鲁迅从中得到启示，从而告诫人们娜拉需要钱来养活自己，她要生存就必须有经济上的权利。

11.4 同位语从句的译法

英语的同位语从句是用以解释说明前面某一名词的内容的，也就是将这一名词的含义具体化，其地位和此名词是同等的。从句常用that或whether来引导。同位语从句常用来说明fact、theory、sense、question、conclusion、news、experience、evidence、proof、condition、law、conjecture、doubt等词的具体含义。翻译此类从句时，一般有两种处理方法：一种把从句译成一个独立的句子，并在其前加即……，这……等词，或在从句所修饰的名词之后加冒号或破折号；二是用“的”字把从句放在它所修饰的词之前。如：

Even though wealth has grown greatly in the United States，there is much concern that its distribution has become increasingly uneven，with the rich getting a great deal richer，while others are being left behind—if true，it is an unhealthy situation breeding social unrest.

结构分析：句子的框架是Even though wealth has grown...there is much concern that...distribution has become uneven，with...。主句是there is much concern that...，that引导了同位语从句作concern的同位语，在此同位语从句中，介词结构with...，while...中包括了while连接的并列分句，while表示对比，相当于whereas，译成“而”；破折号之后是总结句，这里的if true是省略句，完整的句子为if it is true。

虽然美国的财富大大增长，但是有许多人担心美国的财富分配已变得越来越不均衡，富人变得更富，而其他人则落在后面——这种情况如果属实，这将是一种不健康的局面，孕育着社会动乱。

If I ever contribute to the socialist movement，the book I sometimes dream of；I know what I shall name it：*Industrial Blindness and Socialist Deafness*.

结构分析：句子的框架是If I...，the book...；I know what I shall name it...。这是一个并列复合句，两个分句由分号连接；第一个分句的主句是I sometimes dream of the book，the book前置，if引导了条件从句；第二个分句中，what引导宾语从句作动词know的宾语，冒号之后的成分是it的同位语。

参考译文：如果要对社会主义运动做贡献，我有时梦想写一本书，我知道我将给这本书起什么名字，就叫《工业的瞎子和社会主义的聋子》。

It is scarcely surprising，then，that education systems have for several decades past been severely criticized，partly on the ground that education prepares people to live in an already outdated society.

结构分析：句子的框架是It is surprising that education system have...been... criticized，...on the ground that...。这是典型的句型It + is + adj. + that clause。It是形式主语，真正的主语是that引导的主语从句，而主语从句又包含了that引导的同位语从句that education prepares people to live in an already outdated society作介词词组on the ground中ground的同位语，ground这里的意思是根据。

参考译文：那么教育体制在过去几十年中受到严厉的批评，就不那么令人感到惊讶了，批评者的部分根据是，这种教育培养人们在一种已过时的社会中生存。

综合练习

一、将下列名词性从句译成汉语

1. How and when human language developed and whether animals such as chimpanzees and gorillas can develop a more elaborate system of communication are issues at present being researched，but as yet little understood.

2. From the end of the Second World War until very recently，it was generally accepted in Britain that the State should provide a full range of free educational facilities from nursery schools to universities.

3. What we now will describe is how the magnetic nature of iron oxide can uniquely be exploited as a separation process utilizing a magnetic filtration system.

4. What we require is a theory which is based on various experiments and which enables us to explain more complicated phenomena.

5. That the world's first compass was invented by the Chinese people is a well-known

historical fact.

6. It seemed inconceivable that the pilot could have survived the crash.

7. That substances expand when heated and contract when cooled is a common physical phenomenon.

8. Whatever I saw and heard on my trip gave me a very deep impression.

9. A simple experiment will show whether or not air does have weight.

10. He believes that the highly mobile American society leaves individuals with feelings of rootlessness, isolation, indifference to community welfare, and shallow personal relationships.

11. It is necessary for young people to understand how our society depends upon scientific and technological advancement and to realize that science is a basic part of modern living.

12. We fail to learn that pain is the body's way of informing the mind that we are doing something wrong, not necessarily that something is wrong.

13. The result of invention of steam engine was that human power was replaced by mechanical power.

14. This is where the shoe pinches.

15. Men differ from brutes in that they can think and speaks.

16. Our practice proves that what is perceived cannot at once be comprehended and that only what is comprehended can be more deeply perceived.

17. The law of conservation and transformation of energy states that energy is indestructible and the total amount of energy in the universe is constant.

18. He expressed the hope that he would come over to visit China again.

19. She had no idea why she thought of him suddenly.

20. The fact that the gravity of the earth pulls everything towards the center of the earth explains many things.

21. Not long ago the scientists made an exciting discovery that this "waste" material could be turned into plastics.

22. At the end of last century, an important discovery was made that everything was built partly of electrons.

23. The least we can get from what is mentioned above is the conclusion that the world is in constant change and motion.

24. Is this definition quite satisfactory that a thermometer is an instrument for measuring heat and cold?

25. There is only a remote possibility that many other elements will be found.

26. An order has been given that the researchers who are now in the sky-lab should be sent back.

27. But considering realistically，we had to face the fact that our prospects were less than good.

参考译文

1. 人类的语言是如何发展起来的，是什么时候形成的，诸如黑猩猩和大猩猩一类的动物是否会形成一种更加复杂的交流系统，都是现阶段人们研究的课题，但对此人们都知之甚少。

2. 从第二次世界大战结束直到最近，英国人普遍接受这样一个观点，即：国家应该提供从幼儿园到大学的全方位的免费教育设施。

3. 现在我们所要介绍的是如何奇特地利用氧化铁的磁性而提出一种使用磁力过滤系统的分离法。

4. 我们需要的是建立在各种实验基础上的一种理论，它可以为我们解释更复杂的现象。

5. 世界上第一枚指南针是中国人发明的，这是众所周知的事实。

6. 驾驶员在飞机坠毁之后，竟然还能活着，这看来是不可想象的事。

7. 物质热胀冷缩是一个普通的物理现象。

8. 旅行所见所闻，(这)都给我留下了深刻的印象。

9. 空气是否确有重量，做个简单的试验就可以证明。

10. 他认为，流动性很大的美国社会留给个人的感觉是没有根基、孤立、对社会福利漠不关心和个人关系淡漠。

11. 我们的社会怎样依赖科学和技术的进步，科学也是现代生活的基础部分之一，青年人懂得并认识到这两点，是十分必要的。

12. 我们不知道人体只是用疼痛这种方式通知大脑我们的行为出了差错而并一定是健康有问题。

13. 蒸汽机发明的结果是，机械力代替了人力。

14. 这就是症结所在。

15. 人与兽的区别，就在于人有思维而且会说话。

16. 我们的实践证明：感觉到了东西，我们不能立刻理解它；只有理解了的东西才能更深刻地感觉它。

17. 能量守恒和转换定律说明：能量是不灭的，宇宙间能量的总量和是不变的。

18. 他表示希望能再来中国访问。

19. 她不明白自己为什么突然想到了他。

20. 地球引力把一切东西都吸向地心这一事实解释了许多现象。

21. 不久以前，科学家们有了一个令人振奋的发现，即可以把这种废物变为塑料。

22. 上世纪末有一个重要的发现，即一切东西都有一部分是由电子构成的。

23. 据上所述，我们至少可以得出这样的一个结论：世界处于永恒的变化和运动中。

24. 温度计是测量冷热的工具这一定义是否完美呢？

25. 再发现许多新元素的可能性是不大的。

26. 以下命令要求将目前在航天实验室里的研究人员送回来。

27. 但是现实地考虑一下，我们不得不正视这样一个事实：我们的前景并不妙。

二、将下列段落译成汉语

Passage One:

A Nation of Hypochondriacs

—Norman Cousins

The main impression growing out of twelve years on the faculty of a medical school is that the No.1 health problem in the U.S. today even more than AIDS or cancer is that Americans don't know how to think about health and illness. Our reactions are formed on the terror level. We fear the worst expect the worst thus invite the worst. The result is that we are becoming a nation of weaklings and hypochondriacs a self-medicating society incapable of distinguishing between casual everyday symptoms and those that require professional attention.

Somewhere in our early education we become addicted to the notion that pain means sickness. We fail to learn that pain is the body's way of informing the mind that we are doing something wrong not necessarily that something is wrong. We don't understand that pain may be telling us that we are eating too much or the wrong things; or that we are smoking too much or drinking too much; or that there is too much emotional congestion in our lives; or that we are being worn down by having to cope daily with overcrowded streets and highways the pounding noise of garbage grinders or the cosmic distance between the entrance to the airport and the departure gate. We get the message of pain all wrong. Instead of addressing ourselves to the cause we become pushovers for pills driving the pain underground and inviting it to return with increased authority.

参考译文

一个疑病症患者的国度

——诺曼·克森斯

在一所医学院校任教十二年来我获得的主要印象是：当今美国头号的健康问题甚至比艾滋病或癌症都更为严重的问题就是美国人不知道如何去认识健康与疾病。我们的反应是建立在恐惧这个尺度之上的。我们怕最坏的事期待着最坏的事而恰恰就招来了最坏的事。结果我们变成了一个一个虚弱的、自疑有病的国度，一个分不清哪些是日常偶发症状、哪些又是需要医生医治的症状而自己擅自用药的社会。

在我们早期教育的某个阶段我们变得对疼痛即疾病这一概念深信不疑。我们不知道人体只是用疼痛这种方式通知大脑我们的行为出了差错而并一定是健康有问题。我们不明白疼痛可能是在告诫我们或吃得太饱或吃得不当或吸烟太多或饮酒过度或生活中感情煎熬太苦或因每天都得面对拥挤的大街和公路、忍受垃圾粉碎机的撞击声和奔波于从机场入口到登机口之间的长距离而被搞得过分疲劳。我们把疼痛传达的信息全搞错了。我们不去探查其缘由却大服其药把疼痛压下去从而招致它以更大的威力再次发作。

Passage Two:

First impressions are often lasting ones. Indeed, if you play your cards right you can enjoy the benefits of what sociologists call the "halo effect." This means that if you're viewed positively within the critical first few minutes, the person you've met will likely assume everything you do is positive.

How you move and gesture will greatly influence an interviewer's first impression of you. In a landmark study of communications, psychologists discovered that seven percent of any message about our feelings and attitudes comes from the words we use, 38 percent from our voice, and a startling 55 percent from our facial expressions. In fact, when our facial expression or tone of voice conflicts with our words, the listener will typically put more weight on the nonverbal message.

To make your first encounter a positive one, start with a firm handshake. If the interviewer doesn't initiate the gesture, offer your hand first. Whenever you have a choice of seats, select a chair beside his or her desk, as opposed to one across from it. That way there are no barriers between the two of you and the effect is somewhat less confrontational. If you must sit facing the desk, shift your chair slightly as you sit down, or angle your body in the chair so you're not directly in front of your interviewer.

Monitor your body language to make sure you don't seem too desperate for the job, or too eager to please. Keep a Poker face in business situations. Inappropriate smiling is the most common example of a nonverbal behavior that undercuts verbal messages—making you appear weak and unassertive. Good eye contact is also important. One study found that job applicants who make more eye contact are perceived as more alert, dependable, confident and responsible.

参考译文

第一印象常常是持久的印象。的确，如果处理得当，你就能有幸获得社会学家称之为“光环效应”带来的种种好处。这就是说，要是在一开始关键的几分钟里你就给人留下好的印象，初遇者就可能认为你办的事件件都好。

你的一举一动都会大大影响你给面试者的第一印象。在有关人际交流的一项意义重大的研究中心理学家发现，关于情感和态度的信息有7%来自我们的语言文字，有38%来自我们的语音，而惊人的是，竟有55%来自我们的面部表情。事实上，如果面部表情或说话语调与我们所说的话发生矛盾时，听者通常会更加看重那些非语言信息。

为了使第一次面试成功，一开始的握手要坚定有力。如果面试者没有主动伸出手来，你就主动先把手伸出来。要是可以选择座位的话，要坐在面试者桌子的侧面，而不要坐在正对面。这样坐法你们中间就没有障碍了，而且在一定程度上起到减少对立的作用。如果你只能坐在桌子对面，那么坐的时候把椅子稍微挪一下或者把身体坐的角度偏一点，这样你就不是正对着面试者了。

要注意你的形体语言，千万不要表现得对这份工作迫不及待，也不要表现得急于讨好别人。要保持一种办理公事时一本正经的神态。非语言行为可削弱语言信息的力量，从而使你显得优柔寡断缺乏自信，而不合时宜的微笑就是一个最为常见的例子。良好的目光交流也非常重要。有一项研究发现，多用目光进行交流的求职者可给人以更为机警、可靠、自信、负责的印象。

第12章

翻译技巧(八)状语从句译法

状语从句是英汉两种语言中都存在的语言现象。英语状语从句根据功能的不同可分为时间、地点、原因、条件、让步、目的等状语从句，在英汉翻译时一般比较容易处理，不会构成翻译的主要障碍，关键在于怎样将其放入恰当的位置，怎样处理好句与句之间的连接关系。本章举例说明了各种英语状语从句的翻译方法。

在翻译状语从句时，应注意以下几点：第一，应注意各类状语从句在英汉两种语言中的位置差异，在译文中适当调整语序，相应地译成符合译出语表达习惯的状语从句。第二，应注意连接词，分清主句和从句之间的逻辑关系，因为汉语造句多用意合法，一些连接词往往省略。第三，尽量避免机械地照搬连接词的汉语对应词或译义，在准确理解主句和从句间的逻辑关系后，进行相应的句型转换，如将英语的时间状语从句译为汉语的并列句或条件句，地点状语从句译为汉语的条件句等。第四，应注意主语的使用。

状语从句的翻译方法，总的来说遵循以下4点主要原则。

1 状语从句前置

英语中的时间、地点、条件、原因等状语从句可前可后，而汉语中的这类状语从句一般前置；英语中表示条件的状语从句一般位于句首，尤其是虚拟条件句，这类条件句常常采用顺译法，将从句置于句首；英语中的让步状语从句前后均可，而汉语则前置为多。

2 状语从句后置

汉语中表原因、时间、条件、让步的从句一般前置，但有时也将它们放在主句后面，此时，从句含有补充说明的作用。英语中表示比较、结果、方式和目的的状语从句汉译时可后置。

3 状语从句的转换

有些状语从句从形式上看是某种状语从句，但从其主句和从句的逻辑意义来看，却不属于该种状语从句，而属于另一种从句。此时，汉译时就可根据主句和从句的逻辑意义，进行适当的转换，将其翻译成为另一种句型。如将时间状语从句译为条件句或让步状语从句，地点状语从句译为条件句或结果状语从句等。

4 省略连词

由于汉语造句采用意合法，汉语的复合句常常省略连词。因此，翻译英语中有些状语从句中的连词时，省略比译出更符合汉语表达习惯。此时从句和主句之间可能成为并列关系，或与主句紧缩为一个句子。

12.1 时间状语从句译法

英语时间状语从句，一般译成与汉语完全对应的表示时间的状语。有些英语状语从句虽然形式上是由表示时间的引导词(如when、before、until等)引导，但根据句子逻辑意义来判断，应灵活翻译成表因果关系的从句，或者翻译为表条件的状语从句或表目的的状语从句。例如：

When they approached Trenton，lights were still burning in many of the houses and Christmas parties were still going on.

当他们逼近屈兰敦时，许多房子里仍然灯火通明，圣诞晚会还未结束。

Every time you try to answer a question that asks why，you engage in the process of causal analysis—you attempt to determine a cause or series of causes for a particular effect.

每当你试图回答一个问及为什么的问题时，你就是在进行因果分析了。也就是说，你正努力寻找决定某个结果的某个原因或一系列原因。

Not until we have detailed studies of the present movement of traffic and have a clearer idea of how many people wish to travel，where they want to go，at what time of day and how quickly— not until then can we begin to plan a proper transportation system for the future.

只有详细地研究当前的交通流量，比较清楚地了解有多少人想去旅行，要到哪里去，在一天中的什么时候上路，希望以多快的速度旅行，只有到那时，我们才能开始对未来的运输系统进行合理的规划。

When winds blow particles against a large rock for a long time，the softer layers of the rock are slowly worn away.

由于风把砂粒刮起来，碰撞大岩石，久而久之，较松软的岩石层就被慢慢地磨损。

Before manned spacecraft could be sent to space，the problem of getting the spacecraft safely back to earth had to be solved.

为了把载人的宇宙飞船送到太空上去，就必须先解决使飞船安全返回的问题。

Where it is dry so much of the time that few plants can live，the destructive waters have their own way when the occasional rains come.

结构分析：句子的框架是Where it is dry...，the destructive waters have...。where it is dry...是地点状语从句。it是无人称代词，表示自然现象。在这个从句中包含了一个由that引导的结果状语从句，与so相呼应。主句中包含一个由when引导的时间状语从句。the destructive waters不能直译为具有破坏性的水，而应与谓语结合转译成雨水泛滥，造成灾害。

参考译文：在长期干旱以致植物稀少的地方，偶尔降雨便会泛滥，造成灾害。

12.2 地点状语从句译法

英语地点状语从句除译作汉语的地点状语从句外，有时还可译作汉语的条件句。例如：

Make a mark where you have any doubts or questions.

在有疑问的地方做个记号。

Where water resources are plentiful，hydroelectric power stations are being built in large numbers.

哪里水源充足，就在哪里修建大批的水电站。

The materials are excellent for use where the value of the workpieces is not high.

如果零件价位不高，使用这些材料是最好不过的了。

12.3 原因状语从句译法

英语原因状语从句通常由从属连词 as、because、since 引导。由because引出的原因状语从句一般置于句末，也可位于句首，通常用来表示直接原因。由as引导的原因状语从句通常位于句首；若置于句末，前面应有逗号分开。表示的原因或理由为说话的对方所知道，as通常翻译为“由于”。since引出的原因状语从句通常位于句首，把已知的事实作为推理的依据，说明的原因或理由是说话的双方所明知的事实，因此，since往往翻译为“既然”。英语的原因状语从句一般译为汉语的原因状语从句，有时可视情况译作汉语主句。所有的英语原因状语从句在汉语译文中通常位于句首，偶尔亦置于句末。例如：

Because we are both prepared to proceed on the basis of equality and mutual respect，we meet at a moment when we can make peaceful cooperation a reality.

由于我们双方都准备在平等互尊的基础上行事，我们在这个时刻会晤就能够使和平合作成为现实。

It also plays an important role in making the earth more habitable，as warm ocean currents bring milder temperatures to places that would otherwise be quite cold.

由于温暖的洋流能把温暖的气候带给那些本来十分寒冷的地区并使之变暖，因此，海洋在使这个地球更适合人类居住方面也扮演一个重要的角色。

12.4　条件状语从句译法

一般情况下，条件状语从句可译作汉语的假设句或补语从句，例如：

Whatever its underlying reasons，there is no doubt that much of the pollution caused could be controlled if only companies，individuals and governments would make more efforts.

结构分析：句子的框架是Whatever its underlying reasons，there is no doubt that...if only companies，...。whatever引导让步状语从句，谓语may be省略。句子主语为reasons，whatever是may be的表语。its指代pollution's。主句中that引导的是doubt的同位语从句。过去分词caused作pollution的定语。在同位语从句中包含了由if only引导的条件状语从句。整个同位语从句用虚拟语气，表示这种可能性很小。

参考译文：不论污染的根本原因是什么，毫无疑问，只要各大公司、个人和各级政府都能做出较大的努力，所造成的大部分污染是可以加以控制的。

If developing countries feel that industrialized countries are trying to divert attention from their problems by focusing on the problems of poorer countries，then we risk wrestling endlessly over these issues rather than solving our common problems.

结构分析：句子的框架是If developing countries feel that...，then we risk wrestling endlessly over...。if引导条件状语从句。而在此从句中又套了一个由that引导的宾语从句。介词短语by focusing on...作状语。对于这样长的条件句，应采用分译法。we指代前文的developing countries。wrestle不能直译为搏斗，应转译为争论。

参考译文：工业化国家正试图通过强调贫困国家的问题来转移人们对他们的问题的注意力；如果发展中国家意识到这一点，那我们就会冒险把这些问题无休止地争论下去，而没有解决我们共同的问题。

You can drive tonight if you are ready.

你今晚就可以出车，如果你愿意的话。

Any body above the earth will fall unless it is supported by an upward force equal to its weight.

地球上的任何物体都会落下来，除非它受到一个大小与其重量相等的力的支持。

12.5　让步状语从句译法

英语中的让步状语从句可由although、though、...though、...as、even though、even if等引导。一般译成表示“让步”的汉语状语从句。例如：

Although there are these cultural differences the main engine propelling the separatist cause is economic.

尽管有文化差异，但是推动分裂主义进程的主要动力是经济因素。

有时译成表示“无条件”的条件分句。汉语里有一种复句，前一分句排除某一方面的一切条件，后一分句说出在任何条件下都会产生同样的结果，也就是说结果的产生没有什么条件限制。这样的复句里的前一部分，称之为“无条件”的条件分句，通常以whatever、wherever、whoever、whenever、no matter wh-为引导词，通常翻译为“不论”“无论”“不管”等关联词。例如：

While it is true that this competition may induce efforts to expand territory at the expense of others，and thus lead to conflict，it cannot be said that war-like conflict among other nations is inevitable，although competition is.

该句可拆分为三大部分：(While it is true that this competition may induce efforts to expand territory at the expense of others，and thus lead to conflict，) (it cannot be said that war-like conflict among other nations is inevitable，) (although competition is.)。第一部分是While引导的让步状语从句，第二部分是主句，第三部分是although引导的让步状语从句。第一部分的主语是it，指代后面的that从句，实际上，While it is true that已形成固定结构，that从句的主语是this competition，谓语是may induce，宾语是efforts，不定式to expand territory作efforts的后置定语，at the expense of others作expand的状语，and之后的lead to是谓语，与前面的induce并列，conflict是宾语；主句中的主语是it，指代后面的that从句，该从句的主语是conflict，谓语动词是is，表语是inevitable，复合形容词war-like作conflict的定语，among other nations作conflict的后置定语；第三部分although从句的主语是competition，谓语是is，表语是inevitable，承前省略了。该句的第二部分，即主句运用了被动语态，在翻译时要译为汉语的主动语态，这是常用的一条原则，因为英文多被动，汉语多主动。

参考译文：虽然这种竞争会引发以他人利益为代价的领土扩张行动，因此也会引发冲突，但却不能认为类似于战争的国家间的冲突不可避免，尽管竞争是不可避免的。

Although humans are the most intelligent creature on earth，anything humans can do，Nature has already done better and in far，far less space.

虽然人类是地球上最聪明的生物，人能创造一切，但大自然更富于创造性，早已创造出比人类创造的更好更小巧的东西。

No matter how carefully you move your hand toward a fly，the insect will dart off almost every time.

不管你多么小心翼翼地把手伸向一只苍蝇，差不多每次它都飞走。

Lifts stopped working，so that even if you were lucky enough not to be trapped between two floors，you had the unpleasant task of finding your way down hundreds of flights of stairs.

电梯停了，因此即使你幸而没有被困在两个楼层中间，你也得去完成一项不愉快的任务，即摸黑往下走百级楼梯。

12.6 目的状语从句译法

英语目的状语从句一般译成汉语中表示目的的前置分句，常用“为了”“省(免)得”“以免”“以便”“生怕”等词引导。例如：

A rocket must attain a speed of about five miles per second so that it may put a satellite in orbit. 火箭必须获得每秒大约5英里的速度，以便把卫星送入轨道。

We do not read history simply for pleasure，but in order that we may discover the laws of political growth and change.

我们读历史不单纯是为了娱乐，而是为了可以从中发现政治发展和政治演变的规律。

Electricity is such a part of our everyday lives and so much taken for granted nowadays that we rarely think twice when we switch on the light or turn on the radio.

电在我们的日常生活中所占的地位是如此重要，而且现在人们认为电是想当然的事，所以我们在开电灯或开收音机时，就很少再去想一想电是怎么来的。

12.7 注意几种状语从句的译法

12.7.1 连词until引导的时间状语从句

(1) until引导的时间状语从句修饰主句中否定形式的瞬间谓语动词，此时汉语译文中常有“直到……才……”的字样。例如：

We can’t start the job until we have got the approval from the authority concerned.

没有有关当局的批准我们不能开始做这项工作。

He didn’t appear until the party was over.

他直到聚会结束才来。

He wasn’t able to return until the volcano became quiet.

直到火山平息下来，他才得以回去。

(2) until引导的时间状语从句修饰主句中肯定形式的持续性谓语动词，此时汉语译文中常带有“一直……到……”的字样。例如：

He stayed there until the evening was over.

他在那里一直待到晚会结束。

I will wait here until the concert is over.

我会在这里一直等到音乐会结束。

We should continue the struggle until our object is reached.

我们应该继续奋斗，直到达到目的。

He waited until the volcano became quiet.

他一直等到火山平息下来。

(3) 在will not...until的句子中，根据助动词的含义，until译成“如果”效果更好。

A man will not become a fool until he stops asking questions.

如果人停止思考就会变得愚蠢。

Things will not turn up in the world until somebody turns them up.

世间之事物，如果不去发掘是不会自行出现的。

12.7.2 连词since引导的时间状语从句

(1) since引导的时间状语从句中谓语动词为瞬间动词时，汉语译文中常含有“自……以来”的意义。例如：

What have you been doing since I last saw you?

自我上次和你见面以后，你一直在做什么？

It is five years since he joined the army.

他参军已有五年了。

It is two years since we parted.

我们分别至今已有两年了。

(2) since引导的时间状语从句中谓语动词为延续性动词或状态性动词时，汉语译文中常含有“自……结束以来……”的意义。例如：

He has been hunting jobs since he worked in that company.

从那家公司离职后，他一直在找工作。

It is five years since he was a soldier.

他退役已经五年了。

He has been quite well since he smoked.

他戒烟以来身体一直很好。

12.7.3　连词before引导的时间状语从句

(1) before引导的时间状语从句本身意为“在……前”，这时主句与before从句中的两个动作按时间先后依次发生。例如：

Before the rooster crows，you will say three times that you don’t know me.

在公鸡叫之前，你要说三次你不认识我。

You must not count your chickens before they are hatched.

小鸡尚未孵出之前不能算数。

Before they drive any of the buses，they will have to pass a special test.

在他们驾车之前必须通过一项专门的测试。

Before I enter on the subject I have something to say.

在讨论这些问题之前我有些话要说。

(2) 译成“(后)……才”。副词“才”在汉语中表示某事发生得晚或慢。

The train had left before he got to the station.

火车开了他才到车站。

It seemed a long time before my turn came.

似乎过了好大一会儿才轮到我。

The fire spread four streets before the firefighters could control it.

大火蔓延了四条大街，消防队员们才控制住火势。

(3) 连词before与barely、scarcely、hardly连用时还可译成“刚……就”，在汉语中“就”强调事情发生得早或快。例如：

We had barely run out before the house collapsed.

我们刚跑出来，房子就塌了。

We had scarcely reached the school before it began to rain.

我们刚到学校，天就开始下起雨来。

(4) 如果原文的目的在于渲染从句动作发生之前，主句动作已发生，可译成“未……就”或“还没有(来得及)……就”。例如：

The day began to break before we got to the hilltop.

我们还没到达山顶天就亮了。

The girl was drowned before succors did anything.

救援人员还未能采取措施，那个女孩就已经淹死了。

She rushed out like crazy before I could explain anything.

我还没来得及作任何解释，她就发疯似的冲了出去。

Before we could stop him，he had rushed on to a potato plot and dug up one of the potatoes.

我们还来不及阻止他，他已经飞奔到一块土豆地里，挖出了一只土豆。

(5) before还作“与其……(宁愿)”解，通常可译为“宁可……(也)不(肯)”“宁愿……决不”等。例如：

He would die before he lied.

他宁死也不肯说谎。

He would die before he should disgrace himself.

他宁死不受辱。

He said he himself would die of hunger before he stole.

他说他本人宁愿饿死也不愿偷他人钱财。

12.7.4 连词because引导的原因状语从句

because引导的原因状语从句本身意为“因为……”，但如语境有变化，也会有不同的译法。如：

John didn't attend the meeting because he was ill.

约翰没有出席会议，因为他病了。

He does not want to go with us，because he is tired.

他不想和我们一起去，因为他很累。

He doesn't eat because he is hungry，but greedy.

他不是因为饿了，而是因为贪嘴才吃的。

Galileo didn't believe it because Aristotle said so.

伽利略并不因为这是亚里士多德说的，就去相信它。

I didn't criticize him because I hate him but because I love him.

我不是因为恨他，而是因为爱他，才去批评他的。

综合练习

一、将下列句子译成汉语

1. When censorship laws are relaxed，dishonest people are given a chance to produce virtually anything in the name of “art”.

2. Please turn off the light when you leave the room.

3. Mary had scarcely heard the news when she wept aloud.

4. When I reached the beach，I collapsed.

5. They set him free when his ransom had not yet been paid.

6. I was about to speak，when Mr. Smith cut in.

7. Turn off the switch when anything goes wrong with the machine.

8. A body at rest will not move till a force is exerted on it.

9. Until all is over，ambition never dies.

10. The crops failed because the season was dry.

11. As the moon's gravity is only about 1/6 of the gravity of the earth，a 200 pounds man weighs only 33 pounds on the moon.

12. Although its form can be changed，energy can neither be created nor destroyed.

13. Even though robots can do many things than man does，they cannot replace man.

14. Although television was developed for broadcasting，many important uses have been found that have nothing to do with it.

15. Whether the characters portrayed are taken from real life or are purely imaginary，they may become our companions and friends.

16. By many such experiments Galileo showed that，apart from differences caused by air resistance，all bodies fall to the ground at the same speed，whatever their weight is.

17. I still think that you made a mistake while I admit what you say.

18. If one of them dares to lay his little finger on me as we go out，I won't answer for what I'll be doing.

19. If something has the ability to adjust itself to the environment，we say it has intelligence.

20. Granted that this is true，what conclusion can you draw?

21. We won't attack others unless we are attacked.

22. If you get beyond your depth，you'll suffer.

23. A man don't know the difficulty of anything unless he does it personally.

24. Some wild animals are not easily tamed unless caught young.

25. No one，unless he be a lunatic，could do that.

26. If we can't do as we could then we must do as we can.

27. If I could relive my life，I would lead quite a different life，leaving less regrets.

28. Should there be urgent situation，press the red button to switch off the electricity.

29. Yet whenever I stopped by his hospital bedside，he was surrounded by visitors from his church，singing and praying.

30. They support the holding of a summit conference no matter whether this sort of conference will make achievement or not.

31. No matter what misfortune befell him, he always squared his shoulders and said: "Never mind, I'll work harder."

32. He got the same result whichever way he did the experiment.

33. No matter how hard it is raining, I am going out for a walk.

34. All living things, whether they are animals or plants, are made up of cells.

35. They were determined to carry out their plan no matter what obstacles they would have to face.

36. We should start early so that we might get there before noon.

37. Steel parts are usually covered with grease for fear that they should rust.

38. He slammed the door so that his mother would know he was home.

39. The murderer ran away as fast as he could, so that he might not be caught red-handed.

40. The bridge was so well built that it lasted for 100 years.

参考译文

1. 当审查放宽时，招摇撞骗之徒就会有机可乘，在"艺术"的幌子下炮制出形形色色的东西来。

2. 离屋时请关电灯。

3. 玛丽一听到这消息就放声大哭。

4. 我一游到海滩，就昏倒了。

5. 他还没有交赎金，他们就把他释放了。

6. 我正想讲，史密斯先生就插嘴了。

7. 如果机器发生故障，就把电门关上。

8. 若无外力的作用，静止的物体则不会移动。

9. 不到黄河心不死。

10. 气候干燥，作物歉收。

11. 由于月球的引力只有地球引力的六分之一，所以体重200磅的人在月球上仅重33磅。

12. 尽管能量的形式可以转变，但它既不能创造，也不能消灭。

13. 虽然机器人能做人所做的许多事情，但不能代替人。

14. 虽然电视是为了广播而发明的，但是电视还有许多与广播无关的重要用途。

15. 无论书中描述的角色来自真实生活还是来自纯粹的想象，他们都可能成为我们的伙伴和朋友。

16. 伽利略经过多次这类实验证明，一切物体，不论其重量如何，除了因空气阻力引起的差别外，都是以同样的速度落向地面的。

17. 就算我承认你所说的那番话，但我还是认为你犯了个错误。

18. 如果我们出去的时候，他们谁敢碰我一根汗毛，我可就要不客气了。

19. 如果某物具有适应环境的能力，我们就说它具有智力。

20. 假设这是实际情况，你又能得出什么结论呢？

21. 人不犯我，我不犯人。

22. 打肿脸充胖子，吃亏是自己。

23. 不经自己做，一个人不会知晓做事的困难。

24. 有一些野生动物，除非在幼小时被捕获，一般是不容易驯养的。

25. 没有人会那样做，除非是狂人。

26. 如果我们不能如愿以偿也应当尽力而为。

27. 如果我可以重新过日子，我会生活得截然不同，不会留下这么多遗憾。

28. 万一有紧急情况，请按红色按钮以切断电源。

29. 然而，无论我们何时来到他的病床边，他总是被来自他奉职教堂的人所包围，他们又唱又祷告。

30. 他们支持召开首脑会议，不管这种会议有无成就。

31. 不管他遭受什么不幸事儿，他总是把胸一挺，说："没关系，我再加把劲儿。"

32. 无论用什么方法做实验，他所得到的结果都是相同的。

33. 不管雨下得多大，我还是要出去散步。

34. 一切生物，不管是动物还是植物，都是由细胞组成的。

35. 他们决心坚决执行计划，不论他们将面临什么样的障碍。

36. 为了正午以前赶到那里，我们应当早点动身。

37. 钢制零件通常涂上润滑油，以防生锈。

38. 他把门砰的一声关上，好让他母亲知道他回来了。

39. 凶手尽快地跑开，以免被人当场抓住。

40. 桥建得很牢，至少能用100年。

二、将下列段落译成汉语

Why Measure Life in Heartbeats?

Hemingway once wrote that courage is grace under pressure. But I would rather think with the 18th-century Italian dramatist，Vittorio Alfieri，that "often the test of courage is not to die but to live." For living with cancer engenders more than pressure；it begets terror. To live with it, to face up to it—that's courage.

Hope is our most effective "drug" in treating cancer. There is almost no cancer (at any stage) that cannot be treated. By instilling hope in a patient, we can help develop a positive, combative attitude to his disease. Illogical, unproven? Perhaps. But many doctors believe that this must become a part of cancer therapy if the therapy is to be effective.

I have had the joy of two beautiful and wonderful wives, the happiness of parenthood and the love of eight children. My work was constantly challenging and fulfilling. I have always loved music and books, ballet and the theater. I was addicted to fitness, tennis, golf, curling, hunting and fishing. Good food and wine graced my table. My home was a warm and happy place.

But when I became aware of my imminent mortality, my attitudes changed. There was real meaning to the words, "This is the first day of the rest of your life." There was a heightened awareness of each sunny day, the beauty of flowers, the song of a bird. How often do we reflect on the joy of breathing easily, of swallowing without effort and discomfort, of walking without pain, of a complete and peaceful night's sleep?

After I became ill, I embarked upon many things I had been putting off before. I read the books I had set aside for retirement and wrote one myself, entitled *The Art of Surgery*. My wife Madeleine and I took more holidays. We played tennis regularly and curled avidly; we took the boys fishing. When I review these past few years, it seems in many ways that I have lived a lifetime since I acquired cancer. On my last holiday in the Bahamas, as I walked along the beach feeling the gentle waves wash over my feet, I felt a part of the universe, even if only a minuscule one, like a grain of sand on the beach.

Although I had to restrict the size of my practice, I felt closer empathy with my patients. When I walked into the Intensive Care Unit there was an awesome feeling knowing I, too, had been a patient there. It was a special satisfaction to comfort my patients with cancer, knowing that it is possible to enjoy life after the anguish of that diagnosis. It gave me a warm feeling to see the sparkle in one patient's eyes—a man with a total laryngectomy—when I asked if he would enjoy a cold beer and went to get him one.

If one realizes that our time on this earth is but a tiny fraction of that within the cosmos, then life calculated in years may not be as important as we think. Why measure life in heartbeats? When life is so dependent on such an unreliable function as the beating of the heart, then it is fragile indeed. The only thing that one can depend upon with absolute certainty is death.

I believe that death may be the most important part of life. I believe that life is infinitesimally brief in relation to the immensity of eternity. I believe, because of my religious faith, that I shall "return to the Father" in an afterlife that is beyond description. I believe that though my life was short in years, it was full in experience, joy, love and accomplishment; that my own immortality will reside in the memories of my loved ones left behind, mother, brother, wife, children, dear friends. I believe that I will die with loved ones close by and, one hopes, achieve that great gift of God—death in peace, and with dignity.

参考译文

何必以心跳定生死?

海明威曾经写过，勇气就是临危不惧。不过，我更赞同18世纪意大利戏剧家维多利奥·阿尔菲利的观点："对勇气的考验往往不是去死，而是要活。"身患癌症，不仅带来痛苦，而且引起恐惧。抱病生活，并敢于正视这一现实，这就是勇气。

希望是我们治疗癌症最有效的"药物"。几乎没有什么癌症(无论发展到哪一期)是不能医治的。把希望灌输到病人心里，我们就可以帮助他树立起积极与疾病做斗争的观念。也许此话不合逻辑，言之无据，是吗？然而，许多医生认为，要想使疗法有效，这必须成为治疗的一部分。

我有幸先后拥有两位美丽贤惠的妻子所带来的欢乐，体验过为人之父的乐趣，并得到八个子女的爱。过去，我的工作一直富有挑战性，令人有成就感。我一向喜欢听音乐和读书，酷爱芭蕾舞和戏剧。我曾醉心于健身运动、网球、高尔夫球、冰上溜石、打猎和垂钓。我的餐桌摆满美酒佳肴。我的家温馨而又幸福。

可是，当我知道自己大限将至时，生活态度就变了。"这是您余生的开始"这句话对我有了实实在在的含义。对每一个晴天丽日，对鸟语花香，我的感触倍加强烈。平时呼吸轻松，吞食自如，走路毫不费力，一夜安寝到天明，我们几曾回味过其中的乐趣?

患病以后，我着手做以前搁置下来的许多事情。我阅读了本来留到退休后才读的书，而且还写一本题为《外科术》的书。我与夫人玛德琳度假更加频繁。我们经常去打网球，劲头十足地在冰上溜石，还带儿子们去钓鱼。回顾过去几年，从许多方面来看，我似乎已经活了一辈子。上次到巴哈马度假期间，我沿着海滩漫步，海浪轻轻抚揉着我的双脚，此时此刻我蓦然觉得自己与整个宇宙融为一体，尽管我显得微不足道，就像海滩上的一粒沙子。

虽然我不得不限制自己的医务工作量，我感到与病人更加心灵相通。当我走进特别护理室，一种敬畏之感油然而生，因为我知道自己也曾是这里的病人。我明白，在经历了被确诊为癌症的极度痛苦之后，仍有可能享受生活，因此，安慰癌症患者成了一种特别的乐事。一位病人做了喉切手术，我问他是否想喝冻啤酒，而且为他拿来了一杯，这时我看到他眼里闪现出了火花，一股暖流顿时涌上我的心头。

倘若人们意识到人生在世只不过是宇宙的时间长河中转瞬即逝的一刹那，那么以岁月计算的生命就不会像我们所想象的那样重要了。何必以心跳来定生死呢？当生命依赖于心跳这样一种不可靠的功能时，它的确脆弱不堪。而只有死亡才是人们唯一可以绝对依赖的。

我想，死亡可能是人生中最重要的一环。我认为，与那漫长的永生相比，生命是极其短暂的。基于我的宗教信仰，我相信在我身后那难以描绘的时光里，我将回归圣父。我相信，我的生命以年月计算，虽然是短暂的，但经历丰富，充满了欢乐、爱情和成就；我将永远活在我所爱的人，即我母亲、兄弟、妻子、儿女及密友的记忆中。我相信，在弥留之际，我的亲朋好友将陪伴在我身旁：我希望得到上帝的恩赐——带着尊严，安详地告别人间。

第13章

翻译技巧(九)被动语态译法

进行汉英对比，我们会发现英语的被动句显然多于汉语，因为英语重视形态(形式)，汉语不重视形态，重视语感。以汉语为母语的人自古以来有一种主体思维方式，认为“成事者必在人”，施事者“尽在不言之中”。所以很多被动关系不必一定用“被”字句。在英语中，语态是动词的一种形式。英语动词有两种形式：主动语态和被动语态。其中，与汉语句子表达方式相比，英语被动语态是使用频率很高的形式，英语被动语态的译法十分灵活，需要结合上下文语境灵活把握才能翻译出表意准确、流畅通顺的句子。

汉语中可以表达被动意义的主动句式很多，情况比较复杂。这里我们只谈其中一种与被动句关系最密切的形式，就是“意义上的被动句”。这类句子的主语大多表示无生命的事物，是谓语动词支配的对象。汉语这类句子的数量很大，远远超过被动句，这既是为了语言的简洁，更是由汉语人群的思维习惯决定的。以汉语为母语的人注重思维形态上的主体性，认为任何行为都只能是人这个行为主体完成的，所以当表示无生命事物的词语充当主语时，汉语人群会自然感觉到它不可能是动作的执行者，动词动作的执行者一定另有其人。正是这种思维习惯使汉语的被动意义具有隐含性。被动意义的隐含性是汉语句子的特点，英语并没有这样的特点，所以这类句子译成英语时要使用被动句。例如：汉语句子“房间已经打扫干净了”译成英语为“The room has been cleaned”。

汉语是讲究意合的语言，汉语人群很善于通过意义来判断名词与动词之间的施受关系。当无生命词位于句首，汉语人群能自然而然地通过意义来明确主语是动词的受事者，这时汉语无须再用“被”字来标明主谓之间的受事关系，用主动句就可以达到表达的目的。这一点在口语中表现得尤为明显。例如，钱包丢了，饭做好了，煤气用完了。

英语中被动语态的使用范围很广。凡是在不必说出主动者、不愿说出主动者、无从说出主动者或是为了便于连贯上下文等场合，连贯的时候，使用被动语态就方便多了。而且，被动语态把要说明的问题放在句子的主语的位置上，一是更能唤起人们的注意；二是不带感情色彩，简洁客观。这些独特之处，尤其适应科技作品的需要。了解两种语言在被动语态中的异同，以及英语被动语态的应用特点，可以帮助我们准确把握被动结构的句子，获得理想的译文。汉语中虽然也有被动语态，但使用范围狭窄得多，也不像英语那样有固定的或比较统一的构成形式。因此翻译时应注意英汉这方面的差别，根据汉语的语言习惯，忠实、通顺地翻译英语被动句。英语被动语态的句子，译成汉语时，很多情况下都可译成主动句，但也有一些保持被动语态。这种表达形式选择上的不同源于汉语人群与英语人群思维形式的不同。强调主体意识是汉语的特点，而英语的特点是主客体分明。受主体意识影响而形成的思维习惯使汉语人群常常从主体出发进行叙述，即使从客体出发，汉语人群也会自然而然地感受到客体与动词间是受事关系，不必依靠“被”这样的形式标志。所以汉语中许多主动句形式的句子表达的却是被动意义，而听话人在理解上也不会出现困难。

英语中主客体分明，叙述一件事情既可以从主体出发，也可以从客体出发，所以英语存在主动句与被动句两种对应的表达形式供选择。“与只强调主体意识的汉语相比，英语经常强调客体意识的特点非常突出。所以英语被动句使用的频率远远高于汉语被动句。

汉语的被动句主要用在书面语中，口语中比较少。英语“决定(被动语态)出现次数多少的语体上的主要因素似乎与文章是知识性的还是想象性的有关，而不是与口语或书面语有关。”“一般来说，被动语态在知识性文章中比想象性文章中用得多，而在纯客观的一般性语体的科学文献和新闻报道中尤其用得多。”因此英语被动句形成了其典型的使用场合：科技文章和新闻报道。在科技文章中，科学家们总是力图以客观的态度来说明客观事物的规律，在新闻报道中记者也要注重报道的客观真实，被动句表义的客观性正好满足了这种要求。汉语常用的则是受事主语句或无主句等表示被动义的主动句。

谭卫国先生指出：“造成这种汉语被动句使用范围小的原因可能很多，但主要原因有三个：第一个原因是汉语中有许多动词既可以用来表示主动意义，又可用来表达被动意义。第二个原因是汉语是意合语言，即使不用被动句的标志性词语，也可以表达被动意义。第三个原因是汉语大量使用无主句。”因此，英泽汉中的语态转译现象是一种自然现象。

13.1 英语被动语态译为汉语的主动语态

13.1.1 原句中的主语谓语不变，译文中没有表示被动的标志，形式上是主动句表达被动意义

易词而译是指在译文中用一个表示主动概念的动词，代替原文中表示被动概念的动词，例如用“得知”译“are told”，用“得不到”译“aren’t given”，用“收入”译“are paid”，等。这样的翻译不仅读起来自然流畅，而且避免了“被告知”“被问道”等不符合汉语的表达习惯的译文。例如：

She didn’t expect she should be asked to speak before a big audience.

她没想到会让她在一大群听众前讲话。

If you are asked personal questions you need not answer them.

如果有人问你私人问题，无须回答。

His sense of inferiority that acquired in his youth has never been totally eradicated.

他在青少年时留下的自卑感还没有完全消除。

The money will be used to sustain national parks and reserves within the tropical rain forest belt in countries around the globe。

这笔款将用于维持全世界范围内的国家公园和热带雨林地区保留林的发展。

13.1.2 原句中的主语移到谓语之后译作宾语

这种译法适用于翻译英语里无生命名词做主语的句子。英语常用无生命名词作句子的主语，而汉语习惯用有生命的名词作句子的主语。当英语的被动式译成相应的汉语被动式读出来生硬、不很顺口时，翻译时可考虑将原文的主语(即受动者)与原文的宾语(即施事者)互换位置，即原文的主语成了译文的宾语，而原文的宾语成了译文的主语。如：

Heat is constantly produced by the body as a result of muscular and cellular activity.

由于肌肉和细胞的活动，身体不断产生热。

The friendship was tamed to enmity through idle gossips.

流言蜚语使他们之间的友谊变成了怨仇。

13.1.3 英语被动语态惯用法的翻译

在英语被动语态中，有一种以"it"作形式主语，以被动语态作谓语其后接以由"that"引起的主语从句的表达方法。这类习惯用语可一律译成汉语的主动结构，即将原文中的主语从句置于译文中的宾语位置。译文主语或者略去，或者采用"据"字的结构，或则根据上下文补充以"人们""我们""有人""大家"等泛指性代词充之。例如：

不加主语的：

It is hoped that...希望

It is reported that...据报道

It is said that...据说

It is supposed that...据推测

It must be admitted that...必须承认

It must be pointed out that...必须指出

It may be said without fear of exaggeration that...可以毫不夸张地说

It will be seen from this that...由此可见

可以加主语的：

It is asserted that...有人主张

It is believed that有人相信

It was told that...有人曾经说

It will be said that...有人会说

It is well known that...大家知道(众所周知)

It is generally considered that...大家认为

I was told that...我听说

例如：

It is generally accepted that the experiences of the child in his first years largely determine his character and later personality.

人们普遍认为，孩子们的早年经历在很大程度上决定了他们的性格及其未来的人品。

It is estimated that at one time there existed from one to two thousand American Indian languages and at least as many as cultures each different in some respect from all the others.

据估计曾经有一两千种美洲印第安人的语言和至少同样多的文化，每种语言和文化又在某个方面与其他的语言和文化各不相同。

13.1.4 英语被动语态译成汉语带表语的主动语态

英语被动句，有的并非强调被动的动作，只是以被动语态的形式描述事物的过程、性质和状况，实际上与系表结构很相似。这类被动句可译成“是……的”句式。如：

Rainbows are formed when sunlight passes through small drops of water in the sky.

彩虹是阳光透过天空中的小水滴时形成的。

The women were carefully selected from among many applicants.

这些妇女是从众多的申请者当中选拔出来的。

How can a series of motionless or still pictures be blended on a screen to produce emotion pictures?

一组不动的，即静止的图片是怎样在银幕上连到一起合成电影的呢?

13.1.5 英语被动语态译成汉语带句首词的无主句

汉语的无主句与英语相比是一种独特的句式。英语的许多被动句不需要或无法讲出动作的发出者，因此往往可译成汉语的无主句而把原句中的主语译成宾语。一般说来，描述什么地方发生、存在或消失了什么事物的英语被动句以及表示观点、态度、告诫、要求、号召等的被动句汉译时往往采用无主句，有时还可在动词前加上“把”“使”“将”“对”等词。例如：

New sources of energy must be found to avoid causing energy shortages in the world.

必须找到新的能源以避免造成世界上能源的短缺。

Methods are found to take these materials out of the rubbish and use them again.

现在已经找到了从垃圾中提取这些材料并加以利用的方法。

Great efforts should be made to inform young people especially the dreadful consequence of taking up the habit.

应该尽最大努力告诫年轻人吸烟的危害，特别是上瘾后的可怕后果。

此外，英语中有些固定的动词短语如make use of、pay attention to、take care of、put an end to等，变成被动语态时可将其中名词做主语，汉译时可译成无主句把主语和谓语合并译出。

The unpleasant noise must be immediately put an end to.

必须立即终止这种讨厌的噪声。

Attention has been paid to the new measures to prevent corrosion.

已经注意到采取防腐新措施。

13.2 英语被动语态译为汉语的被动语态

英译汉时，汉语也有用被动形式来表达的情况。这时通常看重被动的动作，有时，可以说出动作的发出者，有时则没有这种必要。在把英语被动句译成汉语被动句时，我们常常使用下述几种方法。

(1) 将英语的被动语态译为汉语带“被”或“给”字的句子。例如：

Except in times of drought，water has never been regarded as a valuable natural resource.

除了干旱时期，否则水不会被看成宝贵的自然资源。

Paris was chosen as the national capital in the late 10th century.

在十世纪末，巴黎被选作了法国的首都。

A mess had been made of the house.

房子被弄得一片狼藉。

Vitamin C is destroyed when it is overheated.

维生素C受热过度就会被破坏。

(2) 将英语的被动语态译为汉语带“遭”“受”或“挨”字的句子。例如：

Last year the region was hit by the worst drought in 100 years.

去年该地区遭受了百年来最严重的旱灾。

The driver was blamed for his escape from the traffic accident.

这位司机因为逃逸交通事故而受谴责。

He was set upon by two masked men.

他遭到两个蒙面人的袭击。

(3) 将英语的被动语态译为汉语带“把”“使”或“由”字的句子。例如：

He was obsessed with fear of poverty.

对贫困的担心使他忧虑重重。

Despite their countless capabilities the miracle chips must be programmed by human beings.

尽管这些神奇的集成线路中有数不清的性能，但还需要由人为它们编制程序。

Rivers are controlled by dams.

拦河坝把河水控制住了。

(4) 将英语的被动语态译为汉语中带有“得到、受到……的”“为…… 所”等结构的句子。例如：

Such conduct will be looked down upon by all with sense of decency.

这种行为将会为一切有良知的人所蔑视。

All the buildings were destroyed in a big fire.

所有的建筑物均为一场大火所焚毁。

Good teachers are respected by students.

优秀教师得到学生们的尊敬。

(5) 英语原文中的主语在译文中仍做主语。

在采用此方法时，我们往往在译文中使用了含有“予以”“加以”“经过”“用……来”等词来体现原文中的被动含义。

Mistake must not be covered up. They must be exposed before you can correct them.

错误不应当加以掩饰，而必须加以揭露，才能加以改正。

Nuclear power's danger to health safety，and even life itself can be summed up in one word：radiation.

核能对健康、安全，甚至对生命本身构成的危险可以用个词“辐射”加以概括。

13.3　英语双重被动句的常见译法

英语双重被动句的译法类似于一般被动句的译法，但英语双重被动句在译成汉语时不能生搬硬套，需要根据汉语的习惯采取一些辅助、综合的办法，因为英语中有双重被动句，而汉语中没有相应的句式。

(1) 英语双重被动句译成含有泛指主语的汉语主动句。译句前通常加上“人们”“大家”“我们”等泛指词。原句中的主语与第一个不定式被动结构扩展为一个新的分句。例如：

The river is known to have been polluted.

众所周知，这条河已经受了污染。

The problem is believed to be settled sooner or later.

大家相信这个问题迟早会解决的。

The meeting is suggested to be put off till next Friday.

有人建议会议推迟到下周星期五举行。

(2) 英语双重被动句译成汉语无主句。原句中的主语与第一个不定式被动结构扩展为一个新的分句。例如：

No building is permitted to be built here.

此处不准盖房。

Cars are allowed to be parked over there.

可以把车停在那边。

The mayor was arranged to be met at the airport.

安排在机场接见市长。

(3) 英语双重被动句有时可以按顺序直接译成省略被动语言标志的汉语被动句。例如：

These books weren't permitted to be taken out of the room.

这些书不许带出房间。

That film is banned.

这部影片禁播了。

(4) 有的英语双重被动句在汉译时，可根据第一个被动结构的词汇意义译成“据……”，原句中的主语与第一个不定式被动结构扩展为一个新的分句。例如：

The child is reported to have been found.

据报道孩子已经找到了。

He is said to have been sent to Switzerland.

据说他被派到瑞士去了。

The result is supposed to be announced soon.

据估计成绩不久就宣布。

一般来说，英语被动语态是由“be+及物动词的过去分词”构成的。但是，这并不是被动语态的唯一表示方式。除了用助动词be外，有些动词还可以用来构成被动语态。弄清这一问题，有利于翻译英语被动句。“动词get、become或feel的一定形式+及物动词的过去分词”可表示被动语态。这一结构通常表示动作的结果并非动作本身，也常用来表示突然发生、未曾料到的势态。这类句子常译成汉语被动句或汉语主动句。例如：

I think we may make it unless we get held up.

我想如果不被耽搁的话，我们能按时到达。

We all felt worried about the complication.

我们都为此事的复杂性而感到烦恼。

总而言之，英语被动语态的用法比较复杂，翻译方法又是灵活多样的。随着英语语言的发展和科学技术的不断进步，被动语态会更多出现在语言实践中，我们应进一步细微观察，认真研究它的结构、用法及其翻译，力求把被动语态用好、译好。

综合练习

一、将下列英语句子译成汉语

1. We hold these truths to be self-evident，that all men are created equal.

2. He was seen to enter the house.

3. He was thrown into confusion by the return of his wife.

4. He has been wedded to translation.

5. The news was passed on by word of mouth.

6. Her husband has been made Mayor，and Mayra herself had got a medal for her work for the aged.

7. He was told that two of them seemed unlikely to pass the exam.

8. The jacket was creased，but the creases will wear out.

9. Many streets have been widened.

10. I hoped I may be pardoned by all of you.

11. The subway was completed by the end of last year.

12. The compass was invented in China four thousand years ago.

13. The performance was fully appreciated by the audience，mostly college students.

14. A truly elegant taste is generally accompanied with excellence of heart.

15. To whom nothing is given，of whom nothing is required.

16. The virtue of a man should be measured not by his extraordinary exertions，but by his everyday conduct.

17. It is believed that the future will be better than the present.

18. It will be seen that my reason for thinking the earth is not round are rather precarious ones.

19. It was announced that there will be a new film tomorrow.

20. It is said that the meeting will not be held.

21. It is decided that I will meet them at the airport.
22. It is known that matter is in constant motion.
23. History is made by the people.
24. My first thirty years were spent in Western America.
25. Coffee stains can soon be washed out.
26. The response of the premature to certain drugs should be thoroughly understood.
27. In many countries authority is seldom，if ever questioned.
28. The traffic regulations served are to be observed.
29. Smoking is not allowed in the office.
30. A telephone was fitted up in the pavilion.
31. Three hundred thousand Yuan has been raised for the village children to build a school.
32. The doctor should be sent for right away.
33. Beethoven and Mozart are both rated among the greatest composers of the world.
34. Those young trees were washed away by the flood.
35. The success of the Chinese people is continually lauded.
36. Our foreign policy is supported by the people all over the world.
37. The boy was criticized yesterday.
38. The translation technique should be paid enough attention to.
39. Other questions will be discussed briefly.

参考译文

1. 我们认为这些真理是不言而喻的：所有人生来就是平等的。
2. 有人看见他进了那所房子。
3. 他由于妻子归来而陷入惶惑不安中。
4. 他与翻译结下不解之缘。
5. 众口相传，消息不胫而走。
6. 她丈夫当上了市长，迈拉自己也由于悉心为老年人工作而获得了一枚奖章。
7. 他已得知他们中有两个人好像不能及格。
8. 衣服起了一些褶，但会慢慢消失的。
9. 许多街道都拓宽了。
10. 我希望能得到你们大家的原谅。
11. 这条地铁路于去年年底完工。
12. 中国在四千年前发明了指南针。

13. 观众对演出十分欣赏，他们中大多数是大学生。
14. 真正的审美力与心灵美通常是分不开的。
15. 如果什么东西也没有给人，那就休想从他人那里得到任何东西。
16. 人的品德不能看他一时格外卖力，而要看他的日常行为。
17. 人们相信未来要胜过现在。
18. 人们将看到，我认为地球不是圆的，其根据相当不牢靠。
19. 有人通知明天放映新影片。
20. 据说会不开了。
21. 决定让我去机场接他们。
22. 大家(我们)知道，物质处于不断运动中。
23. 历史是人民创造的。
24. 我的前三十年是在美国西部度过的。
25. 咖啡斑是可以很快洗掉的。
26. 应该全面了解早产儿对某些药物的反应。
27. 在许多国家很少向权威提出质疑。
28. 必须遵守交通规则。
29. 办公室内不许抽烟。
30. 亭子里装了一部电话。
31. 已经筹集了三十万元为村里的孩子们建一所学校。
32. 得马上请医生来。
33. 贝多芬和莫扎特都被为世界最伟大的作曲家。
34. 那些小树被大水冲跑了。
35. 中国人民的胜利不断受到人们的赞扬。
36. 我们的对外政策受到全世界人民的支持。
37. 这孩子昨天挨了一顿批评。
38. 翻译技巧应予以足够的重视。
39. 其他问题将简单地加以讨论。

二、将下列段落译成汉语

Socialism is to remain dominant in China while capitalism is allowed in certain regions like Hongkong and Taiwan. And the concept of “One country，two systems” which proved successful in solving the Hongkong issue could also be used to settle international problems.

Using a collection of Deng’s talks with foreign guests and people from Hongkong and Macao，the article traces the formation of these ideas since they were first discussed after the

Third Plenary Session of the 11th Chinese Communist Party Central Committee(十一届三中全会) in 1978.

If the capitalist system is not guaranteed in Hongkong and Taiwan, Deng is quoted as saying, prosperity and stability there cannot be maintained and a peaceful settlement will become impossible. The idea that the capitalist system in Hongkong should remain unchanged for 50 years after 1997, Deng said, was advanced because China needs 50 to 60 years to realize modernization. According to Deng, the "One country, two systems" policy that has been adopted suits China's position and is not an expedient measure. Deng also said that the unification of China is a national desire and will be realized even if it takes a thousand years. "The "one country, two systems" concept is not my personal idea but a principle and law adopted by the National People's Congress(全国人大) and therefore will not change," Deng said.

The article also quoted Deng as saying that it was possible for other countries to use the same concept to settle difficult problems. There are two ways to settle the issues, peaceful or non-peaceful. Since there are many issues that can not be settled in traditional ways, new methods will have to be found.

参考译文

在中国的某些地区，如香港和台湾，虽然允许资本主义存在，但社会主义依然是中国的主体。在解决香港问题上已经证明行之有效的“一国两制”构想也可用于解决国际问题。

该文引用邓和外宾及港澳人士的一系列谈话，追述了这类构想在1978年中共十一届三中全会上首次讨论以来的形成过程。

该文还引用邓的话说如果资本主义制度在港台得不到保障，那里的繁荣与稳定就不能维持，和平解决问题也就不可能了。邓说，之所以提出自1997年起维持香港的资本主义制度50年不变的构想，是因为中国需要50到60年才能实现现代化。据邓说，采取“一国两制”适合中国国情，并非权宜之计。邓还说，统一中国是全民族的愿望，即使要一千年也要实现统一。邓说：“‘一国两制’构想并非我个人的想法，而是由全国人民代表大会通过的原则与法律，因此是不会改变的。”

该文还引用邓的话说，其他国家亦可使用这一构想解决困难问题。解决问题有两种方法：和平的与非和平的。由于许多问题无法用传统办法解决，他说，就不得不去寻求新的办法。

第14章

翻译技巧(十)英语长句译法

潘文国先生在《汉英语言对比纲要》一书中讲到汉英句子结构的对比，指出英语句子是树式结构，汉语句子是竹式结构。“树式结构的背后是以整驭零的封闭性结构，竹式结构的背后是以零驭整的开放性结构。”也就是说，英语句子犹如一棵枝叶繁茂的参天大树，有树干，有枝叶，枝叶以树干为核心。因此，英语中各种类型的长句、难句比比皆是，长句主要是由基本句型扩展而成，其方式包括：增加修饰成分如定语、状语，用各种短语如介词、分词、动名词或不定式短语充当句子成分，也可能是通过关联词将两个或两个以上的句子组合成并列复合句或主从复合句。在处理英语句子的时候，我们就需要剔除枝叶对我们的干扰，把握好句子的基本的主干结构。而汉语句子就不同了，在表情达意时，往往要借助动词，按照动作的发生顺序或逻辑顺序，逐步交代，层层铺开，结构犹如竹子，一节一节连下去，表义不完，句子不止。因此，在英语语言中，英译汉时，往往要先分析句子结构、形式，才能确定句子的功能、意义。

汉语注重隐性连贯(covert coherence)，是意合(parataxis) 语言。所谓意合是指句子之间不用关联词作纽带而靠内涵意义和语序表明关系，词语之间的关系常在不言之中，词法意义和逻辑关系常隐含在字里行间。而英语句子偏重形合(hypotaxis)。所谓形合是指句中的词语或分句之间用语言形式手段(如连接代词、关系代词、连接副词或关系副词)连接起来，表达语法意义和逻辑关系，因此句子注重显性接应(overt cohesion)，注重句子形式和结构完整，以形显义来表达一定的语法关系和逻辑关系。这些语言形式手段的运用增加了英语主从复合句长度。另外，汉语句子句首开放，句尾收缩，多用松散句、省略句等。这些特征大大地限制了句子的长度。正如王力先生指出：“西洋人做文章把语言化零为整，中国人做文章几乎可以说是化整为零。”

与汉语句子相比，英语主从复合句长而复杂，这是英语自身在发展中形成的特点。F. Crews 认为：“Subordination，the placing of certain elements in modifying roles，is a fundamental principle of writing.”从句子深层语义结构而论，英语句子喜欢头轻脚重而避免头重脚轻，使句子的重心置于句尾，形成尾重(end-weight)。正如刘宓庆先生所言：“英语句首封闭，句尾开放，定语修饰语可以后置。句子多用包孕式主从复合句，句子可以不断向句尾扩展延伸。”这样就形成了复杂的主从复合句。由此可知，汉英两种语言差别很大。在进行主从复合句的翻译时，首先要弄清原文的句法结构，找出主句与从句，理出主句的主语、谓语和宾语。然后分析从句结构，在理解原文内容的基础上分清主次，分清几层意思之间的逻辑关系(时间、因果关系)，再按照汉语特点和表达方式正确地译出原文的意思。一般来说，造成长句的原因有三方面：①修饰语过多；②并列成分多；③语言结构层次多。英语长句都是由基本结构扩展而来的，所以了解英语基本结构的扩展是分析长句的基础。英语句子扩展的主要方式有以下三种。

(1) 增加句子的修饰语。

(2) 增加并列成分或并列句。

(3) 由短语或从句充当句子成分。

在分析语法所表达的意思时，要注意逻辑上的联系，语法不能脱离逻辑。随后，在弄清句子结构的基础上就可以运用各种翻译处理方法进行汉语表达。

长句的翻译应分两步走：第一步为理解阶段，第二步为表达阶段。理解是翻译的第一步，也是最重要的一步，是正确翻译的基础。所谓理解，就是从语法上区分主句和从句，从语义上找出这个句子有几层含义以及各个层次之间的逻辑关系。当我们弄清了一个长句的句子结构后，第一步，也是关键的一步就是尽可能正确地把整个句子的意思表达出来。如上所述，英汉是两种完全不同的语言，在句子结构和表达方式上都有所不同。因此，我们在翻译中要把这些因素考虑进来。除了准确理解原文之外，译文的成功与否很大程度上取决于译者对母语的驾驭能力以及对翻译技巧的灵活运用。如果对一个句子的理解是错误的，译文也绝不可能正确。

英译汉的长句处理一般可分为6个具体的翻译步骤。

理解阶段的三个步骤为：①扼要拟出全句的主要轮廓；②辨清主从结构，并根据上下文领会全句的要旨；③划出句与句之间的从属关系，理清每句原文的意思。

表达也分三步：①尝试性译出每层的意思；②各层意思之间的重组与综合；③润色。在熟悉了长句的翻译步骤后，我们就可以运用不同的方法翻译不同类型的长句。在分析长句时可以采用下面的方法。

(1) 找出全句的主语、谓语和宾语，从整体上把握句子的结构。

(2) 找出句中所有的谓语结构、非谓语动词、介词短语和从句的引导词。

(3) 分析从句和短语的功能，例如，是否为主语从句、宾语从句、表语从句等；若是状语，它是表示时间、原因、结果，还是表示条件等。

(4) 分析词、短语和从句之间的相互关系，例如，定语从句所修饰的先行词是哪一个等。

(5) 注意插入语等其他成分。

(6) 注意分析句子中是否有固定词组或固定搭配。

下面我们结合一些实例来进行分析。

Behaviorists suggest that the child who is raised in an environment where there are many stimuli which develop his or her capacity for appropriate responses will experience greater intellectual development.

分析：①该句的主语为behaviorists，谓语为suggest，宾语为一个从句，因此整个句子为Behaviorists suggest that-clause结构。②该句共有5个谓语结构，它们的谓语动词分别为suggest、is raised、are、develop、experience，这5个谓语结构之间的关系为：Behaviorists suggest that-clause 结构为主句；who is raised in an environment为定语从句，所修饰的先行词为child；where there are many stimuli为定语从句，所修饰的先行词为environment；which develop his or her capacity for appropriate responses为定语从句，所修饰的先行词为stimuli；在suggest的宾语从句中，主语为child，谓语为experience，宾语为greater intellectual development。

在做了如上的分析之后，我们就会对该句有了一个较为透彻的理解，然后根据上面所讲述的各种翻译方法，可以把该句翻译为：

行为主义者认为，如果儿童的成长环境里有许多刺激因素，这些因素又有利于其适当反应能力的发展，那么，儿童的智力就会发展到较高的水平。

总结一下，长句的主要翻译方法有4种：顺译法，逆译法，分译法，综合法。

14.1 顺译法

在一个长句中，当所叙述的一连串动作是按照动作发生的时间先后安排，或是按照逻辑关系排列时，这与汉语表达方式基本一致，因此翻译时可按照原文顺序译出。例如：

For a family of four，for example，it is more convenient as well as cheaper to sit comfortably at home，with almost unlimited entertainment available，than to go out in search of amusement elsewhere.

分析：①该句的骨干结构为it is more ... to do sth than to do sth else，是一个比较结构，而且是在两个不定式之间进行比较。②该句中共有三个谓语结构，它们之间的关系为：it is more convenient as well as cheaper to... 为主体结构，但it是形式主语，真正的主语为第二个谓语结构：to sit comfortably at home，并与第三个谓语结构to go out in search of amusement elsewhere作比较。③句首的for a family of four作状语，表示条件。另外，还有两个介词短语作插入语：for example，with almost unlimited entertainment available，其中第二个介词短语作伴随状语，修饰to sit comfortably at home。

参考译文：譬如，对于一个四口之家来说，舒舒服服地在家中看电视，就能看到几乎数不清的娱乐节目，这比到外面别的地方去消遣又便宜又方便。

Achieving these will depend，in very large measure，upon the mobilization and education of the entire population，in particular，on improving the education of girls and women who are，at once，the most educational deprived part of the population，and that with the greatest unexploited potential and talent.

这是一个结构复杂而又不流散的英语复合句。谓语动词depend后接两个介词短upon...与on...，第二个介词短语是第一个意思的具体与深化，起强调作用。这与汉语的表达习惯相一致。另外，who 引导的定语从句又是对girls and women的补充说明。该从句又有两个并列表语the... part 和that (即the part)。

参考译文：要达到这些目的，在很大程度上依赖于动员和教育全体人民，尤其依赖于改善女童和妇女的教育。在所有的人中，她们既是在教育权利上受剥夺最甚的一部分，又是具有最大的尚未发掘的潜力和才能的一部分。

What begins as penny-ante dishonesty in elementary school-glancing at a neighbor's spelling test—snowballs into more serious cheating in middle and high school，as enrollments swell and students start moving class to class，teacher to teacher.

本句是一个结构复杂的句子。它有两个从句，其中由what引导的从句即为名词性从句中的主语从句，即what引导从句在句中作主语，谓语是snowballs into，另外破折号之间的分句的分词短语是对what引导的主语从句的补充说明，也应译出；另一个从句为由as引导的伴随状语从句，它由两个分句并列而成。

参考译文：一开始在小学只不过是小小不言的不诚行为，比如偷看一眼邻桌的拼写试卷。到初中、高中，随着招生人数的增加，学生不断更换班级、更换老师，逐渐发展成为更为严重的作弊行为。

Dying patients especially—who are easiest to mislead and most often kept in the dark—can then not make decisions about the end of life；about whether or not they should enter a hospital or to have surgery；about where and with whom they should spend their remaining time ；about how they should bring their affairs to a close and leave.

本句结构复杂，同时出现三个同位语从句，它与汉语的句序、内在逻辑关系及表达法基本相似，因而可用顺译法直接翻译。

参考译文：特别是濒临死亡的病人——他们最易受骗，也最易被人蒙在鼓里——因而不能作出临终前的种种抉择：是否要住进医院或进行手术；在何处与何人度过所剩的时光；以及如何处理完自己的后事再与世长辞。

14.2 逆译法

事物发展顺序是先有因后有果，先有假设才有可能，先有条件才有结果。汉语正是按照这种先后、因果、由假设到推论、由事实到结论的事物发展逻辑顺序逐层叙述、层层推进的。信息焦点(即说话人认为最重要的内容) 往往出现在后面，越靠后越显得重要，句子语义结构是“头轻脚重”。汉语通常称复合句为“偏正句”，偏句是指从句，常在句首，而正句是指主句，多在句末，起总结作用。相反，英语在表达多层逻辑思维时，句子语义结构往往是“头重脚轻”，将重要信息放在句首，次要的在句末。英语长句汉译时，不能拘泥于原文形式机械翻译，必须破句重组，逆着原文的顺序翻译以达到译文与原文的“动态对等”，这就是逆译法。在许多情况下，英语长句的表达次序与汉语表达习惯不同，有时甚至完全相反。在这种情况下，我们必须改变原文的句序，从原文后面译起，逆着原文的顺序翻译，使之符合汉语的习惯。例如：

It remains to be seen whether the reserves of raw materials would be sufficient to supply world economy which would have grown by 500 percent.

句中whether the reserves of...by 500 percent 部分为主语从句，it 是形式主语，形成了It remains to be seen whether...的结构，避免了句子的头重脚轻。此句如果按照自然顺序翻译，就无法正确表达，而先翻译which would have grown by 500 percent这一定语从句，并根据本句的逻辑意思，译成条件状语从句，译文就变得通顺流畅。

参考译文：如果世界经济真的以5倍于现有的速度在增长，那么原材料的储备是否能充分满足其需求，尚不得而知。

That our environment had little，if anything，to do with our abilities，characteristics and behavior is central to this theory.

句中That our environment had... and behavior为主语从句，主语很长，若按句子的自然顺序翻译，肯定是一个头重脚轻的句子。不如采取倒译，使句子意思明了。

参考译文：这种理论的核心是，我们的环境同我们的才能、性格特征和行为即使有什么关系，也不会关系重大。

14.3 分译法

在英语长句中，当主句与从句或主句与修饰语之间的关系不那么密切时，翻译时可按汉语多短句的习惯，把长句中的从句或短语化为句子，分开来叙述；有时，也可以适当增加词语以便使语意连贯。在下列情况下，我们常采用分译法翻译英语长句。

He poured into his writing all the pain of his life and the conviction it had brought to him that the world could be made a better place to live in if the people became the masters of their fate.

分析：这句中宾语很长，从all the pain of his life 开始，直至句末people became the masters of their fate为止；宾语conviction后面既受定语从句it had brought to him的修辞，又接一个较长的同位语从句that...of their fate。这句话译成汉语可将定语从句“这种痛苦给他带来的”移在“信念”之前，但无法将这么长的同位语从句放在“信念”之前，在此只需在conviction和同位语从句分译，补充动词“认为”，意思是“这种信念认为……”译文就通顺达意。

参考译文：他在作品里倾诉了自己一生的痛苦给他带来的一种信念，认为如果人民成为自己命运的主人，世界就会变得更美好。

The president said at a press conference dominated by questions on yesterday’s election results that he could not explain why the Republicans had suffered such a widespread defeat, which in the end would deprive the Republican Party of long-held superiority in the House.

本句含有两个宾语从句和一个非限制定语从句。全句共有三层意思：在一次关于选举结果的记者招待会上，总统发了言；他说他不能够解释为什么共和党遭到了这样大的失败；这种情况最终会使共和党失去在众院中长期享有的优势。三层意思都具有相对的独立性，因此，在译文中拆开来分别叙述，译成三个单句。

参考译文：一次记者招待会上，问题集中于昨天的选举结果，总统就此发了言。他说他不能解释为什么共和党遭到了这样大的失败。这种情况最终会使共和党失去在众院中长期享有的优势。

Anyone considering taking part in a work of transformation of those forms of older art which seem to us in many ways unsatisfactory，so that they should be more in turn with the changing times，and anyone who does not quail at the prospect of seeking out new forms of expression for new materials and new building function，will find spiritual kinship，observing Borromini's building.

此句中的两个并列主语anyone带一长串后置修饰语，如果将它们译成长定语放在中心词的前面，不符合汉语的表达习惯。故采用分译法使中心词和谓语动词靠拢，并把后置修饰语拆成短语，另行安排。

参考译文：旧艺术形式在许多方面似乎不能令我们满意，这就有待于我们去变革这种形式以便更好地跟上多变的时代步伐。任何考虑参加这项工作的人，任何用勇于为新材料和新建筑功能探索新表现形式的人，观察一下博罗里尼的建筑，都会发现精神上的血缘关系。

First，attention shifted from the individual worker to the household as a supplier of labor services；the increasing tendency of married women to enter the labor force and the wide disparities and fluctuations observed in the rate that females participate in a labor force drew attention to the fact that an individual's decision to supply labor force is not independent of the size，age structure，and asset holdings of the household to which he or she belongs.

本句由两个并列分句组成，结构相当复杂，同位语从句是the fact后的that... belongs；第二个分句中，主语是由and连接在一起的两个名词短语；observed ...force 是过去分词短语作后置定语，修饰the wide disparities and fluctuations。

参考译文：首先，人们在考虑劳动力的提供者时，把注意力从个人转向家庭，已婚妇女参加工作人数增加的趋势以及妇女劳动力所占的比例呈现的巨大差距和波动使人注意到以下事实：一个人做出参加工作的决定和他生活的家庭的人口、年龄结构、资产等因素不是毫不相关的。

14.4 综合法

我们常常会遇到一些英语长句，翻译时既不能只用顺译法，也不能只用逆译法和分译法。这时就应仔细推敲，或按时间先后，或按逻辑顺序，有顺有逆、有主有次地对全句进行综合处理。例如：

One teacher writes that instead of drawing students' compositions in critical red ink, the teacher will get far more constructive results by finding one or two things which have been done better than last time, and commenting favorably on them.

分析：这个长句含有一个宾语从句，宾语从句中又有一个定语从句which have been done better than last time修饰它前面的中心词things。由介词by和instead of引导的短语作方式状语修饰句子the teacher will get...results。翻译这个句子需要同时运用切段、倒置、拆离几种技巧。

参考译文：如果我们能从学生的作文中找出一两处比上一次做得更好的地方，并提出表扬性评语，而不是用墨水把学生的作文改得一塌糊涂，我们就能从中得到更富有建设性的成果。

New forms of thought as well as new subjects for thought must arise in the future as they have in the past giving rise to new standards of elegance.

分析：此句不算太长，但翻译时却颇费脑力。先拆译原文中的方式状语从句as they have in the past，置于句首，原文中的主语New forms of thought as well as new subjects for thought处理成译文的宾语，即逆译此部分，而全句后半部分的现在分词短语giving rise to new standards of elegance则按原文之序译出。

参考译文：同过去一样，将来必然会出现新的思维方式和新的思维对象，给完美以新的标准。

People were afraid to leave their houses, for although the police had been ordered to stand by in case of emergency, they were just as confused and helpless as anybody else.

分析：该句共有三层含义：①人们不敢出门；②尽管警察已接到命令，要做好准备以应付紧急情况；③警察也和其他人一样不知所措和无能为力。在这三层含义中，②表示让步，③表示原因，而①则表示结果，应按照汉语习惯顺序，我们将该句翻译如下：

参考译文：尽管警察已接到命令，要做好准备以应付紧急情况，但人们不敢出门，因为警察也和其他人一样不知所措和无能为力。

综合练习

一、翻译下列长句

A. 用顺译法翻译下列长句

1. The global economy that boomed in the 1960s, growing at an average of 5.5 percent a year and pushed ahead at a 4.5 percent-a-year rate in the mid-1970s, simply stopped growing in 1981—1982.

2. All services in business such as gift wrapping, delivery, and credit have some amount of costs associated with them, and these costs must be covered by higher prices.

3. Her first impulse was to go round all the rooms looking for the thieves, but then she decided that at her age it might be more prudent to have someone with her, so she went to fetch the porter from his basement.

4. As I lie awake in bed, listening to the sound those rain sharp drops pounding on the pavement, my mind goes reeling down dark corridors teeming with agonizing flashbacks, and a chill from within fills me with dread.

5. One widely held belief is that a sharp fright will end a troublesome bout of hiccups, but many people prefer just waiting for them to go away as this "cure" is often worse than the ailment itself .

6. So, as well as being overworked, a detective has to be out at all hours of the day and night interviewing his witnesses and persuading them, usually against their own best interests, to help them.

7. She could always reflect that all parties concerned had married according to their stations, a prerequisite for their true happiness.

8. When Torvald gave her money for new dress and such things, she never spent more than half of it, and she found other ways to earn money.

9. We hear what they said and view what they did; we see them as if they were really alive; we sympathize with them, enjoy with them, grieve with them; their experience becomes ours, and we feel as if we were in a measure actors with them in the scenes which they describe.

10. The world is undergoing profound changes: the integration of economy with science and technology is increasing, the restructuring of the world economy is speeding up, and economic prosperity depends not only on the total volume of resources and capital, but also directly on the accumulation and application of technological knowledge and information.

11. Power politics and hegemony still exist in international political, economic and

security realms and have further asserted themselves; regional conflicts have erupted one after another; the gap in development between North and South countries continues to widen. Mankind is plagued by transnational problems such as environmental degradation, arms proliferation, international crimes and terrorism.

12. Working for President Ronald Reagan, Mr. Bush was a silent and subservient vice president, a former rival who gave himself the task of proving his loyalty by staying in the background and never speaking out when his beliefs differed from those of his boss.

13. Increasing labor force participation, record homeownership, surging consumer confidence and spending, near record levels of immigration, and urban renewal are all anecdotal evidences that hopes are high.

14. In such case, the public and its political decision-makers get information only of a certain kind, because there is no private, well-funded foundation call The Consortium of Single Mothers on Welfare that bestows similar massive funding to discover the efforts of poverty on the development of children.

15. Even when we turn off the beside lamp and are fast asleep, electricity is working for us, driving our refrigerators, heating our water, or keeping our rooms air-conditioned.

16. In Africa I met a boy, who was crying as if his heart would break and said when I spoke to him, that he was hungry because he had had no food for two days.

17. Prior to the twentieth century, women in novels were stereotypes of lacking any features that made them unique individuals and were also subject to numerous restrictions imposed by the male-dominated culture.

18. It begins as a childlike interest in the grand spectacle and exciting event; it grows as a mature interest in the variety and complexity of the drama, the splendid achievements and terrible failures; it ends as deep sense of the mystery of man's life of all the dead, great and obscure, who once walked the earth, and of wonderful and awful possibilities of being a human being.

19. Owing to the remarkable development in mass-communications, people everywhere are feeling new wants and are being exposed to new customs and ideas, while governments are often forced to introduce still further innovations for the reasons given above.

参考译文

1. 世界经济在60年代很繁荣，每年平均以5.5%的比率增长，到了70年代中期仍以平均每年4.5%的比率增长，但是1981年到1982年间就完全停止增长了。

2. 商业中所有的服务——诸如礼品包装、送货以及赊账——都有相应的成本，而这些成本要靠较高的价格来弥补。

3. 她的第一个反应是逐一搜查所有的房间以寻找窃贼，但她接着又想，自己上了年纪，若是有人来帮着一起干，那就更为稳妥，所以她就从底层那里找了守门人来。

4. 我躺在床上，睡不着，听着雨点儿在路面上啪啪作响。我思绪万千，恍恍惚惚进入了一条幽暗的通道。回想起许多痛苦的往事，心里一阵冰凉，不禁感到毛骨悚然。

5. 一种普遍为人们接受的观点是，猛然的惊吓会止住一阵讨厌的打嗝。但是许多人宁愿等打嗝自然过去，因为这种“治嗝的方法”往往比打嗝本身更糟。

6. 所以除了过度操劳外，警探还需没日没夜地整天在外面找证人谈话，劝说他们往往是要说服他们违背自身的利益来帮助他。

7. 她总可以这样回首往事，她周围的人全都门当户对地婚配成亲，这才是他们真正幸福的必要条件。

8. 每次托伐给她钱买新衣服和其他东西，她起码要省下一半，而且还要想别的路子去挣钱。

9. 我们如闻其声，如观其行，如见其人；我们赞同、支持他们，和他们悲喜与共；他们的感受成为我们自己的感受，我们觉得仿佛自己是在他们所描绘的场景中与他们同台扮演着角色。

10. 世界正在发生深刻的变化：经济与科学技术的结合与日俱增；世界经济的重组加快步伐；经济繁荣不仅仅取决于资源和资本的总量，而且直接有赖于技术知识和信息的积累及其应用。

11. 强权政治和霸权主义在国际政治、经济和安全领域中依然存在并有新的发展，地区冲突此起彼伏，南北发展差距继续扩大，环境恶化、武器扩散、国际犯罪、恐怖主义等跨国问题困扰着人类。

12. 布什先生为里根总统效力时，是一个缄默顺从的副总统，他以前曾是里根的竞争对手，当了副总统以后，他要证实自己对里根的忠诚：他尽量不抛头露面突出自己，在自己的观点与上司相左时，他总是把话放到肚子里。

13. 劳动阶层越来越多地致力于发展经济、国有资产达到创纪录的水平、消费者信心高涨、消费增长、移民数量接近新高纪录以及城市不断更新改造，这些都是栩栩如生的证据，表明人们充满了希望。

14. 在这些事例中，公众和决策者只能获得一种类别的信息，因为根本没有称之为“单亲母亲福利协会”私人基金会，有雄厚的资金，足以拿出相近数额的巨额资金来资助关于贫困对于儿童成长发育影响的研究。

15. 即使在我们关掉了床头灯深深地进入梦乡时，电仍在为我们工作：帮我们开动电冰箱，把水加热，或使室内空调机继续运转。

16. 在非洲，我遇到了一个男孩，他哭得伤心极了，我问他时，他说他饿了，两天没有吃饭了。

17. 在20世纪以前，小说中的妇女都像是一个模式。她们没有任何特点，因而无法成为具有个性的人；她们还要屈从于由男性主宰的文化传统强加给她们的种种束缚。

18. 我们对历史的爱好起源于我们最初仅对一些历史上的宏伟场面和激动人心的事件感到孩童般的兴趣；其后，这种爱好变得成熟起来，我们开始对历史这出“戏剧”的多样性和复杂性，对历史上的辉煌成就和悲壮失败也感兴趣；对历史的爱好，最终以我们对人类生命的一种深沉的神秘感而告结束。死去的，无论是伟大与平凡，所有在这个地球上走过而已逝的人，都有能取得伟大奇迹或制造可怕事件的潜力。

19. 大众通讯的显著发展使各地的人们不断感到有新的需求，不断接触到新的习俗和思想，由于上述原因，政府常常得推出更多的革新。

B. 用逆译法翻译下列长句

1. We were most impressed by the fact that even those patients who were not told of their serious illness were quite aware of its potential outcome.

2. And he knew how ashamed he would have been if she had known his mother and the kind of place in which he was born，and the kind of people among whom he was born.

3. A lion had long watched them in the hope of making prize of them，but found that there was little chance for him so long as they kept all together. —*Esop's Fable*：*The Lion and the Bulls*

4. Such is human nature in the West that a great many people are often willing to sacrifice higher pay for the privilege of becoming white-collar workers.

5. It should be the pressing task in international postal cooperation to actively help developing countries overcome difficulties in their development of postal services and to energetically narrow the gap between the developing and the developed countries in this field.

6. Fourth，severe punishment shall be imposed on those who make use of or instigate minors to smuggle，traffic，transport or manufacture drugs，sell drugs to minors，or lure，instigate，deceive or force them into taking or injecting drugs，and on those who have again committed drug-related crimes after having been convicted of the crime of smuggling，trafficking，transporting，manufacturing or i1legally holding drugs.

7. A great number of graduate students were driven into the intellectual slum when in the United States the intellectual poor became the classic poor，the poor under the rather romantic guise of the Beat Generation，a real phenomenon in the late fifties.

8. Insects would make it impossible for us to live in the world; they would devour all our crops and kill our flocks and herds, if it were not for the protection we get from insect-eating animals.

9. Any man on the street scarcely realizes that whereas the disappearance, or even what we see in some quarters, the continuous neglect and degradation of the teaching profession, must mean a disaster to the entire nation.

参考译文

1. 即使那些病人没有被告知患了重病，他们也十分清楚潜在的后果，这一点给我们留下了深刻的印象。

2. 他出生在这一类人中间，他出生在这种地方，他有这样的母亲；他知道这些要是让她了解了的话，该多么丢人。

3. 一头狮子盯了他们许久，想把他们给捕捉起来。但又发觉，如果他们老是凑在一起，那就很难如愿以偿。——伊索寓言：狮子和公牛

4. 许多人常常宁愿牺牲比较高的工资以换取白领工人的社会地位，这在西方倒是人之常情。

5. 积极帮助发展中国家克服邮政建设中面临的困难，努力缩小发展中国家与发达国家在邮政领域的差距，应成为国际邮政合作的当务之急。

6. 其四，对利用、教唆未成年人走私、贩卖、运输、制造毒品，或者向未成年人出售毒品的，引诱、教唆、欺骗或者强迫未成年人吸食、注射毒品的，因走私、贩卖、运输、制造、非法持有毒品罪被判过刑又有毒品罪行为的，从重处罚。

7. 50年代后期的美国出现了一个任何人都不可能视而不见的现象，穷知识分子以“垮掉的一代”这种颇为浪漫的姿态出现而成为美国典型的穷人，正是这个时候大批大学生被赶进了知识分子的贫民窟。

8. 假如没有那些以昆虫为食的动物保护我们，昆虫将吞噬我们所有的庄稼，害死我们的牛羊家畜，使我们不能生存于世。

9. 如果没有教师这一职业，或者像在某些地区那样，教育事业长期不受重视并且每况愈下，那么就整个国家而言，这必将是一场灾难。这一点一般人很少认识到。

C. 用分译法翻译下列长句

1. A spirited discussion springs up between a young girl who insists that women have outgrown the jumping-on-the-chair-at-the-sight-of-a-mouse era, and a colonel who says they haven't.

2. Tardiness in rising is punished by extra haste in eating breakfast or in walking to catch

the train: in the ling run, it may even mean the loss of a job or of advancement in business.

3. The mother might have spoken with understandable pride of her child.

4. Her complete happiness was marred only by the fact that she knew her marriage would upset her father who disliked change of any kind and that she had unknowingly prepared Harriet for another disappointment. —Jane Austen: *Emma*

5. Human beings have distinguished themselves from other animals, and in doing so ensured their survival, by the ability to observe and understand their environment and then either to adapt to that environment or to control and adapt it to their own needs.

6. The number of the young people in the United States who cannot read is incredible-about one in four.

7. All they have to do is press a button, and they can see plays, films, operas, and shows of every kind, not to mention political discussions and the latest exciting football match.

8. A conflict between the generations—between youth and age—seems the most stupid of all conflicts, for it is one between oneself as one is and oneself as one will be, or between oneself as one was and oneself as one is.

9. There is a tide taken at the flood in the affairs not only of men but of women too, which leads on to fortune.

10. Some men have been virtuous blindly, others have speculated fantastically, and others have been shrewd to bad purposes.

参考译文

1. 一位年轻的女子和一位上校展开了一场热烈讨论。女士坚持己见，即妇女已有进步，看见老鼠就吓得跳上椅子的时代已经过去了，上校则认为没有。

2. 爱懒床的人会得到惩罚：他们得赶着吃早餐、跑着赶火车。从长远来看，这可能意味着失去工作或升职的机会。

3. 母亲在谈到她的孩子时，也许有些自豪感，这是可以理解的。

4. 但她的圆满幸福也有美中不足。她知道自己的婚事会使父亲很不高兴，因为老人不愿生活有丝毫的改变。而且她在不知不觉中又一次使哈里特面临失望的打击。

5. 人类具有观察和了解周围环境的能力，要么适应环境，要么控制环境，或根据自身的需要改造环境。人类就这样把自己和其他动物区别开来并一代代地生存下来。

6. 大约有四分之一的美国青年人没有阅读能力，这简直令人难以置信!

7. 他们所必须做的只是按一下开关。开关一开，就可以看到电视剧、电影、歌剧，以及其他各种各样的文艺节目。至于政治问题的辩论、最近的激动人心的足球赛更是不在话下。

8. 一代人与一代人之间的冲突，也就是年轻人与老年人的冲突，似乎是最可笑的。因为这就是现在与将来的自己，或者是过去与现在的自己之间的冲突。

9. 人生在世，有时会走运，抓住时机，就能飞黄腾达，不但男性如此，女性也一样。

10. 有些人品行端正，但却不去推究为什么要这样做；有些人深思熟虑，但却流于脱离现实；有些人非常精明，但却把精明用于邪道。

D. 用综合法翻译下列长句

1. As far as sight could reach，I feasted my eyes on a vastness of infinite charm，which presents itself in a profusion of color，in verdant luxuriance，in dulcet warbling，in pervading perfume，in rippling undulation，in cataract sprays，in hilly waves，in field crisscross and verily in vitality and variety.

2. What the New Yorker would find missing is what many outsiders find oppressive and distasteful about New York—its rawness，tension，urgency；its bracing competitiveness；the rigor of its judgment；and the congested，democratic presence of so many other New Yorkers encased in their own world.

3. Countless others have written on this theme，and it may be that I shall pass unnoticed among them；if so I must comfort myself with the greatness and splendor of my rivals，whose work will rob my own of recognition.

4. Modern scientific and technical books，especially textbooks，require revision at short intervals if their authors wish to keep pace with new ideas，observations and discoveries.

5. The principal of a great Philadelphia high school is driven to cry for help in combating the notion that it is undemocratic to run a special program of studies for outstanding boys and girls.

6. It was an old woman，tall and shapely still，though withered by time，on whom his eyes fell when he stopped and turned.

7. Law-and-order is the longest-running and probably the best-loved political issue in U.S. history. Yet it is painfully apparent that millions of Americans who would never think of themselves as lawbreakers，let alone criminals，are increasingly taking liberties with the legal codes that are designed to protect them and their society.

参考译文

1. 纵目眺望，我饱览了一片无限娇艳的风光：万紫千红，郁郁葱葱。鸟语悦耳，花香袭人，涟漪荡漾，瀑布飞流，层峦起伏，阡陌纵横。真可谓生机勃勃，气象万千。

2. 纽约的粗犷、紧张，那种急迫感和催人奋发的竞争性，它的是非观念之严酷无情，纽约市的那种各色人等熙熙攘攘、兼容并蓄于各自的天地之中的格局，这一切都使那些非纽约人感到厌恶和窒息；而这一切，又正是纽约人所眷恋的。

3. 有关这个题目的其他著作数不胜数，我写的书可能淹没其间，无人垂顾；倘若如此，那是因为我的竞争对手博大精深，才华横溢，所以他们的著作才会使我的作品默默无闻，我必须借此聊以自慰。

4. 对于现代书籍，特别是教科书来说，要是作者希望自己书中的内容能与新概念、新观察到的事实和新发现同步发展的话，那么就应该每隔较短的时间，将书中的内容重新修改。

5. 费城的一所名牌中学为一些出类拔萃的男女学生开设一套特别课程，有人认为这种做法不民主，结果校长不得不大声疾呼求助人们同这种观念做斗争。

6. 他站住，转过身来，定睛一看，是个年迈妇女，个子很高，依然一副好身材，虽然受岁月折磨而显得憔悴。

7. 法律和秩序是美国历史上持续时间最长、也可能是政治上最热门的话题。然而，如今数以百万计的美国人尽管从来不认为自己会违反法律，更不用说会成为罪犯，却在越来越随意地践踏那些专为保护他们和他们的社会而制定的法规。显而易见，这不能不使人痛心疾首。

二、翻译下列段落

The British Educational System

All over the world mention of English education suggests a picture of the "public schools", and it suggests in particular the names of certain very famous institutions—Eton, Oxford and Cambridge; but people do not always realize what place these institutions occupy in the whole educational system. Oxford and Cambridge are university each having about 12 000 students out of a total of over 250 000 students at all British universities. Eton is a public school, and the best known of the public schools, which, in spite of their name, are not really public at all, but independent and private secondary schools taking boys from the age of thirteen to eighteen years. The public schools in reality form a very small part of the whole system of secondary education; only about one out of 40 English boys goes to a public school, and one out of 1 500 goes to Eton.

Apart from the so-called public schools there is a complete system of state primary and secondary education, which resembles in its general form the state education in most other countries. All children must, by law, receive full-time education between the ages of five and sixteen. Any child may attend, without paying fees, a school provided by the public authorities, and the great majority attend such schools. They may continue, still without paying fees, until they are eighteen. In presenting an overall picture of English education it would be reasonable to concentrate on the state system alone and refer briefly to the public schools. However, although the public schools are not important numerically, they have been England's most peculiar and characteristic contribution to educational methods, and they have an immense influence on the whole of English educational practice and on the English social structure. For a hundred years most men in leading positions in banking, insurance, high finance, some industries, the army, the church and conservative politics have been educated at public schools. Things are beginning to change but it will take time. Among the universities, Oxford and Cambridge hold a dominant position. Of cabinet ministers who went to universities, nearly all went to one or the other of these two, and to Oxford in particular.

A student who receives further full-time education after the age of eighteen, either at a university or at a teachers' training college or at some other college giving training of a special type, can usually receive a grant from the public authorities to cover his expenses, or almost all of them, unless his parents have a large income. But the number of young people who can enter universities is limited by the capacity of the universities, which is less than enough to take all the young people who have the basic qualifications for university admission. In practice, therefore, entry to the universities is competitive. But university degree courses are also available at polytechnics, and entry to the Open University is less restricted.

The academic year begins after the summer holidays and is divided into three "terms", with the intervals between them formed by the Christmas and Easter holidays. The exact dates of the holidays vary from area to area, being in general about two weeks at Christmas and Easter, plus often a week or more at Whitsun, and six weeks in the summer, beginning rather late. Schools outside the state system decide on their own holiday dates, generally taking a month off at Christmas and Easter and eight weeks in the summer. The three terms are not everywhere called by the same names; indeed some schools call the January-March period "the Spring Term", others use "Spring Term" for the period April-July. Some call the January term "Winter Term" (which is logical), others call it "Easter Term".

Day-schools mostly work Mondays to Fridays only, from about 9 a.m. to between 3 and 4 p.m. Lunch is provided and parents pay for it unless they prove to the authorities that they cannot well afford to. All primary school children, including those in independent schools, were given milk free of charge until 1970 when the government abolished this benefit.

参考译文

英国的教育体系

在世界各地，一谈到英国教育，人们就会联想到一幅“公学”的画面，尤其会想到某些非常著名的学府，如伊顿、牛津和剑桥，然而人们未必了解这些学府在英国整个教育体制中占有怎样的地位。英国各大学学生总数为25万多人，而牛津和剑桥两校各自约有学生12 000多名。伊顿是公学中声望最高的一所，这些学校虽名为公学，可事实上根本就不是公办学校，而是独立的私立中等学校，招收13到18岁的男孩入学。事实上，在整个中等教育体系中公学所占比重甚少。仅有1/40左右的英国男孩就读于公学，有1/1500就读于伊顿公学。

除了所谓的公学之外，英国还有一套完整的国立小学、中学教育体系，这同大部分国家的国立教育大体相似。法律规定所有5～16岁的孩子必须接受全日制教育，任何孩子都可免费到由政府当局开办的学校读书。大部分孩子都上这类学校，并且可以一直读到18岁。要全面介绍英国的教育，应单独集中介绍其国立教育体系，同时简要介绍其公学教育。然而，尽管从数量上讲公学所占的地位不算重要，但它对英国的教育方法做出了最特殊、最具特色的贡献，对整个英国的教育实践和社会结构产生了重大的影响。近百年来在银行、保险、高级金融、工业、军队、宗教、保守政见等领域的顶尖人才大都曾在公学接受过教育。尽管近来情况开始有所变化，但短时间内变化还不明显。牛津大学和剑桥大学在大学教育领域处于领先地位。读过大学的内阁大臣中几乎都上过这两所大学中的某一所，特别是牛津大学。

学生满18岁后，若要进一步接受全日制教育，可以选择读综合性大学、教师训练学院或者其他提供专门培训的学院。政府当局通常可以提供给学生助学金以支付其全部或大部分学费，除非学生的父母收入很高不需要资助。但是由于受到大学容量的限制，上大学的青年人的数量是有限的，这些大学的数量不能容纳下所有具备基本入学资格的学生。因此事实上，上大学是有竞争性的。但是学生还可能选择上工科学院的学位课程，而且上函授大学所受限制则小得多。

每学年的开始从暑假后的学期算，并且分为三个“学期”，由圣诞节、复活节两个假期间隔开来。各学校的具体放假时间因地区差异而不同，大致上圣诞节、复活节各两周的假，加上通常一周或更长一点的圣灵降临节假期和六周的暑假，暑假开始得相当晚。不受国家教育体制限制的学校自行决定放假时间，通常是圣诞节、复活节各放一个月，暑假放八周。这三个学期在不同的地区叫法不完全一样。实际上一些学校称一至三月学期为“春季学期”，另外一个称呼是称四至七月学期为“春季期”。另外一个称呼是称四至七月学期为“春季期”。一些地方称一月学期为“冬季学期”(这是逻辑上的叫法)，而有另外一个称呼则是“复活节学期”。

大部分日校周一至周五上课，大约从早晨九点上到下午三点或四点。学校通常提供午饭，但学生父母要付钱，除非他们向官方证明自己负担不起。所有的小学包括私立学校都向学生提供免费的牛奶，直到1970年政府取消了这一福利。

参考文献

[1] Jin Di，Eugene A. Nida. On Translation[M]. 北京：中国对外翻译出版公司，1984.

[2] A. F. Tytler. Essay on the Principles of Translation[M]. Philadelphia：John Benjamins Publishing Co.，1970.

[3] Mona Baker. 翻译研究百科全书[M]. 上海：上海外语教育出版社，2004.

[4] Venuti，Lawrence. The Translator's Invisibility[M]. London and New York：Routledge，1995：132，20.

[5] 陈德彰. 英汉翻译入门[M]. 北京：外语教育与研究出版社，2005.

[6] 陈宏薇. 新编汉英翻译教程[M]. 上海：上海外语教育出版社，2004.

[7] 程镇球. 翻译论文集[D]. 北京：外语教学与研究出版社，2002.

[8] 陈菁，雷天放. 口译教程[M]. 上海：上海外语教育出版社，2006.

[9] 陈小慰. 新编实用翻译教程[M]. 北京：经济科学出版社，2006.

[10] 方梦之. 英汉—汉英应用翻译教程[M]. 上海：上海外语教育出版社，2005.

[11] 方梦之，毛忠明. 英汉—汉英应用翻译综合教程[M]. 上海：上海外语教育出版社，2008.

[12] 冯庆华，穆雷. 英汉翻译基础教程[M]. 北京：高等教育出版社，2008.

[13] 郭著章，李庆生. 英汉互译实用教程[M]. 武汉：武汉大学出版社，2003.

[14] 何刚强. 笔译理论与技巧[M]. 北京：外语教学与研究出版社，2009.

[15] 贾文波. 应用翻译功能论[M]. 北京：中国对外翻译出版公司，2004.

[16] 李昌拴. 非文学翻译理论与实践[M]. 北京：中国对外翻译出版公司，2004.

[17] 连淑能. 英译汉教程[M]. 北京：高等教育出版社，2006.

[18] 刘重德. 英汉语比较与翻译[M]. 青岛：青岛出版社，1998.

[19] 刘和平. 口译理论与教学[M]. 北京：中国对外翻译出版公司，2005.

[20] 刘季春. 实用翻译教程(修订版)[M]. 广州：中山大学出版社，2007.

[21] 刘宓庆. 文体与翻译[M]. 北京：中国对外翻译出版公司，1998.

[22] 罗进德. 非文学翻译理论与实践[M]. 北京：中国对外翻译出版公司，2004.

[23] 潘红. 商务英语英汉翻译教程[M]. 北京：中国商务出版社，2004.

[24] 钱钟书. 文学翻译的最高标准[A]. 翻译理论与翻译技巧论文集[C]. 北京：中国对外翻译出版公司，1985.

[25] 申雨平，戴宁. 实用英汉翻译教程[M]. 北京：外语教学与研究出版社，2002.

[26] 思果. 翻译新究[M]. 北京：中国对外翻译出版公司，2001.

[27] 孙致礼. 再谈文学翻译的策略问题[J].中国翻译，2003(1)：51.

[28] 孙致礼. 新编英汉翻译教程[M]. 上海：上海外语教育出版社，2003.

[29] 王恩冕. 大学英汉翻译教程[M]. 3版.北京：对外经贸大学出版社，2009.

[30] 王振国，李艳琳.新英汉翻译教程[M]. 北京：高等教育出版社，2007.

[31] 王治奎，等. 大学英汉翻译教程[M]. 济南：山东大学出版社，1995.

[32] 魏志成. 英汉比较翻译教程[M]. 北京：清华大学出版社，2004.

[33] 伍锋，何庆机.应用文体翻译理论与实践[M]. 杭州：浙江大学出版社，2008.

[34] 谢群. 英汉互译教程[M]. 武汉：华中科技大学出版社，2010.

[35] 许建平. 英汉互译实践与技巧[M]. 北京：清华大学出版社，2007.

[36] 杨士焯. 英汉翻译教程[M]. 北京：北京大学出版社，2006.

[37] 叶子南. 高级英汉翻译理论与实践[M]. 北京：清华大学出版社，2001.

[38] 曾诚. 实用汉英翻译教程[M]. 北京：外语教学与研究出版社，2002.

[39] 张培基，等. 英汉翻译教程[M]. 上海：上海外语教育出版社，1998.

[40] 张培基. 英汉翻译教程[M]. 上海：上海外语教育出版社，2009.

[41] 张新红. 商务英语翻译[M]. 北京：高等教育出版社，2003.

[42] 赵萱，郑仰成. 科技英语翻译[M]. 北京：外语教学与研究出版社，2006.

[43] 仲伟合. 英语口译教程[M]. 北京：高等教育出版社，2007.

[44] 钟述孔. 英汉翻译手册[M]. 北京：商务出版社，1997.

[45] 庄绎传. 英汉翻译简明教程[M]. 北京：外语教学与研究出版社，2002.